Also by Bruce Chilton

*Rabbi Jesus*
*Rabbi Paul*

# *Mary Magdalene*

A BIOGRAPHY

## BRUCE CHILTON

IMAGE

DOUBLEDAY

*New York   London   Toronto*
*Sydney   Auckland*

*To the memory of Rose Miller*

AN IMAGE BOOK
PUBLISHED BY DOUBLEDAY

Copyright © 2005 by Bruce Chilton

All Rights Reserved

A hardcover edition of this book was originally published in 2005 by Doubleday.

Published in the United States by Doubleday, an imprint of The Doubleday Broadway
Publishing Group, a division of Random House, Inc., New York.
www.doubleday.com

IMAGE, DOUBLEDAY, and the portrayal of a deer drinking from a stream
are registered trademarks of Random House, Inc.

*Book design by rlf design*
*Maps designed by Jeffrey L. Ward*

Library of Congress Cataloging-in-Publication Data
Chilton, Bruce.
Mary Magdalene : a biography / Bruce Chilton.—1st ed.
p.   cm.
Includes bibliographical references (p. 163) and index.
1. Mary Magdalene, Saint.  2. Christian saints—Biography.
3. Bible.  N.T.—Biography.  4. Jesus Christ—Friends and associates.  I. Title.
BS2485.C45  2005
226'.092—dc22          2005045446

ISBN-13: 978-0-385-51318-0
ISBN-10: 0-385-51318-6

First Paperback Edition

146119709

# Contents

# Contents

# MARGUERITE

I S ANYONE THERE? Is there anyone there?" Marguerite called out loudly.

"Yes, right beside you," I replied, trying to reassure her. People who are dying sometimes wonder whether they are still alive and with people they know. As their priest, I have heard this question a number of times during visits with terminally ill patients. But Marguerite repeated her question despite my response: She wasn't calling to me at all, and it took me a moment to realize that.

I had found Marguerite in bed, on oxygen, and far from her normal, alert self. She was one of my favorites among the congregation of the small Episcopalian church that I serve in Barrytown, New York. She proved to be the best critic of sermons I have ever met. A formidable professional, she had been a social worker in Manhattan and possessed a passion for children's rights that did not wane with her retirement. After she passed the age of ninety, congestive heart failure gradually sapped life from her. She couldn't travel to church any longer, but we made it a point to meet at her home late in the afternoon once or twice a month to talk politics, gardening, and religion, drink gin and tonics, and pray together.

As months passed and Marguerite weakened, I started to bring her the bread and wine of the Eucharist. She would haltingly say the Lord's Prayer with me just before we shared this sacred food of Christianity's holiest rite, which she could follow even when her mind became fogged. She had called out her question partway through our little service of the Eucharist.

Later, she told me that she had been in a different place when she had asked, "Is anyone there?" She had wanted to know whether there was anyone there for her on the other side of death. Who was there like her, to accept her into the presence of God? Where were the *women* in the transcendent realm?

Marguerite was an educated and committed Episcopalian. She was familiar with Catholicism, but no saint in that tradition had the same spiritual meaning for her as did the women in the Bible. In some ways, Marguerite was downright anti-Catholic, and that contributed to her problem. She did not pray to Mary, the mother of Jesus, as many of her Catholic friends did and still do. She looked with Protestant suspicion on the devotion to Mary that emerged during the Middle Ages, with its lucrative rewards for the clergy, who received donations in Mary's name and imposed penances on people to win her favor, the proceeds benefiting the Church. All that seemed to Marguerite rooted more in the desire of the medieval papacy to win prestige and profit from its favorite holy patroness than in the text of the New Testament. Marguerite knew a great deal; I really didn't have anything to tell her about women in the Bible or Christendom's female saints. She was after something different and more profound, and she had come up against an obstacle that lay across the path of her faith.

In its formative years, Christianity developed a deep ambivalence toward women at its core. Ancient Christians acknowledged women's vital role from the first days of Jesus' movement and yet systematically diminished their authority in relation to men. References to women in the New Testament and other ancient Christian writings

are fleeting, occasionally dismissive, and lead to understandable confusions. As a result, today people sometimes conflate Mary Magdalene, Jesus' most prominent female disciple, with Mary, the mother
of Jesus, or with other women in the Gospels (several of whom are
also called "Mary"). That confusion is easily sorted out, although the
fact that it occurs at all points to an underlying problem: Women in
the Gospels and Christian tradition often have the look of ornaments
or afterthoughts.

Retelling biblical stories about women in the traditional way could
not answer Marguerite's plea. She wanted to know where women
were built into the fabric of revelation, where—at the end of the day,
at the end of a life—they were welcomed into the presence of God as
more than ancillary support staff for whom men had condescended
to make a place.

Having developed close contact with progressive religious groups
in Manhattan during her working life, Marguerite was familiar with
what she considered contemporary theology's wishful thinking. She
knew that commentators had spun legends about heroic women
from biblical references that were often no more than a mere mention of a name. She had listened to speaker after speaker at fashionable Protestant churches as they tried to make Christianity palatable
by constructing a picture of Mary Magdalene that seemed truer to
modern feminism than to the texts of the New Testament.

Marguerite was well familiar with the "hypothesis" that Mary was
the true Holy Grail, the wife of Jesus, mother of his child, a Jewish
princess from the house of Benjamin and an émigrée to France, an
embodiment of the pagan earth mother, whom the Catholic Church
for thousands of years has sought to marginalize and suppress. This
Mary becomes the great untold story of Western culture, a figure who
has been both reviled and revered, a goddess who has taken many
forms—witch, heretic, tarot priestess, holy whore, the incarnation of
the eternal feminine, her womb the chalice that bears God's child.

Marguerite had no patience with this program. No feverish myth justified by a conspiracy theory, no vague assurance that God has his feminine side or that early believers looked to the leadership of "strong" women satisfied her. I had no direct response to her question—and neither did modern theology. But her question haunted me. I turned it over and over in my mind, and her appeal—as well as the prompting of friends every bit as insistent as Marguerite—eventually led me to analyze the evidence regarding Mary Magdalene and to write this book.

⊸⊷⊶

IN THE YEARS SINCE Marguerite's death, there has been an increased awareness that major teachers in the New Testament—Paul, Barnabas, Peter, and James—were not just empty vessels filled with Jesus' message, but powerful sages in their own right. Their teachings shaped the Gospels and crafted the practices and beliefs that made Christianity into a world religion.

My study of Mary Magdalene has convinced me that she belongs on this list of the creators of Christianity. Writing this biography led me to a new reading of the Gospels. I argue that Mary provided the source of the Gospels' exorcism stories and influenced much of what early Christians believed about how to treat demonic possession. For that reason, she should be recognized as one of the principal shapers of Christianity's wisdom as it concerns dealing with the world of spirits.

Mary's method of exorcism was intimately linked to the ancient Judaic practice of anointing, and she emerges in the Gospels as a model of that practice, as well. Oil served to consecrate people for ritual purposes, to signal celebration, and as a medium for communing with the divine. We shall see that exorcism and anointing involved mastering the ebb and flow of spiritual energy—and, in this arena, Mary was one of Jesus' most gifted adepts and, in turn, a significant influence upon him.

Her mastery of Jesus' wisdom included a profound understanding of what it means for a person to be raised from the dead. Jesus himself bluntly denied—as we will see in detail—that Resurrection involves a simple continuation of physical life on this earth. He said that in heaven people are not married to the spouses they had when they were alive, but become "like angels" (Mark 12:25). Angels no more have mates than they have aunts and uncles. This spiritual view set Jesus apart from other Jewish teachers of his time, many of whom saw the afterlife in a materialistic way, and aligned him with Judaism's spiritual masters.

Mary Magdalene was the disciple who best appreciated Jesus' visionary teaching of Resurrection, and without her, Christianity would have been entirely different. It is not even clear that its core faith in Jesus' victory over the grave could have emerged at all without Mary. That is why she has been known as "the apostle to the apostles" since the second century: It was from her that the apostles first learned that Jesus had been raised from the dead.

By the time the Gospels were written, more than forty years after Jesus' death, Christianity had declared the allegedly "natural" authority of men over women, to this extent conforming to its surrounding society. An increasingly male clergy tightly controlled exorcism and anointing; a literally physical view of Resurrection began to prevail. It is not surprising that after her death Mary Magdalene was nearly written out of the record of Christian memory.

The Gospels in aggregate relate that she was called "Magdalene," indicating where she came from, and that until Jesus healed her, she had been possessed by seven demons. She followed Jesus in Galilee and helped to support him (Luke 8:2–3). She prepared Jesus' corpse for burial in Jerusalem, and on the way to anoint his body, she and her companions were the first to learn of his Resurrection (Mark 15:42–16:8). All four Gospels agree that she had a role in Jesus' interment and that she came to know that he was raised from the dead, but each goes its own way in depicting those scenes. That is what the

Gospels have to say directly about Mary Magdalene by name, although in this book we will find her implicated in several other passages, as well. Had Jesus not insisted that "wherever the message is proclaimed in the whole world, what she did will also be spoken of in memory of her" (Mark 14:9), this effacement might well have been complete.

Christianity's ambivalence about women lies at the source of this near erasure of Mary. We shall explore the repression of women's leadership in the early Church, which sets the stage for reading what Gnostic teachers had to say about Mary from the second through fourth centuries. The Gnostic portrayal of Mary was tragically conflicted: It venerated her visionary power while denigrating her because she was a woman. Gnosticism provides fascinating insights into how images of Mary shaped attitudes regarding leadership of women in the Church, feminine identity in the godhead, and the nature of revelation.

Modern study of Mary Magdalene has inherited the Christian and Gnostic ambivalence toward women and sexuality. As a result, even when an attempt is made to assert Mary's importance, it often comes at the cost of her historical identity. She has become sexualized in popular culture, the consort of Jesus, a tantric adept or holy vessel for his seed, and thus her true influence is marginalized, distorted, or ignored because her whole importance is limited to the argument over whether she had sex with Jesus. She often becomes the figurehead of neopagan theology—the embattled earth mother, a goddess doomed to exile by a malevolent patriarchy, more a generalization than a person. Even such exaggerated claims have their value, but they need to be sifted through the analysis of history to avoid burying Mary Magdalene under the rubble of the twentieth century's broken dreams.

∾

I WISH MY FRIEND Marguerite were still with us. The silence of the Gospels, the increasing patriarchy of the early Church, the Gnostic schizophrenia toward women, Marguerite's own anti-Catholicism, and the tendency of scholars, even some feminist scholars, to treat women in the Bible more as victims than visionaries stood between my dying friend and what she wanted to see. Powerful forces reaching deep into history, stronger and more complicated than a simple conspiracy theory of male dominance, have veiled Mary's vision of the divine. They veiled her from me and from Marguerite and, for a moment in prayer together, shook our confidence in heaven.

But Mary Magdalene is more powerful than that veil. Her methods of reaching into the divine world shaped the practices of women and men for generations, and they can be uncovered. Anointing, exorcism, and vision persisted through the period of the New Testament, the early Church, and beyond, in ways that are central to the religious identity of all those interested in the life of Spirit.

Christianity has often appreciated the power of Mary's spiritual practices, but church after church has distorted their meaning by alienating them from Mary herself. They have become the sole preserve of clergy, alleged experts, or a few illuminati, instead of being the sustaining rituals of discipleship they were intended to be.

Inferring Mary's influence within Jesus' movement is not an exercise in filling in blanks with the images of her one prefers. Since the second century, as we shall see, Mary has been the target of projections. She has been portrayed as the Shulamit, the dark lover of the Song of Songs, whose physical passion symbolized holy ardor. During the sixth century, Pope Gregory the Great wove that symbolism into a narrative in which Mary Magdalene became a converted prostitute; by the Middle Ages, it became fashionable to depict her as a naked penitent meditating in a cave, and religious houses for converted prostitutes were routinely named after "the Magdalene." From the thirteenth century, some people said Mary was really Christ's concubine, and early efforts at photography in Victorian England included posing adolescent girls as partially clad "Magdalenes." Christianity's efforts to engage issues of human sexuality have been perennially undermined by caricatures of women as goddesses and vixens, and Mary Magdalene has been cast in both roles.

Swamped with a myriad of Magdalene legends, it is tempting for professionals in the study of the New Testament simply to debunk both the traditions of the Church and modern revisionism. I think that is unwise. We need to use the texts to get behind them, into the rich tapestry of meaning in which Mary Magdalene played a pivotal role in Jesus' ministry. The legends of later times, and even of our day, frequently reflect the underlying power of Mary's influence, even when they seem distorted by the mirrors of wishful thinking.

By attending to the texts that Mary Magdalene influenced, and keeping an eye on how that influence played out in later legends, we see a person come into focus. The details of Mary's life are often obscure, but the power of a religious personality is unmistakable. I know now that there *is* someone there for Marguerite—a woman of Spirit, prepared to transmit that Spirit bodily into the lives of all those who long to lift the veils that prevent us from seeing the divine vision, which is also the truth of who we are.

# Mary Magdalene

Paris

Vézelay

Danube

GAUL

Danube

ILLYRICUM
(DALMATIA)

Saint-Maximin-
la-Sainte-Baume

Marseilles

Tiber R.

ITALY

Adriatic Sea

Rome

Three Taverns

Beneventum

Puteoli

Brundisium

Tarentum

Apollonia

Tyrrhenian
Sea

Mediterranean Sea

SICILY

MALTA

AFRICA

0 Miles    100    200    300    400    500

0 Kilometers    300    400    500

© 2005 Jeffrey L. Ward

# THE MEDITERRANEAN BASIN

Danube

*Black Sea*

MACEDONIA

THRACE

Sinope

Philippi
Amphipolis  Neapolis
Thessalonica
Beroea
Apollonia

BITHYNIA
AND PONTUS

Troas

*Aegean Sea*    ASIA

Ancyra

Assos

Pergamum

LESBOS

GALATIA

Nicopolis
Actium

Mitylene

Thyatira

Antioch

CAPPADOCIA

Smyrna

Sardis

Philadelphia

Corinth
Cenchreae

Athens

Ephesus

Iconium
Lystra

Derbe

SAMOS

Laodicea  Colossae

PISIDIA

ACHAIA

Miletus

Cilician Gates

CILICIA

COS

Attalia

PAMPHYLIA

Tarsus

Perga

RHODES

Patara

Myra

Antioch

CYPRUS

Salamis

Fair Havens

CRETE

Paphos

*Mediterranean Sea*

Sidon

SYRIA

Damascus

Tyre

Caesarea Philippi

Sepphoris

*Sea of Galilee*

CYRENAICA

Caesarea Maritima

Tiberias

Joppa

Jerusalem

*Salt Sea*

JUDEA

Alexandria

NABATAEAN
KINGDOM

LIBYA

Petra

Memphis

EGYPT

*Nile R.*

*Arabian Desert*

*Orontes R.*

## Chapter One

# POSSESSED

*And there were some women who had been healed from evil*
*spirits and ailments—Mary who was called Magdalene, from whom*
*seven demons had gone out, and Joanna, Khuza's wife (Herod's*
*commissioner), and Susanna and many others who provided*
*for them from their belongings.*

M ARY APPEARS FOR THE first time in the chronology of Jesus'
life in this brief passage from Luke's Gospel (8:2–3). Luke
indicates when she entered Jesus' life and why she sought him out.
Jesus' reputation must have drawn her the ten hard miles from
her home in Magdala to Capernaum, which is where he lived from 24
C.E. until the early part of 27 C.E. She probably came to him alone, on
foot, over rock roads and rough paths, possessed by demons, her
clothing in tatters. By my estimate, she sought him out in 25 C.E., after
Jesus had become known in Galilee as a rabbi who opened his arms to
people considered sinful and did battle with the demons that afflicted
them. Jesus and Mary might conceivably have met when Jesus visited
Magdala prior to 25 C.E., but there is no reference to that.

If she had begun her journey from Magdala with a woolen cloak—coveted by travelers for shelter at night as well as covering in rain and cold—that and any leather sandals she wore might well have been stolen. Cloaks and sandals, however, were not within reach of every family: The poor had to make their way barefoot, warmed only by the thick flax of their tunics. We can only imagine the toughness of these Galilean peasants, by day outdoors, even in the cold winter rains and occasional snow of the region.

Luke does not present Mary as the wealthy, elegant seductress of medieval legend and modern fantasy. In one vivid tale, frequently re-told and embellished in the city of Ephesus in Asia Minor from the sixth century on, Mary was so wealthy that she was invited after Je-sus' death to a dinner with Tiberius Caesar in Rome. She took the opportunity to preach of Jesus' Resurrection, only to be met with im-perial derision. God would no more raise the dead, the emperor said, than he would turn the egg in Mary's hand from white to red. The egg immediately turned red. Orthodox Christians still recount this story at Easter, and Mary and her egg appear in the icons of Eastern Orthodoxy.

Some modern scholarship has attempted to buttress the picture of Mary's wealth by playing on her association with Joanna in Luke's Gospel, since Joanna had married into the prominent household of Herod Antipas, the ruler of Galilee. In one recent reconstruction, Mary and the influential Joanna were friends and colleagues in busi-ness; Mary exploited Joanna's contacts and used her own wealth to host dinner parties at which she employed Jesus as a comic. Revision-ist readings, like medieval legends, can divert and refresh our imag-inations, but they also show us how much the Western religious imagination still wants a rich and powerful Mary to protect the poor, defenseless Jesus.

But Luke's Gospel simply does not say Mary shared Joanna's sta-tus: It *contrasts* the two women. Among the women Luke mentions,

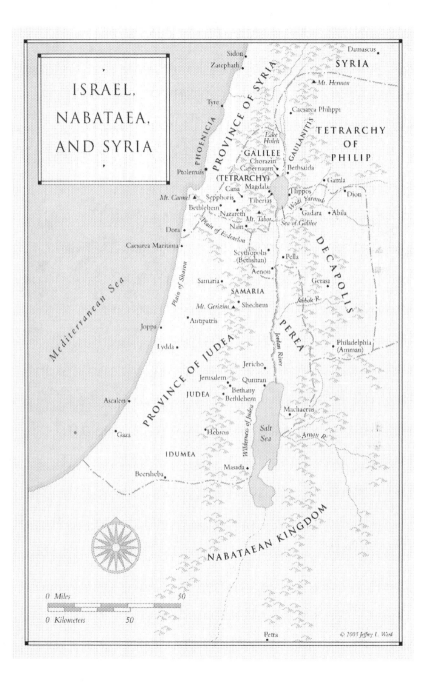

ISRAEL,
NABATAEA,
AND SYRIA

Mediterranean Sea

Sidon
Zarephath
SYRIA
Damascus

Tyre
PHOENICIA
PROVINCE OF SYRIA
Mt. Hermon
Caesarea Philippi

Ptolemais
Lake
Huleh
GALILEE
(TETRARCHY)
Chorazin
Capernaum
Bethsaida
GAULANITIS
TETRARCHY
OF
PHILIP

Mt. Carmel
Sepphoris
Cana
Magdala
Tiberias
Hippos
Wadi Yarmuk
Gamla
Dion

Bethlehem
Nazareth
Nain
Mt. Tabor
Sea of Galilee
Gadara
Abila

Plain of Esdraelon
Dora
Caesarea Maritima

DECAPOLIS

Scythopolis
(Bethshan)
Pella

Plain of Sharon
Aenon
Gerasa

Samaria
SAMARIA
Jabbok R.

Mt. Gerizim
Shechem

PEREA

Joppa
Antipatris

Lydda
Jordan River
Philadelphia
(Amman)

PROVINCE OF JUDEA

Jericho
Jerusalem
Qumran
JUDEA
Bethany
Bethlehem

Ascalon

Wilderness of Judea

Salt
Sea
Machaerus

Gaza
Hebron
Arnon R.

IDUMEA

Beersheba
Masada

NABATAEAN KINGDOM

0 Miles 50
0 Kilometers 50

Petra
© 2005 Jeffrey L. Ward

Joanna, married to a government official, is aristocratic, perhaps wealthy, and well connected. Mary, on the other hand, doesn't have Joanna's status or connections. What she has are demons; no ancient text (nor any reasonable speculation) suggests that Jesus ever moved to Magdala or that Mary owned property there that she put at Jesus' disposal.

LUKE DOES NOT INDICATE how old Mary was when she met Jesus, but she was most likely in her twenties, slightly older than he, mature enough to have developed a complicated case of possession (intimated by the reference to "seven demons"). The Gospels say nothing about her family. She was evidently unmarried at an age when one would expect a woman to have settled and produced children.

Given Mary's demonic possession, there is little mystery about her being single. Possession carried the stigma of impurity, not the natural impurity of childbirth (for example), but the contagion of an unclean spirit. She had no doubt been ostracized in Magdala in view of her many demons. The Jews of Galilee defined themselves, in contrast to the Gentiles around them, by their devotion to stringent laws of purity that were commanded by the Torah, the Law of Moses that was written in Hebrew and passed on in oral form in the Aramaic language. What they ate, whom they could eat and associate with, how they farmed, whom they could touch or not touch, the people they could marry, the kind of sex they had and when they had it—all this and more was determined by this Torah. The Galileans' purity was their identity, more precious and delightful in their minds than prosperity under the Romans or even survival. They resorted to violent resistance sporadically during the first century to expunge the impurity the Romans had brought to their land, even when that resistance proved suicidal.

"Unclean spirits," as Jesus and his followers often called demons, inhabited Mary. These demons were considered contagious, moving from person to person and place to place, transmitted by people like Mary who were known to be possessed. In the Hellenistic world, an invisible contagion of this kind was called a *daimon,* the origin of the word *demon.* But a *daimon* needn't be harmful in the sources of Greco-Roman thought. *Daimones* hovered in the space between the terrestrial world and the realm of the gods. When Socrates was asked how he knew how to act when he faced an ethical dilemma, he said that he listened to his *daimonion ti,* a nameless "little *daimon"* that guided him.

Judaism during this period referred to the same kind of forces, using the language of spirit and distinguishing between good spirits (such as angels and the Holy Spirit that God breathed over the world) and bad spirits. Jesus called harmful spiritual influences "unclean" or "evil" spirits, and the word *daimon* has been used in this sense within both Judaism and Christianity. After all, even a "good" *daimon* from the Hellenistic world was associated with idolatry, and that is why the term *demon* is used in a pejorative sense in modern languages influenced by Church practices.

Everyone in the ancient world, Jewish or not, agreed that *daimonia* could do harm, invading people, animals, and objects, inhabiting and possessing them. While *daimonia* are in some ways comparable to psychological complexes, they are also analogous to our bacteria, viruses, and microbes. People protected themselves from invisible *daimonia* with the care we devote to hygiene, and ancient experts listed them the way we catalog diseases and their alleged causes. Such lists have survived on fragments of papyrus that record the ancient craft of exorcism. The fact that these experts disagreed did not undermine belief in *daimonia* any more than changing health advice today makes people skeptical of science. Then, as now, conflict among experts only heightened belief in the vital importance of the subject.

Some scholars have argued that women in early Greece were

thought more susceptible of possession than men, on the dubious grounds that their vaginas made their bodies vulnerable to entry. Ancient thought was usually subtler than that, and demons do not seem to have required many apertures or much room for maneuver. A person's eyes, ears, and nose were much more likely to expose him to their influences than any orifice below the waist.

⟊

HOWEVER MARY CAME BY her *daimonia,* they rendered her unclean within the society of Jewish Galilee. She was probably very much alone when she arrived in Capernaum.

In antiquity, women without families were vulnerable in ways that we can scarcely imagine. The Gospels typically identify a woman as a sister, wife, or mother of some man. That link was her protection. As happens in many cultures, a wife who was alone with any man but her husband in a private place became liable to the charge of adultery (Sotah 1:1–7 in the Mishnah, the tradition of Rabbinic teaching that put the Law of Moses into practice). Similarly, a man who stayed in his future father-in-law's house could not complain later that his wife was not a virgin, on the grounds that he might well have deflowered her, given half a chance. Women without men did not make themselves available; rather, men availed themselves of them.

From the custody of her father, a woman at puberty (around the age of thirteen) passed by marriage to the custody of a husband. Weddings were arranged between families that sought the advantage to both sides of increasing their families, the fields they farmed, the herds they tended, the labor force they could count on, and the contacts for trade that they could exploit. Marriage was a binding contract, sealed by a written record in literate communities, or by witnesses in illiterate peasant environments. A young woman remained in her father's home for a year or so after the marriage contract was agreed upon. Even with this delay of sexual relations, however, pregnant fourteen- and fifteen-year-old women must have been a relatively common sight.

This whole arrangement was designed to protect the purity of Israel's bloodlines by managing a woman's transition from puberty to childbearing with a husband who knew he had married a virgin. Taking another man's wife was therefore punishable by death in the Torah (Leviticus 20:10). Relations with a married woman constituted the sin of adultery, while seducing a virgin could be punished more lightly (Leviticus 22:16–17), sometimes only by a fine.

Unmarried women past the age of being virgins had a liminal, uncontrolled status, as troublesome to the families that had failed to marry them off as to the women themselves. Both men and women who had Israelite mothers but whose paternity was in doubt posed a particular problem when it came to marriage, because they could not marry most other Israelites. Like Jesus, Mary Magdalene might conceivably have been a *mamzer,* an Israelite whose paternity was doubtful and who was therefore restricted when it came to prospects for marriage.

Modern scholarship continues to parry the medieval tradition of portraying Mary as a prostitute at the time she encountered Jesus. But encouraging one's daughter to become a prostitute was prohibited, even if she was a financial burden. The punishment for promoting or allowing prostitution is not specified (Leviticus 19:29), and the fact is that prostitution did exist in and around Israel. But the practice was blamed for blighting the land. The whole concept behind the rules of purity was that Israel had been given a land to manage with attention and care so that it would continue to be fruitful. Sinful behavior produced impurity and pushed Israel toward annihilation: If Israelites stopped practicing the laws of purity, God threatened that the land itself would vomit them out (Leviticus 18:3–30).

Had Mary turned to prostitution before she met Jesus? Had she been raped or exploited during her journey from Magdala? Those are good questions, although no text or reasonable inference from a text answers them. To affirm or deny these possibilities takes us beyond the available evidence. But we can say that in Mary Magdalene's time and place—as in ours—likely victims of sin were often portrayed as being sinners themselves.

Luke's reference to Mary's seven demons encouraged the Western tradition that depicts her as a prostitute. Typical paintings portray her in lavish dress, arranging herself in front of a mirror, or abased in shame at Jesus' feet. Medieval piety associated vanity with prostitution, on the grounds that women sold themselves only because they enjoyed whoring, and pastoral theologians saw self-abasement, including flagellation on many occasions, as the best cure for this sin. Vanity and lust were kissing cousins within Mary's demonic menagerie prior to her exorcism, which was portrayed in the West as a conversion.

Mary Magdalene became popular as the patron saint of flagellants by the fourteenth century, and devotion to her and to the practice of self-inflicted pain was widespread. In one story of her life, she clawed at her skin until she bled, scored her breasts with stones, and tore out her hair, all as acts of penance for her self-indulgence. She long remained the ideal icon of mortification among the lay and clerical groups that encouraged similar penances. In 1375, an Italian fraternity of flagellants carried a banner during their processions as they whipped themselves; it depicts a giant enthroned Mary Magdalene. Her head reaches into the heavens and angels surround her. At her feet kneel four white-hooded figures, whose robes leave a gap at the back for ritual scourging.

Where did people in the medieval world find the material to produce such an image? Certainly not from the New Testament or from early traditions concerning Mary Magdalene. The woman whom the flagellants venerated was a combination of two different Marys: Mary Magdalene and Mary of Egypt. Mary of Egypt is herself a classic figure of Christian folklore, the whore turned ascetic. In stories that began to circulate during the sixth century, Mary of Egypt, for the sake of Christ, gave up her practice of prostitution during a pilgrimage to Jerusalem in the fourth century and lived in a cave for the rest of her life. This story was spliced into Mary Magdalene's biography.

According to this expanded tale, most famous in the thirteenth-century form in which it appears in *The Golden Legend* of Jacobus de Voragine, Mary traveled to France fourteen years after the Resurrection, founding churches and removing idols. In this lush legend, Mary Magdalene is confused with a completely different person in the Gospels, Mary of Bethany. This confusion provides her with a sister she never had (Martha of Bethany) as well as with a brother she never had (Lazarus). She could count on help in her missionary work from her brother Lazarus and her sister Martha, along with the aid of a boatload of Christians who had come with her and her siblings to Marseilles. Then she retreated for thirty anorexic years to an isolated cave in Provence, where she was fed miraculously during her times of prayer and meditation, when angels lifted her up to heaven.

The deep ambivalence about sexuality held by those within monastic culture did not, however, quite allow them to give up thinking about how desirable this former prostitute must have been after her conversion. She is often depicted as nude in the craggy rocks of La Sainte-Baume. Her long and lustrous hair, covering the parts of her body that modesty conventionally requires to be covered, is a staple of iconography in the West to this day, making Mary Magdalene the Lady Godiva of Christian spirituality.

---

MARY MAGDALENE APPROACHED the right rabbi when she sought out Jesus. He reveled in his reputation for consorting with allegedly loose women (the word *loose* being applicable to any woman who did not bear her husband's or her father's name, or some other token of male protection). There were many unattached women among Jesus' disciples; when people called him "the friend of customs-agents and sinners" (Matthew 11:19), that was not a compliment, and Jesus' critics ranked these female disciples among the "sinners."

Rabbi Jesus didn't mind damning his opponents in his defense of his female followers: "Amen I say to you, that customs-agents and whores precede you into the kingdom of God!" (Matthew 21:31). That is obviously not a general endorsement of tax collection and prostitution as methods of salvation, but a tough rejoinder to people who despised his followers and called his female disciples "whores."

Mary Magdalene's persistent reputation for promiscuity in medieval legend and in many modern novels rests on the mistake of presuming that women with demons were necessarily promiscuous. Exorcism in the ancient world was not only about sex, although scholars sometimes assume that describing a person as possessed denigrates that person, even after the cure. This was not the case: Ancient thinkers knew how to distinguish a person from his or her afflictions in a way their modern counterparts might learn from.

<hr/>

WHEN MARY FIRST met him, Jesus had moved from Nazareth to Capernaum after a near stoning (Luke 4:16–30) convinced him that the parochial hamlet he had known from his childhood would never accept him as a rabbi. In Capernaum, he hit his stride. This fishing town of a couple thousand people provided him with a secure haven, and his reputation as an exorcist grew.

Jesus settled in with two brothers named Simon and Andrew, who had originally come from Bethsaida (John 1:44) and had married into a fishing family in Capernaum. Following a custom in Galilee, they moved in with their in-laws, so Simon's mother-in-law was an important member of a large extended family (Mark 1:29–31). The

sturdy basalt houses of Capernaum were small and packed with people. Most were one-story dwellings, although there were occasional
two-story houses, as well. Few had courtyards, and since some people
kept livestock, animals joined them from time to time in their
cramped homes.

Accommodating Rabbi Jesus was not a routine act of hospitality.
His own needs were modest enough for a prosperous family to support, although he admitted himself (Luke 7:34; Matthew 11:19) that
he did have the reputation of eating and drinking a great deal. The
strain came more from the eager crowds that thronged around him.
Venues where Jesus practiced exorcism and healing could become
so crowded that people were unable to move. The Gospels describe
a scene in a house that was so crowded that four men had to break a
hole through the roof and lower their paralyzed friend to Jesus on a
litter to be healed (Matthew 9:1–8; Mark 2:1–12; Luke 5:17–26). That
scene suggests the environment in which Mary Magdalene first met
the young rabbi. Capernaum was abuzz with Jesus' reputation—you
had to fight your way in to see him.

Time and again in the Gospels, people with unclean spirits and
diseases are portrayed as taking the initiative and demanding Jesus'
attention, often shouting out to him and pushing through crowds to
touch him.

Jesus exorcised and healed by the flow of Spirit that, he said, burst
forth from him and tossed out demons for the sake of God's Kingdom (Matthew 12:28; Luke 11:20). These two forces—the Spirit and
God's Kingdom—were central to his practice, and they were doubtless the two energies uppermost in his mind when he treated Mary
Magdalene.

God's Kingdom was a new social order that, in the mind of Jesus
and his followers, was already beginning to emerge and overthrow
the rule of Rome and its dominance in the territory that it came to
call Provincia Syria Palaestina. Rome's rule through its local under-

lings seemed to break every promise God had made to Israel. The chosen people were supposed to be secure in the Promised Land; the Gentiles, Isaiah had prophesied (Isaiah 25:6–12), would make pilgrimage to Mount Zion as supplicants, not victors.

In the midst of Jewish disappointment at the advent of Roman hegemony, Jesus announced this new, divine supremacy that the Aramaic Scriptures had promised: the *malkhuta delahah,* "the Kingdom of God." Jesus had memorized many of these texts (which differed in significant ways from Hebrew Scripture) when he was a child, embracing the complex, rich oral tradition that was the foundation of peasant life in first-century Syria Palaestina.

Like many other rabbis of his time, Jesus could not read or write. His learning came through oral traditions, and his peculiar genius found expression in his poetry of the divine Kingdom. He gave people like Mary the inner experience of God's power, which they felt was beginning to displace the demons, impurity, poverty, and brutish Roman rule that plagued their land. Jesus taught that God's Kingdom was the revolutionary principle behind the whole cosmos: One day all of life would shimmer with divine fullness and energy. Caesar's might would dissolve and the Kingdom would push past any resistance with a force as natural and mysterious as a sprouting seed, as inexorable as rivers in flood.

People loved to hear Jesus' vision of a new age, a complete transformation of the world as they knew it. They felt themselves transformed by the many parables he wove to take them into the world where divine justice and mercy would reign supreme and transform all humanity. In his exorcisms and healings, Jesus put this vision of the transformative Kingdom into action.

Mary joined these gatherings and participated in festive meals in houses in and around Capernaum, where Jesus talked about God's extraordinary secret *malkhuta.* Rabbi Jesus must have been especially voluble while he drank wine and ate sheep or goat and fresh vegetables provided by accommodating hosts, tracing visions of how God would change everything someday soon and the Israelites who were eating together would banquet with Abraham, Isaac, and Jacob, risen from the dead. If you knew the Kingdom was at hand, you could celebrate its arrival, lying back on a couch of straw (or a real couch, if your host was wealthy), even while Caesar still ruled.

It is easy to imagine how Mary, an outsider who herself had been marginalized and ostracized, without a place in the social web of Galilee, might have responded to these parables of vindication and the vanquishing of Israel's oppressors. She may have had to push her way through crowds to see Jesus, but once she got his attention, he attended to her, as is clear from Luke's Gospel. We don't know what that first meeting would have been like, but it proved auspicious, for both the rabbi and the possessed woman in rags, very much alone, who was destined to become one of his most important disciples.

*Chapter Two*

# THE MAGDALENE

⁂

*M*AGDALENE.

The name has reverberated—with overtones of sensuality, penitence, and devotion—for nearly two millennia. It echoes today in the cloisters and churches of Vézelay in Burgundy and Saint-Maximin in Provence.

Thousands of pilgrims and tourists still throng up winding roads to Vézelay's lush hilltop, where its Romanesque basilica—simple, welcoming, austere—houses what the Benedictine monks who lived there during the eleventh century and later said were the Magdalene's earthly remains. All that is left of what is supposed to be Mary's body is a bit of bone in a glass cylinder, framed by metallic angels and cherubim, in a darkened underground chapel. While researching this book, I made my own pilgrimage to Vézelay; the Romanesque crypt draws the quiet curiosity of tourists as well as the devoted prayer of worshipers. The sense of devotion seems to vibrate in resonance to the elegant architecture of the site. But a little written notice beside Mary's relics adds nothing new to her story, except for a complaint about the Reformation and the French Revolution disrupting her remains. That is a leitmotif of antimodernist devotion to the Magdalene in France.

The building at Saint-Maximin, in the south of France, is grander and more recent, the scale accentuated by the flattish sun-baked land and smaller buildings that surround it. This thirteenth-century Gothic complex, comprising both basilica and cloister, was deliberately designed to put Vézelay to shame. The Dominican friars of Saint-Maximin said that the bones they had unearthed in their ancient cemetery were the true relics of Mary Magdalene, whatever the Benedictines up north claimed. The crypt still boasts several sarcophagi and inscriptions, and the work of excavating the nearby cemetery, displaying ancient artifacts, and offering tours to pilgrims and visitors occupies Dominican friars to this day. Guided tours focus on a complete glass-encased skull, allegedly Mary Magdalene's.

During the Middle Ages, Vézelay and Saint-Maximin were prominent, although far from unique. Pilgrims streamed every year to scores and scores of sites that venerated the Magdalene, and many of them also claimed her earthly remains, the holy relics of flesh transformed by Jesus. When Jesus said to Mary, "Do not touch me" (John 20:17), legend adds that he touched her on the forehead to ward her off. The Dominicans at Saint-Maximin still repeat the claim that the bit of skin that received Jesus' touch never did decay, but clings tenaciously to her skull. That was a sight worth a long pilgrimage; becoming a pilgrim earned an indulgence from the Pope to escape many years of purgatory, and seeing Mary's flesh on her skull, however shriveled, confirmed the promise of life beyond the grave.

During the Middle Ages, penitents made their way to sites that venerated the Magdalene, from Constantinople to Exeter. Many of these sites offered worshipers the opportunity of seeing the Magdalene's relics, usually bones or cartilage, but several churches boasted her skull, and her alleged fingers and locks of hair were scattered throughout Europe. However a saint died, the anniversary of his or her death became that saint's feast day, marking the transition from this earth to the realm where the saint would be with Jesus forever. Since the eighth century, Orthodox tradition has recognized July 22 as the anniversary of Mary Magdalene's death, and the Catholic calendar fell in with that custom.

Bishops, archbishops, priests, and Popes, civic authorities, kings, and peasants took part in solemn ceremonial parades, known as processions, in her honor. (Both Vézelay and Saint-Maximin continue this tradition on July 22 of each year.) Processions filled cathedrals and churches, whose dedicated purpose was pilgrimage and festival. Dignitaries carried Mary's relics, displayed them on palanquins, and paraded inside the basilica and outside, then pushed through the streets of towns, where worshipful crowds of pilgrims and local people sang, chanted, and danced. Opportunistic vendors sold food and holy trinkets; the inevitable pickpockets, petty thieves, and thugs posed a constant threat. But in the midst of all the danger and noise and expense of pilgrimage and procession, if you could gaze in adoration upon Mary Magdalene's relics as they moved through the streets and churches, and if you had followed the penitential disciplines of the Catholic Church, you felt that your own flesh was being transformed in the way the Magdalene's had been. Each day spent in pilgrimage, every penny dispensed for the glory of Mary's memory, the heavy toll miles on dangerous roads exacted from travelers—all were recompensed by the knowledge that these payments bought a personal lease on heaven.

There were darker claims about the Magdalene—difficult to document or date, but without doubt circulating by the thirteenth century—which claimed she had been Jesus' wife or concubine. On July 22, 1209, Crusaders dispatched by the Pope torched the town of Béziers, punishing the heretical teaching that Mary and Jesus had had sexual relations. One pious chronicler of the time rejoiced "that these disgusting dogs were taken and massacred during the feast of the one that they had insulted." Some fifteen thousand people died that day, including the heretics and those who protected them.

A recent spate of books has connected the legend that Jesus and Mary were lovers with the myth of the Holy Grail, the cup Jesus allegedly used at his last supper. The Grail myth has always been ripe for deconstruction, since it usually involves some sort of metal beaker, a far cry from the earthenware vessels accessible to people of Jesus' time and class. In any case, the real Grail wasn't a cup at all, according to this new variant of the myth; rather, the Grail was Mary's womb—the holy vessel that gave birth to Jesus' children. Esoteric stories of this kind need mysterious names and suppositions of conspiracies to keep them going—and "the Magdalene" (frequently spelled "Magdalen" for added cachet) invokes this whole theory by synecdoche in the minds of many people.

These stories and their variants, whether recounted in the hushed crypts of Vézelay and Saint-Maximin or filmed for the entertainment and curiosity of pilgrims who do not need to leave their couches, blend the memory of Mary Magdalene with the religious sensibilities of the storytellers. The skull at Saint-Maximin, with its alleged patch of skin, and the published genealogies of families claiming lineal descent from Jesus on the basis of forged documents don't tell us much about Mary Magdalene, but they do illuminate the deep attraction she exerts on people of very different orientations. Amid the claims and counterclaims, the common element driving each and every legend forward is the sense of an intimate association between Jesus and Mary. However outlandish the results may seem, that instinct proves accurate. From 25 C.E. onward in Capernaum, Mary was part of Jesus' inner circle. She became his disciple, dedicated to learning his wisdom.

Women as well as men became Jesus' disciples and gathered around him in Capernaum between the years 24 and 27 C.E. The Gospels name several of these female followers, and their place in Jesus' movement is beyond doubt. Nonetheless, many churches have ignored these women, claiming that Jesus chose only twelve disciples, all of them male.

This confusion is due, in part, to the common tendency to confuse disciples with apostles, and to attribute a stature to apostles that doesn't really reflect their role in Jesus' movement. Mary should not be denied the standing within nascent Christianity to which she is entitled simply because she wasn't one of the Twelve.

After the end of his time in Capernaum, during the year 29 C.E., Jesus selected twelve of his disciples, all men, to be his delegates. He whittled his disciples down to that all-male company in response to a specific threat. By exorcising demons and preaching the triumph of God's Kingdom, Jesus took up the protest against Herod Antipas and the forces of Rome that his rabbi, John the Baptist, had pioneered. Herod Antipas, who governed Galilee and Peraea under Roman authority, had ordered Jesus' arrest and execution.

Galilee became a place of mortal danger for Jesus as a result of Herod's threat, so he chose twelve of his disciples to be his envoys or "apostles," the *apostoloi* of the Greek Gospels. He sent them out to preach, heal, and exorcise in the same way he did. They spread Jesus' message while at the same time acting as decoys. This gambit could only work with mature men who could double for him and were capable of traveling quickly and lightly, handling themselves on dangerous roads, and eluding Antipas's agents. Rabbi Jesus' exclusion of women from this company reflects the desperate circumstances he faced and the stark reality that travel in Galilee could be perilous.

Jesus' use of disciples as envoys to befuddle Antipas was a move of strategic genius. But without the larger cohort of disciples in Capernaum who were familiar with him and his teaching, his maneuver would have been impossible. In Capernaum, he gathered more than twelve disciples; they numbered around thirty—and they weren't all men.

---

THE FACT THAT MARY bore the nickname "Magdalene" among Jesus' followers supports the impression that she became part of his inner circle in Capernaum. He gave such names to his closest disciples, after he had known them for an extended period of time. But in looking for the meaning and tenor of the sobriquet "Magdalene," we should not automatically assume it was a compliment; that simply wasn't Jesus' style.

Jesus enjoyed his students' company and loved to tease them. Although Simon was a fisherman, Jesus dubbed him "Rock" (Kepha in Aramaic, Petros in Greek). This name made fun of the instability of Simon's boat when Jesus used it as a platform to preach to crowds on the shore. (Given Simon Peter's sluggishness in understanding what Jesus said on several occasions, "Rock" might allude to some mental density, as well.) The two other leading apostles, James and John, were obviously a noisy pair: Jesus called them *"Boanerges,* that is, Sons of Thunder" (Mark 3:16–17).

The Gospels don't report that Jesus personally gave Mary the name Magdalene. No one can prove he called her that, if that means finding a text that says that in so many words. But by inferring that he identified one Mary among the several other Marys the Gospels mention by calling her "Magdalene," we can explain why that name appears so consistently. Handing out monikers was characteristic of him, and this one stuck. How much less romantic might later legends of Mary's wealth, elegance, and seductiveness have been had scholars and fabulists alike remembered that Magdala was a fishing town, known throughout the region for its fish?

Instead of a portraying her as peasant fishmonger in a stained tunic, portraits of Mary Magdalene during the Renaissance typically depict her as a stylish urban lady prior to her encounter with Jesus, with jewelry, a low-cut dress, and beautifully coiffed hair. To make it unmistakable how vain she was at this stage, she is also shown staring into a mirror; a famous painting by Caravaggio provides one example among many. Church dogma considered that wealth often prompted self-indulgence and indolence, sins to which women were particularly prone and which were gateways to promiscuity.

This theology explains why the medieval Mary Magdalene as well as her successors in later times became a prostitute despite all her wealth. Sexual excess was considered the result of the sin of *luxuria*— too much love of pleasure and too much time to indulge it. According to this way of thinking, women didn't prostitute themselves from necessity; rather, they enjoyed sexual indulgence, which was considered to be sinful even within marriage. Outside of marriage, it was theoretically beyond the pale, although the behavior of those in the royal houses of Europe shows there were different pales for different people.

The Magdalene became a poster girl for female aberration because her sexuality, and the drive to repress female sexuality in particular, took precedence over the evidence of the Gospels and over the commandment in the Torah that humanity should "be fruitful and multiply" (Genesis 1:28). At the same time, inventing and heightening her excesses perpetuated the myth that women were more inclined toward illicit sex than men were. Mary Magdalene became a working girl for the same reason she became rich—so that she could be depicted as the epitome of female indulgence.

By getting the converted Magdalene away from her mirror, out of bed, and into postures of penitential prayer, proponents of Christian piety during the Middle Ages and the Renaissance provided a powerful model for appropriate feminine behavior. At the same time, this image of the Magdalene offered a model of sanctity that covered the spectrum of human behavior, from degradation to the height of religious fervor. A penitent prostitute, however many times she might relapse, could join the procession for Mary, and there are reports of prostitutes in medieval cities who were required to do just that, sometimes after they had been stripped half-naked. At the other end of the spectrum, a cloistered nun could also take Mary's name as her own, a reminder to herself and others of the sexuality that she had left behind in order to follow Christ on her ascetic path. The symbolic power of the Magdalene was so great that even male ascetics took her name.

⸺

THE DESIGNATION "MAGDALENE" distinguishes Mary from the other Marys who were associated with Jesus. Several women named Miriam, the Semitic name anglicized as Mary, were close to Jesus, including his mother and the mother of the disciples James and Joses (Mark 15:40). Moses' sister was called Miriam, and Jews in Galilee and elsewhere proudly embraced that name for their own daughters. But only one of the Miriams in Jesus' group was identified as coming from a town called Magdala in the Aramaic spoken there.

Magdala was important both practically and symbolically for Jesus and his disciples. The name Magdala derives from the term *migdal,* a low stone tower for keeping fish. Holding facilities were part of the complex of stone breakwaters, docks, and reservoirs that distinguished this town of about three thousand residents. Local fishermen netted fish from the Sea of Galilee, especially trying for the plentiful sprat, a small bony fish about six inches long that could be dried for export. They dragged loads of live fish into stone holding tanks and then stockpiled them for drying and salting.

The Galilean sprat was one of Rabbi Jesus' favorite foods, as it was for many of his countrymen. Dried fish was also popular among his followers long after his death and far from Galilee, because Jews and non-Jews in Jesus' movement could eat fish together without raising the question of whether it was kosher, always an issue in cases when meat was involved. In fact, the fish became a symbol for Christians during the second century: The letters of the word *fish* in Greek were an acronym for "Jesus Christ, God's Son, Savior" and stood for Christ.

Fish meant currency, trade, and prosperity for Magdala's Jews. Their dried and salted fish was sold inland in Galilee and across the water in the self-governing Gentile region of Decapolis (a confederation of ten cities). But most significantly, Magdala supplied Tiberias, a vast city that Herod Antipas started building in 19 C.E.

Tiberias proved central to Mary Magdalene's identity all her life. Antipas wanted a new capital for Galilee to replace the garrison town of Sepphoris inland. He chose a spot along the Sea of Galilee, three and a half miles south and somewhat east of Magdala, and named it after Tiberius, the reigning Roman emperor (Josephus *Antiquities* 18.36–38).

The city was built in the Roman style, with aqueducts, temples, baths, theaters, and a stadium. Pious Jews reacted negatively, to say the least, to this monument to Roman values arising in their midst. Temples for idols like Mars, Apollo, and Diana were bad enough. Statues of Venus in the baths made them trysting places for lovers and aspiring lovers of all kinds of tastes, a flagrant example of exactly the kind of behavior that the Torah abhorred. As if this wasn't enough, Antipas desecrated a cemetery to make room for his sprawling metropolis. Devout Jews contended that this made the whole place unclean. In short, the new city of Tiberias was a monument to impurity and idolatry, far worse than the incidental uncleanness involved in doing business with its Gentiles or coping with their slaves.

In the early years of Tiberias, Antipas had to *give* land away to Galilean Jews to get them to live there. The first-century Jewish historian Josephus says that the Jews who moved to the city were the flotsam of Galilee, trash washed up on the shore (Josephus *Antiquities* 18.36–38). The offer of free property drew debtors, drifters, runaway slaves, common criminals, and *mamzerim*. These marginal types had a chance to improve their lot by living alongside the dead and becoming service personnel to the Roman and Herodian occupation forces. Those whose purity was already suspect had little to lose, but from the point of view of the standard practice of Judaism, these settlers became vehicles of the uncleanness that Herod Antipas had released throughout the Galilean region.

Tiberias's proximity to and economic domination of Magdala subjected Mary's town to the forces of impurity. Tiberias produced contagion, and this contagion is what Mary carried in her body. Beyond its obvious association with fish, *this* is what the cognomen "Magdalene" meant to Mary's contemporaries.

Mary's nickname, "Magdalene," also resonates with a name applied to Jesus, linking the two of them in key Gospel texts with a verbal echo. Jesus "the Nazarene" (Nazarenos in Greek) is the grammatical equivalent of "Magdalene" (which also represents the Greek usage), allowing for a change of gender. (In Aramaic, which both Jesus and Mary spoke, the antecedents would have been the equally resonant Natsaraya and Magdalata.) English pronunciation conceals a rhyme that would have caught the ear of any Greek or Aramaic speaker who heard these names spoken aloud: The texts reverberate with an implicit connection between Jesus and Mary.

To call Jesus "the Nazarene" naturally evokes Nazareth as his native village, just as the designation "Magdalene" evokes Magdala on the Sea of Galilee. The verbal echo between the names reflects the geographical proximity between the two villages and their contacts with each other. Mark's Gospel, the earliest of the Gospels and the closest to the Aramaic idioms of Jesus' movement, preserves the resonance between Rabbi Jesus' nickname and Mary's.

The use of "Nazarene" also resonates with the traditional word usage "Nazarite" (Nazir in Hebrew), which means "consecrated." The name Nazarene, paired with the designation "the holy one of God," evokes Jesus' consecration and reinforces his spiritual threat to the world of the demons in the dramatic opening exorcism in Mark's Gospel (1:23–27):

> *And at once there was in their synagogue a person with an unclean spirit. He cried out and said, We have nothing for you, Nazarene Jesus! Have you come to destroy us? I know who you are—the holy one of God! Jesus scolded it and said: Shut up, and get out from him! The unclean spirit convulsed him, sounded with a big sound, and got out from him. And all were astonished.*

The epithet "Nazarene," repeated in Mark's Gospel and echoed in the name "Magdalene," is a constant reminder of the disconcerting sanctity that challenges the whole realm of unclean spirits and at the same time reveals Jesus' identity.

Just as Jesus' contemporaries are "astonished" when the demons in Capernaum shudder in the presence of his purity, the Magdalene and her companions are "completely astonished" by a vision of a young man who tells them Jesus "the Nazarene" has risen from the dead (Mark 16:1–8). Here, too, revelation perplexes those it comes to, and that disturbance echoes through the names Nazarene *and* Magdalene.

To Jesus' mind, Mary was the Magdalene, the woman who had embodied the impurity to which Herod had subjected Magdala. To Mary, Jesus was the Nazarene, the force of Galilean rural purity that could vanquish her demons. Together, these names invoke the way Jesus and Mary became joined, the enduring link between them, and the disturbing thought that the force of the holy cannot be contained by the ordinary conventions of this world.

*Chapter Three*

# SECRET EXORCISM

⬦⬦⬦⬦⬦

Luke's Gospel says that Jesus exorcised Mary of "seven demons" (8:2). That number invited hagiographers during the Middle Ages to imagine Mary being afflicted with all seven Deadly Sins when she first met Jesus. In *The Golden Legend* of Jacobus de Voragine, the compendium of stories of saints compiled during the thirteenth century, Mary was so wealthy that she owned the towns of Magdala and Bethany, near Jerusalem. But her wealth, beauty, and youth brought temptations, and she descended to living as a common prostitute, following a path of degradation that medieval teachers feared for all women.

The number seven resonates with a symbolism broader than the medieval fascination with sin and sexuality: In ancient Hebrew, Babylonian, and Persian numerology, seven represented totality—the eternally reverberating rhythm in Genesis of creation and repose. Israelite fascination with the number represented a version of Babylonian wisdom, rooted in the observation of the heavens. In the lunar calendars of the ancient Near East, the seven-day week marked the phases of the moon: four quarters waxing and waning during the month. Israel embraced this calendar, and Genesis embeds the seven-day week in the structure of nature itself (Genesis 1:3–2:3).

Seven is the symbolic number of totality and fullness, which is why medieval Catholicism conceived of seven Cardinal Virtues to balance the seven Deadly Sins. The seven chakras of Hinduism similarly represent the points at which spiritual energy connects with our physical bodies. Mary's "seven" demons should be viewed in this light. The inherent symbolism of seven in the ancient mind was so strong that the reference to seven demons in Luke's text need not be taken literally.

The multiple exorcisms that Mary underwent probably took about a year, and it was through this process that she emerged as one of Jesus' key disciples. Unlike other exorcists of his time, Jesus freely admitted the difficulty and danger of dealing with unclean spirits. We don't know how many times Jesus met with her, and Luke and the other Gospels are silent about what went on during these sessions. Elsewhere in the New Testament (as in many other ancient literatures), narrators relished tales of demonic possession. The possessed shriek, shred their clothing, and rip their flesh—displays storytellers found hard to resist. Evidently, Mary Magdalene's exorcism did not involve this kind of public drama. Jesus apparently treated her privately.

During this prolonged cure, Jesus initiated Mary into his particular understanding of exorcism. Exorcism is a window into how Rabbi Jesus understood the role of divine Spirit in the world. He called demons "unclean spirits," an unusual way of referring to them picked up by later Christian writers. For Jesus, people taken on their own were as clean as God had made Adam and Eve. If a person became unclean or impure, that was not merely because of contact with exterior objects. Instead, impurity was a disturbance in that person's own spirit, the "unclean spirit," which made him or her want to be impure. To his mind, uncleanness did not arrive from material contagion at all, but from the disturbed desire people conceived to pollute and do harm to themselves.

Uncleanness had to be dealt with in the inward, spiritual personality of those afflicted. "There is nothing outside the person proceeding into one that can defile one, but what proceeds out of the person is what defiles the person" (Mark 7:15). That was why contact with people considered sinners and impure did not bother Jesus, an attitude that scandalized conventional Pharisaic teachers.

Jesus believed that God's Spirit was a far more vital force than the unclean spirits that disturbed humanity. Against demonic infection, a greater force, or countercontagion, could prevail, the positive energy of God's purity. Defilement was an interior force of uncleanness, which needed to be identified and banished by the energy of Spirit.

When Jesus taught his disciples about the practice of exorcism, he specifically recognized the problem of serial possession in a way that mirrors Mary's experience. In Luke's Gospel, this teaching appears shortly after the reference to Mary's possession (11:24–26; see also Matthew 12:43–45): "When the unclean spirit goes out from the person, it passes through waterless places seeking repose, and finding none, then it says, I will return to my house, whence I went out. It goes and finds it swept and adorned. Then it proceeds and takes along other spirits more evil than itself—seven!—and entering dwells there. And the endings of that person become worse than the beginnings."

Rabbi Jesus the exorcist speaks in this passage on the basis of a practitioner's familiarity with demonic behavior. He knows that an unclean spirit, once out of a person, will try to find someplace to go ("seeking repose"), and perhaps will decide to return to the person it came from ("my house"). An exorcist was hardly a success if a person was left like a clean furnished house with open doors and windows waiting for a squatter. That just invited demonic repossession.

Jesus pulls back from any sweeping claim of instantly effective exorcistic power and disparages the results of quick-fix exorcisms. In contrast, the Gospels sporadically make general statements to the effect that Jesus effortlessly exorcised demons. His own words belie that claim. His reference to the demon joining up with "other spirits more evil than itself—seven!" echoes the description of Mary's possession. We can't conclude that Jesus had Mary in mind here; after all, she was possessed by a total of seven demons in Luke's description, while Jesus spoke of seven additional demons. But her case exemplified his concern: a possession that an incautious exorcist might make repeatedly worse.

Wiping out that spiral of possession, Jesus taught, involved installing divine Spirit where demons had been. Mary herself must have been aware both of how desperate she had once been and of the triumph her cure involved. She needed intelligence, insight, and sympathy to follow Jesus' long treatment through to successful completion. The Magdalene felt herself healed by an inner seismic shift that was literally cosmic in its consequences, because it signaled the world's transformation by the arrival of God's Kingdom according to Rabbi Jesus' teaching.

Jesus was not always a gentle therapist. He and his followers insisted on ultimate combat with each and every demon, because each unclean spirit represented them all. Mary became the living, breathing embodiment of the ascendance and power of Spirit. And for all the twists and turns of Christian legend, she has always stood for personal victory over evil.

⚬⚬⚬

IN THE STARK PORTRAYAL of the evil she had overcome, Mary sometimes seems to be the mirror image of Jesus. *The Golden Legend,* which has been mentioned previously, says Christ "embraced her in all his life" and emphasizes that she became his intimate friend, his constant companion, and a source of help on his journeys. Petrarch called her "the sweet friend of God" (*"dulcis amica dei"*). Here legend develops in a way that helps us see better what is already implicit in the most ancient sources: a bond between Jesus and Mary that was close and lasting.

The link between Mary and her rabbi even factored into the way Jesus' opponents responded to him. Mary was said to be possessed by multiple demons; similarly, her rabbi was charged with wielding power that came to him by invoking "Beelzebul," known in Galilee as the prince of all spirits and anglicized as "Beelzebub." In other words, the opposition charged that Jesus was too intimate with the powers of darkness: His practices put him in league with them. That, they said, is why devils did his bidding.

In origin, Beelzebub's name reaches back into the deep pagan past of the Middle East. Beelzebul, god of the underworld, was invoked in spells and sorcery during the period when Jesus lived to drive away demons of disease. In the context of exorcism in first-century Galilee, this accusation against Jesus by his Jewish opponents amounted to a charge of black magic.

Rabbi Jesus responded with a characteristic flash of temper and disregard for logic. He insisted that his exorcisms were beneficial, just like those of the Pharisees who opposed him (see the reference to "your sons" in the passage cited below). He then said that his exorcisms were unique because they signaled the nearness of God's Kingdom, which would overturn Satan's dominion (Matthew 12:24–28):

> *The Pharisees heard and said, He does not throw out demons except by Beelzebul, ruler of the demons! He knew their thoughts and said to them, Every kingdom divided against itself is wasted, and every city or house divided against itself will not stand. And if Satan throws out Satan, he is divided against himself! So how will his kingdom stand? And if I by Beelzebul throw out demons, by whom do your sons throw them out? For this, they themselves will be your judges. But if I throw out demons by God's Spirit, then the kingdom of God has arrived upon you!*

As far as Jesus and his followers were concerned, sensitivity to the world of the spirits, clean and unclean, did not disqualify Mary Magdalene as a disciple, any more than her rabbi's reputation for tackling demons with Beelzebul's authorization disqualified him as an exorcist. In fact, Jesus taught that engaging impure spirits, for all the danger involved, was what dislodged Satan from preeminence in the world, as God's Spirit ushered in God's Kingdom. Contact with the divine in Jesus' teaching transformed unclean spirits with God's Spirit and removed their impure influence. Mary became a living symbol in Jesus' movement of the Spirit by which Jesus removed unclean spirits and brought the divine Kingdom into the human world.

DURING THE TWELFTH CENTURY, a commentator noted that Mary's companionship with Jesus would not have been permitted in the Church of the commentator's own day. He explained that "among the Jews," women were allowed "to go about with religious men," showing that he understood Judaism better than some modern interpreters have. Although the study of history has advanced in many ways since the Middle Ages, in this case there has been a backward movement in the understanding of the place of women and of the feminine within Judaism. Modern Christians still repeat the false claim that women had no place within the leadership of Jewish worship and learning, although that has been disproved again and again.

Mary's gender presented no obstacle to her growing influence among Jesus' disciples. In fact, being a woman was consonant with her emerging power and authority as an expert on exorcism. Rabbi Jesus conceived of divine Spirit, the force that dissolved unclean spirits, as *feminine*.

From the time of the book of Proverbs (that is, the sixth century B.C.E.), Spirit had a firm place in Israelite theology as Yahweh's female partner. The force of Spirit that rushed out from God at the beginning of the cosmos and filled the entire universe was feminine both in the noun's gender (*ruach* in Hebrew) and in the life-giving creativity with which Spirit endowed creation. This divine feminine was closely identified with Wisdom, the eternal consort of Yahweh (Proverbs 8:22–31):

> *Yahweh possessed me in the beginning of his way,*
>> *Before his works of old.*
> *From everlasting I was established,*
>> *From the beginning, before the earth . . .*
> *When he established the heavens, I was there,*
>> *When he drew a circle on the face of the deep.*
> *When he made firm the skies above,*
>> *When the fountains of the deep grew strong,*
> *When he placed the boundary of the sea,*
>> *And waters did not transgress his command,*
>> *When he marked the foundations of the earth,*
> *I was beside him as an architect, and I was daily his delight,*
>> *Pleasuring him in every time,*
> *Pleasuring the expanse of the earth,*
>> *and my delight was with the sons of men.*

The intimacy between Wisdom and Yahweh was so deep and enjoyable that it could be described in erotic terms, and the human delight in Wisdom also promised a life of deep, rewarding pleasure. Just as God might appear by means of the three men who visited Abraham and Sarah at Mamre (Genesis 18:1–15), so divine Spirit conveyed herself with a woman's traits. God's majesty was inconceivably great and varied, and it incorporated feminine as well as masculine identity.

Jesus said he spoke on behalf of Wisdom (Sophia in the Greek text of Luke), and counted himself among her envoys to the world (Luke 11:49): "For this reason also the Wisdom of God said, I myself will delegate to them prophets and apostles." Just as Jesus sent his delegates into Galilee, so he believed Wisdom had delegated him to repair a broken world. In Rabbi Jesus' mind, his whole movement amounted to an apostolic message from Spirit, and therefore from Wisdom.

Western Christianity's fixation since the Middle Ages on an exclusively masculine deity tragically departs from Jesus' conception of God. Even the term for Spirit, which is feminine in Hebrew, becomes neuter in Greek and masculine in Latin, as if the process of translation itself conspired against his thought. Yet at the wellspring of his movement, male and female together reflected the reality of the divine image (Genesis 1:27), and God's Spirit conveyed the full feminine force of divinity.

*Chapter Four*

# MARY'S SIGNATURE

W**E HAVE SEEN THAT** during the year or so it took Jesus to exorcise Mary Magdalene, she came to know his techniques of exorcism better than anyone else. She emerged as one of his key disciples; in the art of dealing with unclean spirits she was an authority who embodied Jesus' bold claim (Matthew 12:28): "If I throw out demons by God's Spirit, then the kingdom of God has arrived upon you!" That gave Mary a privileged position among his disciples; she symbolized the arrival of God's Kingdom, yet Mary's role as a teacher who related Jesus' exorcisms and their significance remains unacknowledged in the Gospels and in scholarship.

In other cases in the Gospels, when a prominent disciple, say Peter, has this kind of close connection to Jesus in relation to stories about him or teachings he crafted and passed on to his followers, scholars identify a source within the Gospels that they attribute to Peter. For example, Peter heads the list of the three premier apostles who were present at the Transfiguration and saw their rabbi transformed with heavenly light and speaking with Moses and Elijah (Mark 9:2–8). Peter was evidently the principal source of this story, the teacher within Jesus' movement who passed it on and shaped its meaning within Christianity's oral tradition until it made its way to the written Gospels.

The Gospels do not identify their authors. Each is simply called "According to Mark," "According to Matthew," "According to Luke," and "According to John," without any indication of who Mark, Matthew, Luke, or John were. How the Gospels were produced, by whom, and in what communities of early Christians has to be inferred from the texts themselves.

Despite the uncertainties involved, thoughtful readers from the start of the second century onward have recognized that the Gospels are not simply books written by individual authors working in isolation. Rather, they are composite editions of differing sources that different communities put together in the generations after Jesus' death.

The Gospels emerged a generation after Jesus' death in the major centers of Christianity. Although certainty eludes any attempt to specify when and where the Gospels were composed, a consensus of scholars agrees that Mark was produced in Rome around 73 C.E.; Matthew in Damascus around 80 C.E.; Luke in Antioch on the Orontes around 90 C.E.; and John in Ephesus around 100 C.E. Both to get at the best evidence about Jesus and to understand how the Gospels developed as literature, it's vital that we identify and analyze the Gospel sources.

Peter provided one of these crucial sources. He and his circle of followers prepared people for baptism by reciting an oral narrative of what God had accomplished with Jesus. Preparing would-be converts to Christianity involved a complex and potentially dangerous process in the Greco-Roman world, unlike the routine baptism of infants in much contemporary practice. The worship of Jesus was, at best, barely tolerated during the first century; sometimes civic-minded enthusiasm burst out against the strange new Christian "superstition" (as the Romans categorized Jesus' movement) in the form of violent local pogroms. Because Christianity was perceived as a strange form of Judaism, Christians could also be swept up in outbursts of violence against Jews. A person who claimed to want to be baptized in Jesus' name might, in fact, be an informer for the magistrate of a city or, worse still, for a gang of narrow-minded thugs.

A good year of probation usually awaited converts, not only to test their sincerity before they learned the identities of everyone in the congregation and joined fully in services of worship but also to ensure that they had learned the congregation's patterns of behavior and ritual and prayer, had refused idolatry and trusted single-mindedly in the one God, and had dedicated themselves to the life of the Spirit and therefore resisted the lures of the material world. All those things had become part and parcel of the Christian message. Each Gospel sets forth that message for its community on the basis of oral sources of evangelism from earlier times.

Peter was especially involved with preparing converts for baptism, and it makes good sense to see him as the source of passages in the Gospels that name him explicitly or that directly concern his baptismal agenda. When scholars tie together a disciple's name with the ritual agenda of that disciple and the oral source he developed, they establish what amounts to that disciple's *signature* within the source. In the case of Peter, he is named repeatedly within passages that were crucial to preparing converts for baptism, so it is widely agreed he had a profound influence on the formation of the Gospels.

If we apply the same logic and refer to the same kind of evidence that has been applied to Peter, Mary Magdalene also emerges as the author of a source of stories that bear her oral signature. She was the single most important conduit of stories concerning Jesus' exorcisms.

Simply by following Jesus, the Magdalene evidenced the purifying presence of Spirit; her experience and her standing put her in an ideal position to craft the detailed exorcism stories we read in the Gospels. Read in order, these three stories amount to a manual of how to cope with unclean spirits (Mark 1:21–28; 5:1–17; 9:14–29): by identifying them, confronting them with divine Spirit, and proclaiming their defeat. They also reflect a progressive development as Jesus honed his craft to deal with increasingly difficult cases of possession.

The first story in the Magdalene source comes from near the beginning of Jesus' time in Capernaum, after 24 C.E. (Mark 1:21–28); the second reflects the period starting with his flight from Herod Antipas in 27 C.E. (Mark 5:1–17); the third appears after Jesus' Transfiguration in 30 C.E. (Mark 9:14–29). Once we recognize these three stories of exorcism as the mainstream of Mary's source, other stories naturally find their place as tributaries.

⸎

THE FIRST EXORCISM STORY, set in the Capernaum synagogue, depicts unclean spirits whose threat dissolves once they are confronted with purity (Mark 1:21–28). Read in detail, this account clearly reveals Mary Magdalene's oral signature. Her perspective governs the presentation of the story, reflecting an insider's knowledge of the deep inner struggle that exorcism involved for a person who was possessed.

Capernaum was a wealthy enough town that its Jewish population could afford to build an actual structure for its "synagogue," a designation that referred in the first century to a congregation of Israelites, with or without a building. This first public act of Jesus in the Gospel According to Mark therefore unfolds in a comparatively dignified space, a small building fitted with benches, where the assembly could comfortably settle local disputes, hear and discuss Scripture, delegate the priestly duties that local Levites fulfilled in Jerusalem, arrange for the collection and transfer of taxes to the Temple, and participate in rituals such as circumcision and burial.

In Mary's story, however, any such routine is derailed when an unclean spirit accosts Jesus. The demon "speaks," but the people in the synagogue hear only inarticulate shrieks. Jesus alone understands the meaning of the sounds. The demon identifies itself with all unclean demons of the spirit world in a fascinating switch of pronouns in the text (here italicized; Mark 1:24): "*We* have nothing for you, Nazarene Jesus! Have you come to destroy *us*? *I* know who you are—the holy one of God!"

The slip back and forth between plural and singular has surprised many readers of Mark's text. Multiple demons—like Mary's seven and the demon who found seven colleagues to repossess a person in Jesus' saying (Luke 11:24–26; Matthew 12:43–45)—signaled the resistance of the demonic world as a whole. Like a military commander who claims that acts by insurgents only prove they are desperate, Jesus viewed the violence of demons as part of the impending defeat of their regime. In addition to its identification with unclean spirits as a whole, the demon in the synagogue also specifies the purpose of Jesus' exorcisms: not simple banishment, but their definitive removal from power. That is what the demon fears on behalf of the whole realm of unclean spirits: regime change instigated by Jesus as the agent of God's Kingdom, the kind of demonic retreat Mary Magdalene had experienced.

Fearing destruction, the unclean spirits act before Jesus speaks, initiating a preemptive strike by naming him. The word *exorcise* (*exorkizo* in Mark's Greek) means to adjure or "to bind with an oath" (which is the aim of an exorcism). The oath was a formula that exorcists usually used to invoke divine power and force demons to obey their commands. Such spells were more effective when they identified a demon by name. In this case, however, the demon jumps in with a spell and a naming of its own. In effect, it is exorcising the exorcist, a notable departure from the well-documented form of exorcism stories in the ancient world.

Mary's source describes this as a very noisy event. The demon "cried out" (Mark 1:23). Jesus shouted back in the rough language of the street, "Shut up, and get out from him!" (v. 25). The demon's obedience came under protest; it "convulsed" its nameless victim and departed with a scream (v. 26).

These acute observations all point toward a storyteller with keen knowledge of the deep combat with evil that Jesus' exorcisms involved, their raucous quality, and the danger that the exorcist would be defeated. Moreover, the storyteller knew how Jesus interpreted the demons' wordless shout (Mark 1:34), as an admission of ultimate defeat. Whoever conveyed this story had to have known both what went on and what Jesus thought about it. Mary Magdalene best fits the description of that storyteller.

⸻

By taking Mary's influence into account, we can understand why, unlike most ancient stories of exorcism, Mark's narratives depict the demons' violent resistance to Jesus instead of portraying him as a self-confident exorcist. This comes out most vividly in the second story from the Magdalene source, which is set in Decapolis, just on the other side of the Sea of Galilee from Magdala.

There, Jesus confronts a horde of demons that have taken up residence in a man who inhabits a cemetery because of his affliction (Mark 5:1–17; Luke 8:26–37; Matthew 8:28–34). When Jesus demands to know the demons' names (a standard feature in exorcisms of the time), they say they are "legion," the designation for a six-thousand-man Roman military unit. The story is related in the same simple, vigorous, abrupt voice of the Capernaum exorcism (Mark 5:1–13), although the action is more complicated:

*And they came to the opposite side of the Sea, into the area of the Gerasenes. He got out from the boat, and at once there met him from the tombs a person with an unclean spirit. He had the habitation among the tombs, and no one was any longer able—even with a chain—to bind him. (For many times he had been bound with fetters and chains, and the chains were torn apart by him, and the fetters smashed, and no one was capable of subduing him. And all night and day he was among the tombs and in the hills, shouting and wounding himself with stones.) He saw Jesus from a distance, and ran and worshipped him, and shouting with a big sound he says, I have nothing for you, Jesus Son of the highest God! I adjure you by God, do not torment me! Because he had been saying to him, Unclean spirit, get out from the person! And he interrogated him, What is your name? And it says to him, Legion is my name, because we are many. And they summoned him a lot, so that he would not dispatch them outside of the area. Yet there was there by the hill a big herd of pigs grazing. They summoned him and said, Send us into the pigs, so that we may enter into them. And he permitted them. The unclean spirits got out and entered into the pigs, and the herd rushed over the cliff into the sea, about two thousand, and they were choked in the sea.*

Several stark images (the victim's habitation in a cemetery, his habit of wounding himself to the point of bleeding, his residence in Gentile territory) indicate that this exorcism targets uncleanness as the evil Jesus addressed in all his exorcisms. The possessed man embodies everything unholy and is named "legion" just in case a hearer or reader might miss the point of where the contagion came from. When Rabbi Jesus drove demons out of people, he acted on behalf of those possessed, but we can clearly see that he was also acting against the source of impurity—Rome and Rome's collaborator, Herod Antipas. Mary Magdalene, whose town lay adjacent to Antipas's new capital, knew the reality of this uncleanness. With equal clarity, the narrative drives home the theme of the struggle involved in this exorcism. The demons were numerous, talked back to Jesus, and did not obey a direct command.

It was unusual in the ancient world to insist that the demons formed a violent, coordinated front of impurity, and bizarre to depict them as dictating how an exorcist should handle them. The legion story deliberately engages in exaggeration, to the point that no commentator has been able to draw the line between the story's symbolic meaning and the literal event it depicts. Still, the symbolic meaning remains clear no matter how literally we take the details: As the divine Kingdom takes root, Rome will be dislodged. Roman demons are no more threatening than panicked pigs; they will neutralize themselves in God's encompassing purity, which is as deep as the sea.

⸙

DEFINITIVE EXORCISM SIGNALED an ultimate change in humanity within Jesus' vision and in Mary's experience. In her narrative, the man who had been possessed with a legion of demons went on to become the first messenger of Jesus in Gentile territory (Mark 5:18–20). After his return from Decapolis to Galilee (in 29 C.E.), Jesus sent out twelve of his disciples. They acted on his behalf, announcing the Kingdom, healing people, cleansing them of impurity, throwing out their demons. When they did so, Jesus said (in a passage I do not assign to the Magdalene source) that he saw Satan fall like lightning from heaven, robbed of his old power (Luke 10:18). Removing impurity by naming it made Satan fall, and other teachings of Jesus unconnected with the stories Mary told confirm this perspective.

The Gospels insist on the violence of the confrontation between Jesus and unclean spirits precisely because it demonstrates the cosmic significance of his actions. As Jesus pressed home the significance of removing demons from people, he evolved as a religious persona. He became increasingly prophetic—his words and deeds took on the character of signs, indicating how God was acting or about to act in the world. Jesus and Mary Magdalene explained why demons shouted at Jesus, and he back at them: They resisted him, crying out his name and spiritual identity, because their encounter with him was a war of worlds.

Mary told the story of the legion of demons from the sympathetic perspective of someone who could speak from firsthand experience of being exorcised. A legion consisted of some six thousand soldiers, and auxiliary troops co-opted by the legion could equal that number. Although Mary's seven demons were by no means literally legion, she could tell this story because she knew the real depth of the cosmic antagonism involved in Jesus' exorcism and had felt that antagonism in her own body.

⤜⋙⋘⤛

IMMEDIATELY BEFORE THE third principal exorcism story in the Magdalene source, Jesus—transformed in divine glory and talking with Moses and Elijah (Mark 9:2–8)—appears to Peter, James, and John. Just as he manifested himself to his disciples in the visionary experience of the Transfiguration as a master comparable to Elijah and Moses, so the story in Mary's source (Mark 9:14–29) expresses Jesus' vehement insistence on the power of Spirit in contrast to the tentative quality of the efforts of his disciples, who had been unable to deal with the demon at hand. Jesus explained to them (Mark 9:29): "This sort can go out by nothing except by prayer." By this time, he was heading toward his final days in Jerusalem, and Jesus had become a master exorcist, locked in cosmic struggle with Satan in a way that was beyond his followers' capacity to emulate and sometimes even to understand.

As his own spirituality evolved, Jesus had found ways to magnify awareness that all impurity dissolves in the holiness of Spirit, and Mary Magdalene was there to trace that development. She knew Jesus' method in this domain inside and out, and exorcism stories from her source reflect this knowledge. In the first story, set in Capernaum's synagogue, the demon defeated itself by acknowledging the purity it confronted in Jesus, "the holy one of God," and Jesus' technique could involve—as in the case of the "legion"—giving unclean spirits what they said they wanted to speed their departure.

In the third principal story, which involves a grievously possessed child, Jesus explains to the distraught father that "everything is possible to one who believes" (Mark 9:23). Faith established the setting of successful therapy, and Mary's faithful discipleship, evidenced by her following Jesus from Capernaum to Jerusalem, symbolized the environment of effective treatment.

Scholars have not yet examined Mary's influence on the Gospels with the same vigor that they have investigated Peter's, Paul's, James's, or Barnabas's. They have had access to the relevant information in the Gospels, and they have honed their analytic tools where other disciples and their sources are concerned. But they have ignored or downplayed Mary's explicit connection with Jesus' exorcisms and disregarded evidence that it was Mary who shaped and conveyed the stories of Jesus' exorcisms in the Gospels. Mary Magdalene's voice has echoed anonymously in the Gospels for nearly two millennia. Now it is time to identify the speaker and appreciate her words.

⸺⸺

LISTENING TO MARY MAGDALENE's source can help us to understand not only Mary herself but also a deeply charismatic and prophetic strand of Christianity. Rooted in Jesus' practice, this impulse adamantly confronts the forces of uncleanness with the power of God's Spirit.

Not all his followers embraced the violence of Jesus' exorcisms all the time. We learn of this not from the Magdalene source but from another run of material that spells out Jesus' exorcistic theory in his own words and represents his conflict with those around him. This teaching confirms, from Jesus' point of view, exactly the sense of cosmic struggle and resistance that the Magdalene source narrates.

Mark's Gospel indicates that once Jesus' family tried to seize him physically; he seemed to them "beside himself" (3:21). If you did not share Jesus' vision, he could easily seem to be out of his mind. Rabbis of this period also characterized another mystic, Simon ben Zoma, as "beside himself" because he was prone to ecstasy in the midst of daily life.

His family's well-meaning, conventional concern for Jesus only stoked his insistence on confrontation with Satan (Mark 3:22–27). He wasn't crazy or possessed by Beelzebul at all, he insisted. Rather, he battled directly in his exorcisms with "the strong man," the honcho of all demons. Rabbi Jesus said, "No one, however, can enter the home of the strong man to rob his vessels unless he first binds the strong man, and then he will rob his home" (v. 27). Once he was bound, Jesus could pillage his goods! Jesus didn't want to leave a possessed person's body open for unclean spirits to return to with ever more impure companions; instead, he would sweep Satan out of house and home.

He was convinced that Satan's defeat completed the Kingdom's arrival; one implied the other, and the Spirit of God effected them both. When the Spirit—conceived of as female in Jesus' theology—moves in this world, she displaces demons and installs divine justice. That is why, speaking about his exorcisms, Jesus said that denying the Holy Spirit was the one sin that would not be pardoned (Mark 3:28–30): "Everything will be forgiven people, sins and curses (as much as they curse), but whoever curses the Holy Spirit will never ever have release but is liable for a perpetual sin." The unpardonable sin is to deny the Holy Spirit as she transforms the world by dissolving evil. The consistency of Jesus' thinking about exorcism is striking, and echoes the Magdalene source.

Luke's naming of Mary in personal connection with repeated exorcism enables us to say that Mary Magdalene told stories about Jesus—especially the detailed stories of his exorcisms—that we can read today in the Gospels. She then takes her place beside apostles who also influenced how the message about Jesus was preached and taught. The exorcism stories in the Gospels bear her signature. One of the most vital and enduring teachings of Jesus she helped craft concerned how the power from God could dissolve evil by letting it name itself for what it was, and she showed how he put that teaching into practice. Medieval legend conveyed its awareness of Mary's importance within this field in its own way. Gherardesca da Pisa, who died in 1269, spoke of Mary as intervening in her own bloody battle with a demon, then as helping her care for her wounds.

Mary knew that the demons' most fearsome weapon, deployed to resist Jesus' exorcism, was their unique knowledge of his identity. Up until the point of the first exorcism story in Mark, no one in the Gospel has called Jesus "the holy one of God." No one will ever call him that again. The demons express insight into Jesus' mysterious identity, what scholars for more than a century have called "the messianic secret." By telling this story and stories like it, Mary indicated that she knew this secret. The nameless man in Capernaum's synagogue alone named Jesus as "the holy one of God"; the man with the legion of demons uniquely called Jesus "Son of highest God" (Mark 5:7). Mary Magdalene, Jesus' companion in exorcism, understood the secret that his struggle with the demons involved.

These inarticulate demonic cries beg a question: If the demons uniquely knew Jesus' spiritual identity, and he alone understood what they said, to whom did he disclose this knowledge? Once again, Mary Magdalene's oral signature leads the way to an answer. The first exorcism in Mark uniquely identifies Jesus as "the holy one of God," and then defines what the phrase means. The demon, as elsewhere in the Gospels, is an "unclean spirit." As we've seen, in Jesus' analysis, uncleanness resides within a human being, rather than in exterior objects. That which defiles comes from within and moves out, rather than the reverse. That conception is crucial to this story. Possession in Rabbi

Jesus' view happened only with a person's tacit consent or inadvertence, so that uncleanness could be removed by conscious intention.

The unclean spirit in the synagogue—a source of impurity—designated Jesus as a source of purity, "the holy one of God." That is why Jesus' presence was a threat to that demon, and the demonic world as a whole. The unspecified number of demons in the synagogue, the "legion" in the cemetery, the demon who resisted Jesus' disciples, the "seven" who departed from Mary Magdalene—all in their different ways signal the demonic axis as a whole. The spiritual combat between Jesus and the forces of impurity was resolved because the unclean spirits recognized purity when they experienced it. Violent though their rebellion seemed, the demons ultimately recognized their own nonexistence. Their only power was denial. They could rebel against God's pure purpose, but only with the empty complaint of their own impotence. Finally, the demons had no power at all. They drowned in their own knowledge as surely as the legion did once they revealed themselves in the pigs. In Mary's telling, Rome itself headed toward the same fate.

The Gospels present only three detailed stories of the exorcisms of Jesus. In each of them, the emphasis on Jesus' assertion of the purity of Spirit, the resistance of the demonic world, impurity, struggle, and the possessed person's breakthrough to integrity come to vivid, precise expression. This oral source, which shines through the tightly coordinated but different versions in Matthew, Mark, and Luke, is the nearest approach there is to Jesus' actual technique of meeting the challenge of uncleanness and evil. Not only in cases of exorcism, which have a long history in the West, but also in Christian approaches to the miseries of addiction, compulsion, aimless violence, and purposeful wrongdoing by people and nations, the basic faith that evil named is evil removed has animated the conduct of millions of people who have read the Gospels. Mary Magdalene, anonymously but effectively, has instructed them all.

⸎

THE PERSPECTIVE FROM WHICH the detailed stories of exorcism in the Gospels are told reveals Mary Magdalene's own experience. She had known the violent contention within her own body between the demons and Jesus' desire to expel them from her forever. The opening demonic scream, "We have nothing for you," is echoed in the story of the man with a legion of demons. The tortured man cries out, "I have nothing for you" (Mark 5:7), and soon it is clear that "I" conceals a demonic multitude. Within her body and mind, contrary and convulsive forces had once put Mary at odds with herself, so that she was controlled by impulses not her own. When one is confronted by the knowledge of purity, however, what seems threatening in impurity simply dissolves. Obsessions stop, replaced by conscious choice among the desires a person might or might not assent to. Purity within means bodily integrity and cleanness in action. That is the wisdom behind Jesus' exorcisms. It was wisdom hard won by Mary from her own experience. The truth of it made her proudly bear the nickname "the Magdalene."

Mary's role in the development of the Gospels has been passed over. The time has come to put that right, and to understand that she was a principal source in understanding Jesus' legacy. Marguerite would have been intrigued by the Magdalene's crucial contribution to the way people in the first century understood Jesus' teaching about confronting evil in this world with the Spirit that heralds the Kingdom of God. Mary's influence on how the founders of Christianity saw Spirit moving in the world would have assured Marguerite that someone was indeed there for her, both on the other side of heaven's gate and in the daily struggle of being alive.

*Chapter Five*

# NAMELESS ANOINTER

By virtue of what she did, what she taught, and who she was, Mary Magdalene emerged as the most influential woman in Rabbi Jesus' movement. She also proved his persistent partner during the most fraught period of his life.

In 27 C.E., Jesus was forced to flee from Capernaum under threat of death from Herod Antipas. He began four years of wandering and flight, experimenting at first with forays into Gentile territory east of Galilee (around Decapolis) and later to the west (near Tyre and Sidon). As the story of the man with the "legion" of demons shows, however, Rabbi Jesus did not get along well—to say the least—with the impurity of Gentile living. By the end of that story, the damage he caused to a herd of swine resulted in the local people asking him to leave (Mark 5:17). The same kind of incompatibility emerged when he met a Gentile woman near Tyre and Sidon. When she asked him for healing on behalf of her daughter, he rebuffed her at first, saying, "It is not fair to take the bread of the children and throw it to the dogs" (Mark 7:27). Although the nameless woman got the better of Rabbi Jesus' hostility to foreigners on that particular occasion, his practice and temperament proved incompatible with sustained residence among non-Israelites. He returned to Galilee, whatever the risks involved.

During this period, Mary must have traveled with Jesus—she witnessed his exorcism in Decapolis, for example. But the extent of her travel was limited by her vulnerability as a woman.

Jesus coordinated his movements with his other disciples, the dozens who were not included among the Twelve but who nonetheless had mastered his teaching and practice. They lived in the towns and villages of Galilee, healing in the way Jesus had taught them, casting out demons, announcing the Kingdom of God, and meditating on the presence of God's Spirit in their midst as they prayed and shared meals together. Mary was part of this group. Most of Jesus' movement kept undercover; the peasant countryside of Galilee camouflaged them, while the twelve apostles and Jesus kept up a hectic pace of movement, diversion, challenge, and flight in order to avoid Herod Antipas.

Mary probably remained around Magdala while the Twelve fanned out through Galilee from the year 29. But in 31 C.E., Rabbi Jesus changed strategy. The opposition of Herod Antipas had only strengthened Jesus' appeal to Galilee's disenfranchised Jews, some of whom wanted the charismatic rabbi to head a violent onslaught against Antipas and his Roman protectors. The story of Jesus' Temptations, when Satan lured him with the promise of ruling "all the kingdoms of the world" (Matthew 4:8; Luke 4:5), encapsulates Jesus' visionary experience at this time. Jesus rejected the satanic offer. Instead of an army, he led a pilgrimage to Jerusalem for the Feast of Tabernacles, and Mary Magdalene was among the pilgrims. Jesus' target was not a Roman installation, but the Temple in Jerusalem, where he believed he and his followers could change the world and welcome God's Kingdom into the land of Israel by offering sacrifice on Mount Zion in the way that the God of Israel desired. Following the prophecy of Zechariah (chapter 14), Rabbi Jesus believed that true sacrifice would bring both the end of Israel's oppression and the opening of the Temple to all humanity, both Jews and non-Jews.

Mary Magdalene was with him when Jesus arrived in Jerusalem, galvanizing the festal crowds during the feast of Sukkot (or Tabernacles) in the autumn of 31 C.E. She saw his reaction when he learned that Caiaphas, the high priest of the time, had authorized trading in the Temple, instead of maintaining the ancient practice—and Zechariah's prophecy—that Israelites offer the work of their own hands there. She would have observed the planning in Bethany for Jesus' onslaught on the Temple, when a small army of disciples and enthusiasts, some 150 or 200 men, joined Jesus one morning to drive out the vendors and the animals Caiaphas had allowed in the Temple's twenty-five-acre southern outer court. She would have been aware of Jesus' reaction when he discovered that one of his sympathizers in Jerusalem, a thug named Barabbas, had committed murder during the Temple raid.

⸙⸙⸙

DURING THE WHOLE of this tumultuous period, from Jesus' early success in Capernaum until his last days in Jerusalem, Mary Magdalene was much more than a skilled practitioner of exorcism. She was also an adept of other spiritual practices. Jesus, Mary, and the other disciples practiced anointing, which was associated with exorcism and healing. When Jesus sent out the twelve apostles to heal, there is reference to anointing, as if it were self-evident that this was part of their standard practices (Mark 6:13). It was exactly that during this period in Judaism, and there is excellent evidence that oiling skin was a routine ritual in Jesus' movement, and that Mary Magdalene was its preeminent practitioner.

Over the course of his last weeks in Jerusalem, Jesus designated Mary as his movement's paradigmatic anointer. Christianity in its modern form has all but forgotten this sacrament of unction as well as its indissoluble link with Mary Magdalene. But the Gospels still preserve her connection with a pivotal sacramental moment in Jesus' life. Mark's Gospel provides the earliest, most richly textured account of this ritual event, in an anointing set in Bethany, the base of Jesus' movement during the last months of his life (14:3–9):

> *He was in Bethany in the home of Simon the scabby [not really a "leper," as in the traditional translation], recumbent, and there came a woman who had an alabaster of genuine, expensive nard ointment. Smashing the alabaster, she poured over his head. But there were some angry among themselves. Why has this waste of the ointment happened? Because this ointment could have been sold for more than three hundred denarii and given to the poor! And they were upbraiding her. But Jesus said, Leave her: why are you making problems for her? She has done a fine deed with me. Because you always have the poor with yourselves, and whenever you want, you can do them good, but me you do not always have. She acted with what she had; she undertook to oil my body for burial. Amen I say to you, wherever the message is proclaimed in the whole world, what she did will also be spoken of in memory of her.*

"What she did will also be spoken of in memory of her." Jesus obliges us to remember the woman's gesture, but at the same time Mark's Gospel withholds her actual identity. This blatant ambivalence is crucial to understanding the text. Does the text in some way let us know who she is, or does it make Jesus' command impossible to fulfill? Mark's Gospel puts the integrity of Jesus' message on the line. By Jesus' own words in Mark, the first known text to bear the name "Gospel," the woman belongs in his announcement of God's Kingdom, Jesus' oral gospel. He calls those who hear him to believe in this gospel (Mark 1:15). The term *euangelion* in Greek reflects the Aramaic word *besora,* a message of triumph of the victory of God's Kingdom. Hence Jesus' clarion preaching as Mark recounts it (1:15): "Time has been fulfilled, and the kingdom of God has approached: repent and believe in the gospel." By Jesus' specific command, that message includes reference to the woman who carried her alabaster to Jesus.

The woman's identity evidently did not remain a secret to those who first heard Mark's Gospel. Her name and personality were hidden only temporarily, until Mark's hearers could become acquainted not only with the Gospel as recited to them, and which we know in its written form, but also with the now-lost oral gospel that enriched their instruction. Baptism, the goal that drew the people who heard the Gospel, opened wide the doors of recognition that the written text had only pushed ajar. In the communities where each Gospel was written (Rome in the case of Mark), master teachers, some of them personally acquainted with Peter, Mary Magdalene, and other disciples, filled in the instruction available in written form with oral memories.

Trace references to these oral memories surface in the Gospel According to Mark. Relying on Mark alone, we would not know that Jesus taught his disciples the Lord's Prayer, that he personally appeared to them alive after his death, or that there was a controversy about his birth. This Gospel contains no overt mention of these topics. Yet, as written, Mark's Gospel also assumes that people prepared for baptism will know how to pray, understand that Jesus' disciples experienced his living presence after his death, and appreciate that Jesus was not an ordinary child who grew up in a conventional family. Primitive Christianity was an oral movement, not a book club, and therefore some of its deepest truths were not committed to writing. The identity of the nameless anointer is a case of Mark intimating more than is literally said.

Mark's Gospel displays a mastery of the rhetoric of the unspoken.

It is a finely balanced text, a hybrid of oral wisdom and literary naïveté that relies on inference. One such inference is that Mary Magdalene is the nameless anointer, which Eastern Orthodox and medieval interpreters correctly surmised—unlike many of their modern counterparts. She is not named, but the clear implication of the Gospel overall when it is read from beginning to end (as it would have been recited to those who prepared for baptism) is that she anointed Jesus prior to his death, and that he wanted her name remembered.

The key to her identity appears later in Mark's text (which we look at in more detail later). What's important to understand at this point is that Mark identifies Mary Magdalene as the principal figure among the women at the mouth of Jesus' tomb after his Crucifixion, and that she undertakes a key ritual action associated with interment— anointing (Mark 16:1): "And when Sabbath elapsed, Mary Magdalene and Mary of James and Salome purchased spices so they could go anoint him." Among these three women, Mary Magdalene foremost had observed where Jesus had been interred by Joseph of Arimathea (Mark 15:47). Mary is the indispensable character in Mark's account of the Resurrection, the pivot of the action around whom the final events turn. She, by name and by action, embodies the connection between Jesus' interment and the angelic announcement to the same Mary Magdalene (16:6–7) that Jesus has been raised from the dead. She connects his death and Resurrection, not only by who she is but also by what she does: Mary Magdalene established the place of anointing as a central ritual in Christianity, recollecting Jesus' death and pointing forward to his Resurrection.

In this way, Mark implies, rather than states, Mary's identity as the woman with the ointment, so our inference is not a deductive certainty. An implication is just that and shouldn't be confused with proof: It leaves traces for the audience of the Gospel to infer its meaning. But read without this inference, Mark breaks Jesus' promise that "wherever the message is proclaimed in the whole world, what she did will also be spoken of in memory of her" (Mark 14:9). By permitting ourselves this inference, we allow the Gospel not to contradict the very saying of Jesus that it takes pains to convey.

Before we turn our attention to the vitally important scene of the women present at the mouth of Jesus' tomb, to which Mary Magdalene's anointing points, we need to appreciate the sense of ritual anointing as practiced within Jesus' movement. It is to an examination of this practice, and its impact on how legend would look at Mary, that we now turn.

*Chapter Six*

# "THY NAME IS AS OIL POURED FORTH"

⌘

Olive oil was the universal solvent of antiquity, a pervasive and valued commodity throughout the Mediterranean basin. Lye soap was for beating into dirty clothes (on those occasions when clothing was washed thoroughly), and did human skin no good. Oil was a prized substance to cleanse and treat skin, to dress wounds, to serve as a base for differing scents, and to condition hair and beards, as well as for preparing and cooking food.

Anointing expressed the lush enjoyment of life; oil running down a man's beard all the way to the "skirts of his garments" (Psalms 133:2) celebrated physical well-being and the pleasure of God's blessing. The king from the house of David was rubbed with oil in a special rite to designate him as sole monarch of Israel, and the high priest enjoyed a similar ritual designed for him alone. Prophets sometimes anointed their successors, and the dead were anointed at burial, an expression of the care and attention by those who mourned their passing. Healers and magi throughout the ancient world knew how to convey their particular techniques of curing disease by their distinctive practices of unction.

Women featured prominently among practitioners of anointing in ancient Judaism. They ran their households, and their domestic arts included unction as a medium of healing. Experienced healers recited therapeutic formulae as they applied oil to relatives or friends. The Talmud of Jerusalem, a Rabbinic commentary on the Mishnah finalized during the fourth century C.E., is an especially rich source for appreciating these traditional practices. The cases involved were sometimes life-threatening, but anointing also dealt with benign conditions. A person with pain in the lower body (Talmud of Jerusalem, Shabbat 14:3, 4) could have the ache treated with oil without fear of breaking the prohibition against work on the Sabbath.

Luke's Gospel says that Mary Magdalene and other women "served" or "ministered to" Jesus and his disciples (8:3). In the Greek of this Gospel—and the Hellenistic mentality it represents—this service included financial support, lodging, work with one's hands for the immediate needs of the fellowship, and labor for the divine Kingdom. The needs of both practical support and evangelical action were met by Mary's anointing, a form of provision at least as valuable as money.

Household practices of anointing led some rabbis to charge women in general with practicing magic. Why did the Law of Moses say that one should not permit a *witch* to live (Exodus 22:18), rather than any sorcerer, whether male or female? The answer to that question was obvious enough (Talmud of Jerusalem, Sanhedrin 7:13): "Torah has taught you how things really are, for the vast majority who practice sorcery are women."

Rabbi Jesus nonetheless endorsed the practice of anointing and provided the ritual with a theory all his own. His anointing with oil carried a precise significance, specifically conveyed in the Gospel According to Luke, and designed to be enacted by his followers. In his native Nazareth during prayers on the Sabbath, he paraphrased a passage from the Book of Isaiah, changing its meaning to apply to his own experience. (In this quotation, I have emphasized terms that he altered in the text from Isaiah.) Here is what he said in the most ancient form of his words (Luke 4:18):

> *The Spirit of the Lord is upon* you, *on account of which*
> *he has anointed* you *to announce triumph to the poor;*
> *And he has delegated me to proclaim to the captives release,*
> *and to the blind sight*
> *—and* I *will free the broken with release . . .*

Jesus' anointing with Spirit moved him to preach, liberate his contemporaries from their unclean spirits, and heal: He himself designated the Spirit as the source of this whole program of revelation.

In the synagogue, Rabbi Jesus did not quote the familiar words from the Book of Isaiah: "The Spirit of the Lord is upon me . . ." (61:1). Instead, he insisted on changing the words, implying that he enjoyed a special relationship with God, and that since his time with John the Baptist, the Holy Spirit had anointed him. This provoked a scandal, and the congregation very nearly stoned him. After all, Jesus was a *mamzer,* an Israelite without a publicly recognized father, and therefore, according to the Torah (Deuteronomy 23:2), without right of entry into the local congregation.

He barely escaped the violence of the congregation that day, and after that experience he always spoke more discreetly of his spiritual anointing. But with or without this painfully learned discretion, he recognized that Spirit was the engine of his action and teaching, the driving force of his exorcisms in particular.

The words of Peter, quoted in the book of Acts, similarly identify Jesus as the one whom God "anointed with Holy Spirit and power, who proceeded to do good and heal those oppressed by the devil, because God was with him" (10:38). Mary Magdalene and her companions took up this programmatic activity, as did the more famous apostles. Mark's Gospel (6:13) reports that when these disciples went out to offer Jesus' healing therapy in his name, "they threw out many demons and anointed with oil many who were ill, and healed them."

Anointing conveyed Spirit, to Jesus' mind, and he wanted his followers to anoint people. Even those texts that attempt to reduce or ignore Mary Magdalene's crucial role among Jesus' disciples confirm her importance within this crucial ritual.

⸺∞⸺

WARY OF MARY MAGDALENE's influence, the Gospel According to Luke ignores her anointing of Jesus prior to his death. A different anointing scene altogether, involving a different woman (7:36–50), takes the place in Luke of Mark's account of Mary's anointing. Jesus laced this woman's act with special significance, and I have no doubt that here Luke gives us an authentic scene from Jesus' life, although the decision to repress Mary Magdalene's anointing is egregious. Nonetheless, the story helpfully illustrates that women other than Mary Magdalene practiced anointing within Jesus' movement.

In Luke's anointing story, a Pharisee named Simon hosts a meal for Jesus in Capernaum (Luke 7:36–50). The whole scene runs counter to the bias against Pharisees in the Gospels, proving that not all Pharisees were Jesus' enemies. Many of them respected him and were curious about his teaching; some even welcomed him into their homes.

Simon must have been wealthy, perhaps a merchant dealing in olive oil from Galilee, which was treasured by Jews as far away as Syria for its quality and because it was kosher. The Pharisee's house would have been large and well appointed, but without the decadent Hellenistic opulence of the homes whose ostentatious wealth Rabbi Jesus criticized.

By inviting Jesus into his home, Simon also opened his doors to Jesus' disciples, followers, and others who came to listen to the rabbi and eat with him out of simple curiosity. One of the curious was a woman described in Luke as "sinful." When she saw Jesus and heard him speak, she cast herself at his feet, repenting of her sins. She wept and "began with tears to wet his feet and with the hair of her head she wiped and kissed his feet" (Luke 7:38). Her act doubtless silenced the chattering, rambunctious crowd. His feet would have been filthy from Capernaum's streets—and the washing of his feet with her hair and tears remains a beautiful, haunting image.

Legends developed after the time of the New Testament have portrayed her as a prostitute, but there is no evidence of that. The fact that the woman is simply called "sinful," without explanation, conceivably intimates that somehow she had been known for sexual impropriety. But there are many, many sins that do not involve sex; Peter calls himself "sinful" in Luke 5:8, yet commentators do not accuse him of prostitution. At any rate, even in cases where women were blamed for their sexual conduct, prostitution was often not at issue. Perhaps the woman in Luke had had a series of spouses, as the Samaritan woman had (see John 4:5–42). Another possibility is that she had flouted the rules that sought to govern whether an Israelite from one social group could marry someone from a different group. Given the elegant gesture with her hair, it is more likely she pursued the proscribed profession of a hairdresser, which many rabbis saw as bordering on prostitution, since touching in private or semiprivate was involved. After all, although the Pharisee objects to her touching Jesus, she is not barred from his house, as a truly notorious sinner might have been.

The Pharisee was offended that Jesus accepted the touch of someone considered a sinner, but Jesus pronounced that her sins had been forgiven, articulating one of his core principles (Luke 7:47): "Her many sins have been released, because she loved much: but to whom little is released, loves little." Those who are unaware of how much they have been forgiven love only a little. By contrast, those who consciously accept divine forgiveness, which releases them from their self-imposed shackles, are alive to the bounty that comes from God alone and are willing to extend that forgiving power to others by performing generous, spontaneous acts like the hairdresser's. Her lavish embrace of Jesus was itself an extension of divine compassion, proof that she had been taken up and purified by God's love.

Centuries after the New Testament was written, Christian teachers such as Pope Gregory the Great identified this woman as Mary Magdalene and stamped her as a woman of ill repute:

> *Mary Magdalene, "who had been a sinner in the city" [Luke 7:37], loved the Truth, and so washed away with her tears the stains of wickedness. Thus was fulfilled the voice of the Truth who said, "Her many sins have been forgiven her, because she loved much" [Luke 7:47]. . . . She had abandoned her wicked ways, and washed away the stains of heart and body with her tears, and touched the feet of her Redeemer.*

That identification, from a sermon preached in 594, fed Mary's reputation as a prostitute during the Middle Ages.

In fact, Luke refers to Mary Magdalene by name only *after* this story, as if she had not been mentioned before. In chapter 8 (v. 2) of this Gospel, Luke introduces Mary Magdalene without any reference back to the story of the woman who anointed Jesus' feet. Critical scholarship since 1517 has formally refuted the confusion between Mary and the woman in chapter 7 of Luke's Gospel. They were obviously two different women, although confused in the West for a thousand years (and more, as we shall see).

Unfortunately, confusions can become dogma. After he proved that the anointer in Capernaum was not Mary Magdalene, Jacques Lefèvre d'Etaples saw his teaching banned by the University of Paris, which went on to pursue him as a heretic in 1523. Instead of successfully making the telling but modest point he had in mind, he found his argument taken up as a key point of contention during the sixteenth century; in France critical discussion of Mary attracted nearly as much opprobrium as the works of Martin Luther.

While marginalizing Mary Magdalene, Luke's Gospel paradoxically winds up confirming the centrality of unction within Jesus' movement. (Luke's desire to erase Mary's anointing scene reflects a pattern within the Gospels as a whole, as we shall see.) Pope Gregory's sermon was obviously wrong in identifying the nameless woman as Mary, but in the way of many medieval theologians, he showed himself more sensitive to the poetics of the Gospels than some modern commentators. The act of the anonymous anointer in chapter 7 of Luke's Gospel does *take the place* of Mary's unction in Mark's Gospel; the hair and tears wiping Jesus' feet represent the anointing he desired and practiced all through his ministry.

⎯∽∾∽⎯

MARY AND HER NAMELESS COLLEAGUE in chapter 7 of Luke's Gospel both show what other ancient documents also demonstrate: Women in Jewish antiquity, particularly within the folk mysticism practiced in Galilee, exercised a prominent role as anointers. Their domain extended far beyond the conventional household, and there is evidence that significant groups of practitioners looked to these women to guide them in their quest to leave this world behind them and experience the divine world.

A work called *The Testament of Job,* which circulated during the first century, enhances the portrait of the biblical Job and designates his daughters as heirs of his mystical practice. He becomes a model of patience (rather than of the kind of complainer he seems in the Bible) and an expert in the practice of the mystical Chariot of God, the *Merkavah* that conveyed the swirling energy of divine presence to those who meditated on this master symbol of Judaic mysticism.

Prior to his death in the *Testament of Job,* Job is taken up to heaven in his vision and given three sashes that shimmer with the light of the sun. Each of them has a title that corresponds to the wisdom it accesses when a person wears the sash: the "Spirit," the "Creation of the Heavens," and "The Paternal Splendor" (*Testament of Job* 46:1–51:4). Job gives these sashes to his three daughters as an inheritance, enabling them to speak in the language of angels. They became the authors of *Merkavah* hymns, much as Enoch is named as a seer of the *Merkavah* in the first-century book named after him. *The Testament of Job* completely overturns the modern assumption concerning women's roles in Judaism, especially in the context of mysticism. (The daughters of Philip in Acts 21:8–9 evidence the continuing role of women prophets in Christianity.) Finally, we come to an intriguing association with Mary: Job's three daughters are said in Rabbinic literature to have settled and eventually to have died in Magdala.

Ancient Jewish literature permits us to see that women pioneered the popular practice of the *Merkavah,* and that Magdala was an important center of that tradition. Along with her vessel for unction, Mary Magdalene carried with her a mystical teaching of the Spirit that her anointing art conveyed.

⟊⟊⟊

WHEN MARY ANOINTED JESUS near the end of his life, the other disciples were angry with her (Mark 14:4). They understood that anointing signaled celebration, a far cry from the somber meals they shared with their rabbi after his failed raid on the Temple. But Jesus himself explained the significance of what Mary Magdalene had done. Anointing the dead was a traditional part of Judaism, and he saw that Mary—by anointing him—connected the spiritual healing of his days in Galilee with the possibility of his execution in Jerusalem. Just as human life could be transformed by the inflowing of Spirit, so death itself could become the vehicle of God's presence.

What is recalled "in memory of her" is an essential aspect of Jesus' entire gospel (Mark 14:9): the insight that suffering can become a medium of divine presence.

Jesus taught his disciples that they had something to learn from Mary's unction. That is not at all surprising, because he had already learned from it himself, both when she anointed him in Bethany and long before that.

When Jesus had crossed back across the Sea of Galilee from Decapolis, a woman came up behind him and touched him, so that a flow of blood that had made her unclean was cured (Mark 5:25–34):

> *And a woman who had a flow of blood twelve years (and had suffered a lot from many physicians and had expended everything that was hers and had not improved, but rather got worse) had heard things concerning Jesus. She came in the crowd from behind, touched his garment. Because she was saying that: If I touch even his garments, I shall be saved. And at once the fountain of her blood dried up, and she knew in the body that she was cured from her plague. Jesus at once recognized in himself the power gone out from him and turned back in the crowd; he was saying, Who touched my garments? And his students were saying to him, Look at the crowd pressing you around, and you say, Who touched me? And he glared around to see the woman who had done this. But the woman was afraid and trembling: she knew what had happened to her. She came and fell before him and said all the truth to him. But he said to her, Daughter, your faith has saved you; depart in peace and be healthy from your plague.*

This story probably comes from the source that Mary Magdalene crafted. It speaks of a woman who lived close to where Mary was brought up, and it specifies her illness as a blood flow—a persistent impurity such as had once afflicted Mary. Indeed, the woman's touching Jesus exemplifies Mary Magdalene's own practice.

Jesus endorsed what the woman did, much as he later endorsed Mary's anointing of him, despite the confusion all around him, the incomprehension of his own disciples, and his own initial resistance to being touched. Gestures such as the woman's enacted faith, as he said, displaying trust in the Spirit he conveyed to others.

Rabbi Jesus' own practice changed after this encounter, as we can see in two further stories from the Magdalene source. Both of them are set on the eastern side of the Sea of Galilee, the region from which Mary's story of the legion of demons came. They both date from the year 31 C.E., when Jesus made his way to Jerusalem for the last time with his disciples. One involves a deaf-mute (Mark 7:31–37) and the other a blind man (Mark 8:22–26). Mark's Gospel alone includes these stories; Matthew and Luke ignored them both. The reason for the repression has been recognized for centuries: Jesus uses his own spit to heal the afflicted organs. This is a record of the magical dimension of his practice, which the later Gospels preferred to repress.

The Talmud of Jerusalem also speaks of anointing with spit with the intention to heal. Women were typical practitioners of this type of healing. In one case, the woman applies her unction of saliva seven times, much as Jesus had to repeat his therapy to clear up the blind man's sight (Mark 8:22–26). Matthew and Luke repressed these stories of healing with spit not only because they involved more magic than they were comfortable with but also because Jesus was following a practice of women's household sorcery that he had learned, in all probability, from his most prominent female disciple—Mary Magdalene.

⸺

BY THE TIME RABBI JESUS signaled the significance of Mary's anointing during his last weeks in Jerusalem, he had learned from her practice and had made aspects of it his own. It was not simply a ritual of healing, but an assurance of divine presence in the midst of danger. Confronting the tangible danger of death, he saw in Mary's anointing a persistent contact with God's Spirit that could transcend his mortal life.

For Rabbi Jesus, being raised from the dead involved a new, spiritual form of life, not just a prolongation of physical existence. In his mind, the Resurrection God promised his people went beyond survival and meant that they would share his immortality. Cases such as that of Lazarus and Jairus's daughter are healings, restorations to life that are unlike the Resurrection of humanity as a whole that Jesus described. Being raised from the dead for him was not a literal resuscitation. It did not mean, for example, that one was able to continue one's marital relationship with a spouse. His teaching in this regard is explicit: "Because when the dead arise they neither marry nor are they given in marriage, but are like angels in the heavens" (Mark 12:25). Life on the other side of death was an existence "like angels," a complete and spiritual transformation of physical life.

Near the time of his anointing by Mary Magdalene, Jesus forged another distinctive teaching: that one's neighbor represents the divine on earth. Jesus quoted two well-known commandments—love of God and love of one's neighbor—as the primordial foundation of the Law and the Prophets. Jesus innovated when he linked the two commandments, pronouncing that the first was "like" the second (Matthew 22:39). While arguing with other teachers in Jerusalem, he had come to the realization that the love one owed the *Merkavah* was exactly what one owed one's neighbor (Mark 12:28–34; Matthew 22:34–40; Luke 10:25–28). Love of God (Deuteronomy 6:5) and love of neighbor (Leviticus 19:18) were basic principles embedded in the Torah. Jesus' innovation lay in the claim that the two were indivisible: Love of God *was* love of neighbor, and vice versa. Every neighbor belonged within God's presence. That is the basis of Jesus' distinctive and challenging ethics of love in the midst of persecution. He linked his ethics to the transformed society that prophets such as Isaiah and Ezekiel and Zechariah had predicted. His words promise that individual suffering can achieve transcendence, provided the "other" is seen not as threat or stranger but as a mirror of the presence of God in the world.

In Mary Magdalene's anointing, she lavished on Jesus exactly that love he called for among Israelites, and she poured oil on him that symbolized the Spirit, which promised a Resurrection to a life "like angels." Resurrection implies that an element of human identity does not disappear at death; for Jesus, this element was comparable to angels who served in the divine presence in heaven. A person who loves another, who incarnates this indestructible element, loves God at the same time. Love of a person and love of God represent the same eternity and flow solely from the divine Spirit. Jesus taught during this same time of his life that in comparison to this Spirit, flowing from God and animating his children eternally, the flesh is weak (Mark 14:38). Carnal weakness can't be avoided; mortality is a cross to be borne to the end of life at the same time that it celebrates God's creativity in the physical world. The suffering that comes with separating from the flesh reveals that which one never loses—the Spirit and an existence like angels.

Anointing for Jesus and Mary conveyed divine selection, the celebration of life, and the transition that made death into the doorway of living. Above all, unction suffused a person with Spirit as effectively as it carried the scent of perfume, symbolizing an inner, intimate transformation that included a person's entire body. The Song of Songs makes scented oil the emblem of the sensuality it celebrates (1:2–3), and—although this is often overlooked—Pope Gregory in his famous sermon invoked this passage in the Song of Songs to speak of Mary's relationship with Jesus from Mary's point of view:

> *He shall kiss me with the kisses of his mouth;*
> *For thy caresses are better than wine.*
> *Because of the aroma of thy fine unctions,*
> *Thy name is as oil poured forth,*
> *Therefore maidens love thee.*

Love, wine, aroma—anointing includes them all, especially when a woman practiced unction on the lavish scale that Mary Magdalene did. The Song of Songs conveys that sensual range with an intimate precision of language that I have attempted to put in English here.

The Song of Songs ran into resistance among Jewish and Christian theologians when it came time to list formally which books belonged in the canon of the Bible. It is a frankly erotic poem, and its association with Solomon—notorious for his seven hundred wives and three hundred concubines (1 Kings 11:3)—only underscores that. An allegorical subterfuge saved the poem for us; the rabbis of the second century declared that the Song of Songs spoke of God's love for Israel, while the Fathers of the Church saw it as a reflection of Christ's love for his Church and Protestants later interpreted the imagery in terms of Christ's love for the individual soul. Those who heard the book read, and who loved anointing as well as the sensuality it represented, didn't let the clouds of allegory obscure its direct meaning.

Just as the woman who speaks at the beginning of the poem praises her lover's unction, so he responds with a detailed descant of what he smells on her body, and where (Song of Songs 4:9–15):

*Thou hast given me heart, my sister, bride,*
*Thou hast given me heart with one of thine eyes,*
    *With one chain of thy neck.*
*How beautiful thy caresses, my sister, bride,*
*How much better thy caresses than wine,*
    *And the smell of thy unctions than all spices.*
*Thy lips, bride, drip—honeycomb!*
    *Honey and milk are under thy tongue, and*
    *The smell of thy clothing is like the smell of Lebanon.*
*A locked garden is my sister, bride,*
*A locked spring, a fountain sealed.*

*Thy plants are a paradise of pomegranates,*
  *with choice fruit; hennas with nards.*
*Nard and saffron; calamus and cinnamon,*
  *With all trees of incense;*
    *Myrrh and aloes with all the main spices.*
*A fountain of gardens, a well of living waters,*
  *And streams from Lebanon.*

The Song of Songs catalogs the fragrances of love in their rich variety.

The lover is invited finally to enjoy the garden he has surveyed. His lover replies to him (Song of Songs 4:16):

*Awake, north wind, and come, south wind,*
*And blow upon my garden, that its spices may flow out.*
*My beloved shall come into his garden,*
  *and eat its choice fruit.*

By pouring expensive oil all over her rabbi—perfumed with nard, as in the Song of Songs—Mary Magdalene treated him like Solomon, and invited people to see her as his lover, whatever the exact circumstances of their relationship, playing out the erotic anointing of Israel's greatest love poem.

The other disciples objected to her action on the grounds of propriety, and because of the waste involved. Their reaction goes hand in hand with the strong tendency of the Gospels to deemphasize the importance of anointing in the exorcisms and healings that Jesus and his followers performed. Mary Magdalene knew better. She had been anointed at his hands, and had anointed him with her own hands. That by no means proves that they replayed the Song of Songs whenever they were in private, but the poem does illustrate the deeply physical pleasure that anointing involved. In Jesus' practice, and therefore in Mary Magdalene's, that pleasure signaled the presence of Spirit, expelling the impurities of a bodily system gone wrong.

Mary Magdalene brought the wisdom of faithful touching into the teaching of the primitive Church, and the Gospels acknowledge her spiritual practice. They dampen it down, to be sure. The physical conveyance of Jesus' power, sensuous and direct, fed into the charge by his opponents that he consorted with promiscuous women, and Mary's own gesture with the alabaster jar must have looked to some like flagrant eroticism. Unction is inherently sensuous, and the Church in many periods has found it essential to control or repress the practice.

By anointing Jesus prior to his burial, Mary prepared and prefigured his death and the suffering that was going to accomplish his Resurrection in the form of an angel. She celebrated that accomplishment with the unction that had been her trademark since her days with Jesus in Galilee.

Natural curiosity makes us ask this question: Did their mutual and sensuous recognition of Spirit tip into erotic relations between them? Neither the Gospels nor their sources tell us, although they do suggest that people at the time asked that same question.

If Jesus were to have had a sexual partner, Mary remains the best candidate. But the frequently repeated argument that as a Jewish man, and above all a rabbi, Jesus must have been married misses the mark. Jewish law required a man to support his wife near her own original family. The earliest compilation of Rabbinic law, the Mishnah (Ketuvoth 13:10), explicitly states that a husband should not move his wife from Galilee to Judea, or from Judea to Galilee, or from city to country, or country to city, or from a rich to a poor setting. More often than not, within the context of rural Galilee, this meant a husband lived with his wife's parents. There is no indication that Jesus did anything of the sort. His constant travel, irregular birth, and unstable economic status made him nobody's ideal husband or son-in-law.

But our inability to specify how intimate Mary and Jesus were in sexual terms should not distract us from the intimacy the sources do make powerfully evident: Anointing was a principal means in Jesus' movement of conveying Spirit and removing impurity. Jesus confirmed the practice of that touching as a sign of faith, and he praised the active contact initiated by Mary and the woman with the flow of blood, as well as by the anonymous anointer in Luke 7.

Many teachers in the early Church were wary about oil and touching. The practice, when recounted in relation to Jesus and Mary, inevitably awakened suspicion that their relations might have been sexual as well as ritually intimate. Since neither of them was married, the accusation of adultery was moot, but by the end of the first century, Christian teachers condemned all sexual relations outside marriage as fornication. Although the Church relaxed the kosher laws when food was at issue, illicit sexuality emerged as the primary form of uncleanness in Christian literature from the time of the New Testament and remained so long after.

Mary and Jesus had both borne the stigma of impurity—Jesus by his birth as a *mamzer* and Mary by her demonic possession—so it became crucial for early Christian teachers to insist that any criticism directed against Jesus or Mary derived from false understandings of uncleanness, not from any fault in them or in their relationship. (This is also one reason the doctrine of the Virgin Birth developed, and why the Magdalene's private contact with Jesus is never specified in the Gospels.) But the simple fact is that the mores and expectations of the Church at the end of the first century and later differed from those of first-century Judaism in Galilee. Even Mary's sevenfold possession must have seemed scandalous in retrospect, a case comparable to that of the woman in the book of Tobit (6:13–17) who was said to have killed each of seven husbands on the night of the marriage. That is a world early Christianity wished to distance Mary from.

A relationship that once would have seemed irregular but understandable became unthinkable, and a considerable tendency emerged to write Mary Magdalene out of the memory of the Church. To this extent, later legends and theories that make Mary Jesus' lover have some basis in the best available evidence, although their baroque complications undercut their basic plausibility. Nonetheless, even the most extreme theories along these lines at least open the door to an investigation of Mary's influence and teaching. That is a service to critical inquiry, because when it comes to Mary's teaching of the Resurrection, as we shall see, the Church's early theologians found all the more reason to sideline Mary Magdalene. She challenged their entire view of how God would save the world.

*Chapter Seven*

# TRANSFIGURATION
# AT THE TOMB

J ESUS' RESURRECTION OCCURRED before anyone could grasp its
significance: That is the unequivocal message of Mark, the earliest
Gospel, in its original form. The Gospel's climax presents a visionary
experience, which Mark evokes with its spare poetry. Three women,
led by Mary Magdalene, saw a vision and heard angelic words. Mark
conveys their bewilderment in the face of revelation (16:1–8):

*And when Sabbath elapsed, Mary the Magdalene and Mary of
James and Salome purchased spices so they could go anoint him.
And very early on the first of the Sabbaths they came upon the
tomb when the sun dawned. And they were saying to one another,
Who will roll the stone away from the opening of the tomb for us?
They looked up and perceived that the stone had been rolled off
(because it was exceedingly big). They went towards the tomb and
saw a young man sitting on the right appareled in a white robe,
and they were completely astonished. But he says to them, Do not*

*be completely astonished. You seek Jesus the crucified Nazarene.*
*He is raised; he is not here. Look—the place where they laid him.*
*But depart, tell his students and Peter that he goes before you into*
*Galilee; you will see him there, just as he said to you. They went*
*out and fled from the tomb, because trembling and frenzy had*
*them. And they said nothing to any one; they were afraid,*
*because—*

This abrupt ending climaxes the primitive but effective art of Mark, signaling how hard and disruptive it was, even for those intimate with Jesus, to grapple with the vision that signaled he had overcome death.

From a prosaic point of view, this truncated finale makes the Gospel seem defective. How could anyone end a story by saying "they were afraid, because—"? In later manuscripts of Mark, this apparent gap was dutifully filled in with now-familiar stories culled from the other Gospels of the risen Jesus appearing to his disciples. Pious scribes frequently harmonized the texts of the Gospels, making them look alike. These additions are transparent, and Mark's stark, primitive ending, the apogee of its art of revelation, stands out because of its powerful originality.

---

IN THE GOSPEL'S ORIGINAL form, the three women are the first to know that Jesus had been raised from the dead. Mark names Mary Magdalene first in this account and her cognomen, "the Magdalene," resonates, as I mentioned in chapter 2, with Jesus'—"the Nazarene." Mary is on her way with Mary of James and Salome to anoint Jesus' corpse, and that reinforces the point made in chapter 5—that the Magdalene had been the nameless anointer who prepared Jesus before his death for burial.

Mary's every action and response are crucial to an understanding of her realization that God had raised Jesus from the dead. It was customary, as well as a commandment of the Torah, that Israelites attend to the corpses of relatives and friends, even victims of crucifixion. A first-century ossuary, discovered outside Jerusalem in 1968, contains the bones of a young man named Yochanan. An iron spike with an attached piece of wood is embedded in his right heel. Properly tending to the dead was incumbent on every Israelite, and any Roman official would court rebellion by deliberately flouting that imperative. The Jerusalem prefect must have released Yochanan's broken body for burial; his ossuary indicates that the Romans honored Israelite tradition.

Following ancient practice, those who received Yochanan's crucified corpse bathed and anointed it, wrapping the body in linen and placing it in a funerary cave. According to usual burial practice, they deposited the bones in a limestone box after a year and carved Yochanan's name on the ossuary's side.

This discovery directly contradicts the claim, fashionable for more than a century, that Jesus' body was tossed to the dogs after his execution. Foundational texts of Judaism give precise instructions for dealing with corpses after crucifixion (see Deuteronomy 21:22–23; the document from the Dead Sea Scrolls known as 11Q64:11–13; Josephus *Life* 421; Mishnah Sanhedrin 6:5–6); a dead body that was exposed was a source of impurity and offended God. Mary and her companions returned to Jesus' tomb in order to fulfill the Torah's commandment, having waited until sundown on the Sabbath so that they could buy materials for anointing Jesus' corpse. Modern readers often express disgust and incredulity at the thought of returning to a corpse that had already been interred for some thirty-six hours. But mourners in antiquity were not squeamish: Death had not yet been banished to the mortician's ghetto and anointing featured importantly in customs of burial in the ancient Near East. Death's impurity had to be dealt with, and people accepted the temporary uncleanness of handling the corpse in order to ensure the purity of the land and the community of Israel.

The Talmud describes not only practices of cleaning, anointing, and wrapping the dead but also the custom of visiting the tomb each day for three days after a burial to make certain that the deceased was truly dead, not simply unconscious. The Talmud in question is the Babylonian Talmud (also called the Bavli), which is later than the Talmud of Jerusalem but nonetheless constitutes the pivotal text of Rabbinic Judaism. The story of the resuscitation of Lazarus in John 11:1–44 presupposes that custom. The Talmud speaks of people going on to lead healthy lives, as Lazarus did, when dedicated relatives and friends discovered they had, in fact, been interred alive.

The moment of natural death can seem strangely uncertain, as anyone who has visited the terminally ill and their families knows. A woman once asked me to come to her home, unsure of whether cancer had at last claimed her husband's life. That kind of doubt is natural; the recovery of the supposedly dead sometimes defies medical technology. I gave the man last rites but stayed with his family until a medical practitioner could confirm his death. Until then, the family lived through the same limbo that ancient Jewish mourners endured for three days—more in the case of Lazarus. This concern—to be sure a living person is not treated as dead—stems from a deep regard for life. In the ancient Israelite ethos, caring for a person extended to taking care of his body until the transition from life to death was complete.

Crucifixion at the hands of the Romans left virtually no room for uncertainty over the fact of death and required the treatment of a badly damaged corpse. Puncture wounds leaked blood and lymphatic fluid, and bits of broken bone extruded; victims who had been flogged prior to crucifixion were covered with deep gashes. In Jesus' case, a javelin had also been thrust into his body. The Roman Empire was in the business of death, using crucifixion as the supreme punishment to terrorize recalcitrant subjects in its dominions between Spain and Syria. They had learned this technique of state terror from the Persian Empire, then went on to master and monopolize it. Crucifixion was a punishment that only the Roman authorities themselves— rather than their client kings or other petty rulers—could inflict. These executioners knew what they were doing, and theories that Jesus somehow physically survived the cross represent a combination of fantasy, revisionism, and half-baked science.

The women did not go to the tomb to confirm that Jesus was dead, but to anoint and care for what they knew all too well was a corpse. The women had joined Joseph of Arimathea, a sympathetic rabbi who offered his own familiy's burial cave to be used for Jesus' interment (Mark 15:42–46). But the observance of the Sabbath (which arrived at sunset) prevented them from purchasing or preparing anointment at the time Jesus was buried. Their delay was therefore natural, calibrated to the rhythm of observant Judaism.

---

To COMPLETE THE dutiful care of their dead rabbi, Mary and the women made their way to the tomb. Perfumed oil for rubbing on the dead was scented with the resin of myrrh and the leaves of aloe (John 19:38–39). The astringent properties of the aloe helped to seal skin made porous by death. The smell of myrrh was associated in the mind of any dedicated Israelite with the aroma of the Temple. Both these scents were also used in the luxurious perfume that a lover might enjoy on the body of the beloved (Song of Songs 4:14). Suspensions of myrrh and aloe were delicate mixtures, produced by seething them in oil and aging the unction in stone containers. In the case of Jesus, a rabbi named Nicodemus saw to the expense so that Mary Magdalene and her companions could purchase the salve from a sympathetic vendor in Jerusalem, who was willing to make the sale as soon as the setting sun brought an end to the Sabbath. They bought their oil and spices so that they "could go anoint" (*elthousai aleipsosin;* Mark 16:1) the body of Jesus.

To say they had to "go" (*elthousai*) for that purpose suggests they walked a distance; one ancient manuscript of the New Testament (the Codex Bezae) says they "proceeded" (*poreutheisai*), implying an even longer journey. This choice of words embarrassed later copyists, who eliminated any reference to the women's travel because it contradicted the tradition that Jesus was buried in the Church of the Holy Sepulcher, one of Christianity's greatest pilgrimage (and hence tourist) sites since the fourth century. Modern archaeology has discredited the notion that this church is the site of Jesus' grave.

Mary Magdalene and her companions found Jesus' tomb in a recognized cemetery well outside the city—a place where prominent people, such as Joseph of Arimathea, purchased caves for family burial. The archaeological evidence for the existence of such sites is now secure. In 1990, on a hill dotted with natural caves in the Arab hamlet of Abu Tor, a mile and a half south of the Temple, the ossuary of Caiaphas, the high priest at the time of Jesus' execution, was discovered. There is little doubt whose ossuary this is: The limestone box was found in situ, with Caiaphas's name written on it twice. A coin discovered in the same cave bears the imprint of Herod Agrippa I, which shows that burial took place in the mid-forties of the first century. The carving on the box picks up the symbolism of the Temple, signaling Caiaphas's status as high priest.

Was it in this cemetery that Joseph of Arimathea, a member of the same council to which the high priest belonged (the Sanhedrin; Mark 15:43), interred the corpse of Jesus? Certainty escapes us, but it is clear that the women as described in Mark went to a private and remote place, much more like Abu Tor than the site of the Church of the Holy Sepulcher inside the city.

Taking place well outside the city, far from earshot or the prying eyes of opponents, the experience at the mouth of the tomb was the women's alone. The three women met there privately with Jesus, just as three men—Peter, James, and John—did on the mountain of the Transfiguration (Mark 9:2–8). In the experience of both female and male disciples, revelation came as a communal vision that intensified each individual's insight. Vision crystallized the women's conviction that Jesus was alive, a vibrant spiritual presence despite his shameful death. It was their Transfiguration. Ancient Judaism conceived of visionary reality as an experience that could be shared—and it was this Transfiguration at the mouth of the tomb that emerged as the force that ultimately turned Jesus' movement into a new religion.

⸺

THE TRANSFIGURATION AND Jesus' Resurrection provoked astonishment and awe. Mark's Gospel intentionally highlights the mystical qualities of these encounters with the divine. When Mark describes the impact of the exorcism Jesus performed in Capernaum's synagogue, he says of the people there that "all were astonished" (1:27). That scene, from the Magdalene source, establishes a clear pattern in the Gospel.

Astonishment and awe provided a litmus test of revelation. The peasants of Galilee ached for transformation into the Kingdom of God, which some rabbis of the time called *ha-olam haba,* "the age to come," when the power of God's eternal Throne would transcend all divisions, heal all ills, and overpower the petty tyrannies of a broken world. Any experience or sign that offered a glimpse into this ultimate reality provoked awestruck joy.

Visionary prophets such as Ezekiel, and mystical practitioners of Judaism after him, conceived of this divine power as "the Chariot." The divine Chariot was nothing other than the Throne of God, which Moses and his companions—Aaron, Nadab, Abihu, and seventy elders of Israel—saw in its sapphire glory (Exodus 24:9–11). Like the Resurrection of Jesus, the Chariot was open to communal vision and could unveil itself anywhere, anytime.

Jewish texts from before, during, and after the first century—the books of Enoch and Jubilees, "The Angelic Liturgy" from Qumran, the Rabbinic tractates called "Chagigah" in the Mishnah, the Tosefta, and the two Talmuds—show that rabbis practiced the unveiling of the Chariot in this world by means of disciplined meditation. Visions were not just spontaneous experiences that burst in on passive recipients; adepts could realize the Chariot through their dedicated practice.

Rabbi Jesus trained his disciples—including Mary Magdalene, from the time she met him in Galilee through the period of his final pilgrimage to Jerusalem—in the tradition of the *Merkavah,* the Chariot. They attuned themselves to the divine Chariot, helped by Scriptures they memorized, disciplines they handed on by word of mouth, and examples of their master's teaching and practice that they emulated. Astonishment in God's presence became their way of life.

This astonishment strikes Peter, James, and John during the Transfiguration, when Jesus is transformed before them into a gleaming white figure. They see him speaking with Moses and Elijah, the two most powerful prophets of Israel's Scriptures (Matthew 17:1–9; Mark 9:2–13; Luke 9:27–36). Jesus' visions began as his own personal revelations, but years of communal meditation made his experiences transparent to his disciples. On the mountain of his Transfiguration, Jesus followed in the footsteps of Moses, who took three of his followers (Aaron, Nadab, and Abihu) up Mount Sinai (Exodus 24:1–11), where they sacrificed and banqueted to celebrate their vision of the God of Israel on his sapphire Throne.

But unlike what happened on Sinai, Jesus' disciples, covered by a shining cloud of glory, also heard a voice: "This is my Son, the beloved, in whom I take pleasure: hear him." When the cloud passed, Moses and Elijah had disappeared. Jesus stood alone as God's Son. Divine "Son" was the designation that Jesus had heard when, as an adolescent, encamped on the River Jordon with his rabbi, John the Baptist, he had practiced mystical ascension; now his own disciples saw and heard the truth of his personal vision. Jesus' true genius lay in the transparency of his visionary experience.

When Jesus immersed in accordance with John the Baptist's teaching, the voice that came from heaven did not speak in the exclusive language of the later doctrine of the Trinity, which made Jesus into the only (and only possible) "Son of God." Rather, Jesus' immersion in Spirit enabled him to initiate others into that experience. Likewise, the voice from the luminous cloud in the Transfiguration signaled that the divine Spirit, which had animated Moses and Elijah, was present in Jesus and that Jesus could pass on that Spirit to his followers, each of whom could also become a child, or "Son," of God. The whole Gospel According to Mark is designed as a program to train its hearers and readers for the moment of baptism, when they, too, will experience the Spirit within them and call upon God as their *Abba,* their father and true source.

According to Mark, when Jesus came down from the place of the Transfiguration, all who saw him "were completely astonished" (9:15). That confusion again signals a divine disclosure. It is a confusion that is part of revelation, where one is jolted out of ordinary experience into a different reality.

Confusion overwhelms Jesus himself in Mark. Immediately prior to his arrest in Gethsemane, Jesus searches inside himself for his deepest understanding of God, seeking to discover whether he truly has to drink the cup of suffering and death—which he prays will pass him by. When he learns that this suffering is necessary (Mark 14:33), Jesus, too, is "completely astonished."

The presentation of Jesus in the Gospels is much more robust than the pale teachings of modern theology. There is no embarrassment about Jesus weeping and praying to avoid death. Luke even portrays him as sweating blood at this point (22:44). (Predictably, some Greek manuscripts omit the verse.) Jesus' humanity was no scandal to Christian faith at its primitive stage. He was not omniscient or cut off from normal human doubt, emotion, and sensation. Jesus' purpose was to tear the veil that separates people from God and obscures the ultimate reality of our lives.

Jesus knew that everyone's perceptions, including his own, had to change and adjust to this transcendent vision. As God's own Son, he was as confused as every Son who would ever follow the path he marked, taking up a cross and crossing over into the world of glory.

This pattern of confusion in the face of revelation climaxes in Jesus' Resurrection. This experience manifested what theologians often refer to as the "presence" of God in this world, although the word *presence* scarcely conveys the inexhaustible dynamism of the Chariot, which welded human consciousness to God's as he founded the universe, maintained its precarious existence moment by moment, and was poised to sweep it all away at will.

Christianity became highly philosophical and often abstract from the second century onward, but Jesus and his Judaic contemporaries did not share the abstractions that have become common currency in the language of the divine world. For Rabbi Jesus, the word *God* conveyed not a philosophical idea but the ultimate reality—beautiful and fearsome and overpowering. At the mouth of the tomb, Mary Magdalene and her companions were taught definitively by Jesus that God was the only, ultimate truth—the omnipotent, swirling vortex of creation.

*Chapter Eight*

# ECSTATIC VISION

Aʟᴛʜᴏᴜɢʜ ᴛʜᴇ Tʀᴀɴsꜰɪɢᴜʀᴀᴛɪᴏɴ itself and the vision of the women at the mouth of the tomb obviously reflect different experiences, both revealed Jesus' divine identity and thoroughly unnerved his disciples. Fear silenced the apostles on Mount Hebron (Mark 9:6), as though they were caught in a dream, unable to speak. Their silence prefigures the silence of the three women at the mouth of the tomb (Mark 16:8; see also the description of the disciples in Gethsemane, 15:32–42). In these cases, the disciples' astonishment signals a vision of the heavenly court, where the Chariot Throne of God is clouded in awe and radiates divine power. Mark indicates that the women left our world and fearfully entered this realm.

Both the Transfiguration and Mary's vision intimately connect Jesus to the Throne of God. In the Transfiguration, he appears in an altered form, shining in brilliance with Moses and Elijah, prophets who, it was understood in the first century, had "not tasted death," a turn of phrase shared among Jewish, Christian, and Gnostic texts. The phrase does not refer to escaping physical death, but to transcending its consequences. Vision gave access to a world where death no longer had dominion. Instead, dying marked an entry into God's presence. This is what the angelic youth at the mouth of the tomb announced: Jesus' victory over death, his permanent transformation to the stature of Moses and Elijah in Israel's divine panoply.

—∞∞—

WHEN THE WOMEN LIFTED their eyes at the mouth of the tomb, they "perceived that the stone had been rolled off" (Mark 16:4). The verb *perceive* represents a precise choice of words. *Theoreo* in Greek (from which our English word *theory,* the equivalent of *theoria,* is derived) refers to the women's deliberate perception, a moment filled with both anxiety and hope. The women had just posed the desolate question, "Who will roll the stone away from the opening of the tomb for us?" (Mark 16:3). A bleak description of the rock follows: ". . . it was exceedingly big" (Mark 16:4). Caught between their own despair and the size of the rock, they lifted their eyes and "perceived." This moment of extraordinary perception opened them to the announcement of Jesus' Resurrection, and their vision became the vessel of Christian hope.

Precisely because it represents the core of Christianity's message, the Resurrection of Jesus continues to touch off controversy and misunderstanding. What the texts say about the events concerned is persistently distorted—as much by the exaggerations of those who impose their own wishes for afterlife onto Jesus as by the dismissal of those who resent the influence of Christianity in the modern world. The result is that treatments of Jesus' Resurrection conform either to the doctrines of a church or to the secular denial of any life after death. Either way, modern presuppositions torment the meanings of ancient texts to the point that even scholars find it difficult to specify what the documents say. In no other question have modern dogmas, both ecclesiastical and secularist, so obscured ancient wisdom.

Mary Magdalene's experience in Mark's Gospel gives us access to her encounter with the risen Jesus, an account independent of our presuppositions, whether pious or skeptical. Before there was any religion called Christianity to believe in or not believe in, before there was any question of influencing theological opinion, the beliefs that people adhere to, or their views regarding life after death, Mary's vision and voice sounded true and clear, waiting to be heard in their own terms.

The distortion of Mary's vision—sometimes willful, sometimes inadvertent—has plagued the interpretation of the New Testament. Her experience conflicts with a later belief widely assumed to be part and parcel of Christianity—the belief in Jesus' physical resuscitation from his grave. Because her experience came first, those who came after her manipulated what she said in her source to accord with their own views. In this case as in others, when a teacher sets in motion a powerful idea or tradition—which the Resurrection of Jesus undoubtedly is—the bitter price of this primacy is often paid in the form of the misinterpretations that come later. At long last, let us step beyond this manipulation, hear a clear voice, and watch the unfolding of a pristine vision.

By the word choice of *theoreo,* rather than *horao* (the verb for physical seeing), the women's visionary discernment literally becomes a matter of deep perception rather than ordinary vision. Mark's awareness that the women's insight was supernatural shines through several elements in the account of what happened at the tomb. The women's apprehension of heaven was so important to them that physical circumstance no longer mattered. Mark says that they moved in the direction of Jesus' corpse. But did they advance "to" the tomb or "toward" the tomb? Or might it be "up to" the tomb or "into" the tomb? The preposition *eis,* the word chosen by Mark in the native language of the Gospel, Greek, might bear any of those meanings, because it refers to direction without exactly specifying extent (Mark 16:5). An author who wanted to specify the physical proximity of the women to the exact place where Jesus' corpse had been deposited would have to say more, as actually happens in the other Gospels (as we shall see). Instead, Mark chooses succinct ambiguity.

Mark places the women at the mouth of the tomb when their vision transfixes them. The Gospel does not concern itself with telling us how far the women go into the tomb. It does not say whether the giant rock they "perceived" to have been rolled away had been literally removed or not. We might want to know whether these visionary events happened in the material world, but for Mark, exterior facts of that sort do not matter. Rather, the women's experience pivots on their apprehension of the angel who speaks to them (Mark 16:5): "a young man sitting on the right appareled in a white robe." The women leave the corporeal realm when Mark says that "they were completely astonished."

What causes their astonishment? It is not, as is expressed by a tiresome and inaccurate convention, "the empty tomb." "The empty tomb" is a bad heading for this passage, although it is the designation frequently provided in printed Bibles. For the simplest of reasons, we have to let that heading go: In Mark's Gospel, the women do not actually enter or inspect the tomb. They or their replacements do so in later Gospels (which also reduce Mary's importance, as we shall see), but not here. At the tomb's mouth, Mary Magdalene and her companions see an angelic "young man." *That* is what astonishes them.

In their astonishment, they do not say (and might very well not have known) whether they were in the door, beside it, or inside the tomb. Visions often occluded a sense of ordinary circumstances. Once, Saint Paul referred to a visionary experience when he was "taken up into the third heaven." He said he could not even tell whether he was "in the body or outside the body," a phrase that derives from Jewish mystical practice. So it was with Mary and her colleagues: The force of vision was upon them, and they don't say whether they went into the tomb or searched for Jesus' corpse.

The youth they perceived was no ordinary adolescent, but "a young man sitting on the right appareled in a white robe," clothing reminiscent of Jesus' Transfiguration (Mark 16:5). This young man is the antithesis of another anonymous youth (a *neaniskos* in Greek), who at the time of Jesus' arrest (Mark 14.51–52) left his linen garment behind when he fled naked from the contingent that had come to seize his rabbi. This is a case of liturgical practice resonating within the Gospel. The hearers who prepared themselves for baptism, following the example of Jesus at the outset of Mark, encounter an image of what it is to be baptized—stripped, laid bare in one's fearfulness, and then reclothed in angelic garments at the Gospel's close.

The symbolic resonance of this youth with baptism complements his central place in the announcement of Jesus' Resurrection. He is key to the experience of the women. What he said convinced them that Jesus was alive despite his death, and their vision—the beginning of the message that God had raised his Son and wanted to raise all his children—set in motion a sequence of visions among the disciples, encounters with the risen Jesus that are reported in the other Gospels after the story of what the women saw and heard at the mouth of the tomb.

<hr />

COMMENTATORS HAVE FREQUENTLY said that Mary Magdalene was the first person to encounter the resurrected Jesus. As a reading of Mark (and not only Mark, as we shall see), that is not quite right. The women do not encounter their rabbi himself, but a messenger who announces that Jesus has been raised. That is both more and less than an encounter with Jesus: less because Jesus himself does not appear, as he does in visions presented in the other Gospels; more because the experience explains what the Resurrection means better than do Jesus' own appearances in those later Gospels.

The "less" of the women's vision helps explain an oddity in what

Paul says about Jesus' Resurrection in the earliest written reference to that event, which appears in his First Letter to the Corinthians (written around 56 C.E.). In his list of those by whom the risen Jesus "was seen" (1 Corinthians 15:3–8), Paul makes no mention at all of the women at the tomb. In this letter, he had just insisted that women keep silent in the churches (1 Corinthians 14:33–34), and this list does effectively silence them. Because the women did not encounter the risen Jesus (as did the apostles and others whom Paul mentions), but instead saw an angel who announced Jesus was risen, Paul could rationalize his omission. He excluded any reference to Mary Magdalene, despite her pivotal role in provoking the experiences of the disciples whom Paul does mention.

Alongside the "less" of Mary's experience and its exploitation by Paul, the "more" also echoes through the texts of the New Testament. Although the women did not see Jesus, they understood without equivocation—instructed by the youth in their vision—that Jesus had been raised from the dead. In every other Resurrection account in the Gospels, those who encounter Jesus express confusion about his identity or the truth of his resurrected existence. These two kinds of doubt are often knitted together in stories of the risen Jesus. Only the women, on the basis of what they directly "perceived," knew the significance of what they saw, and they knew it immediately. That is the "more" of their account.

The visionary youth tells the secret that is the core of their special knowledge. Even before he speaks, the women are "completely astonished," as Mark says and then underscores (16:5–6). The repetition is deliberate—modern translators are wrong to try to soften it. This is the same verb (*thambeomai*) that has modeled human response to revelation from the beginning of the Gospel, and it is repeated here to mark the apogee of its meaning. The exorcism in Capernaum (Mark 1:27), the Transfiguration (Mark 9:15), and Gethsemane (Mark 14:33) all echo through the astonishment of the women, because the revelation of the Gospel culminates in their experience. No less than Jesus in Gethsemane, they are silenced in fear and ecstasy. What is unveiled through the medium of the women for the hearer or reader of Mark expresses Mary's insight into the ultimate significance of who her rabbi was and what his life *and* death truly mean.

In the written text of Mark, all this is powerfully conveyed. Yet any information concerning Mary's eventual meeting with the risen Jesus is sealed in the women's silence. This Gospel is intended as instruction for noninitiates prior to baptism. Once initiated (into the experience of embracing and being embraced by Spirit, which is never forgotten during the recitation of Mark), those baptized were promised deeper instruction, in a protected, oral form, hidden from the eyes and ears of those in the Roman world who wished them ill. Knowledge of Jesus' Resurrection implicitly followed baptism in Mark's presentation: The hearer was promised a wisdom that is not written in the text.

Mary Magdalene's vision is the key to the Gospel as written—and, at the same time, it extends the promise of an esoteric truth. Clues to her secrets emerge when one considers why the later Gospels marginalize her. By getting at what they wanted to suppress, the topic of the next chapter, my hope is that Mary can finally be recognized as the woman whom Marguerite called out for on her deathbed. I want to show that Mary was one of the prime catalysts and shaping forces of Christianity—the role for her that Mark's text intimates.

⸺

MARY'S CONCEALED SIGNIFICANCE in the past, however, does not justify the many projections that have been foisted onto her. Several of these are unmistakably male fantasies. In *The Last Temptation of Christ,* Martin Scorsese pictured Mary Magdalene servicing large numbers of clients in her one-woman Galilean brothel, the kind of establishment that could never have survived in a small Jewish enclave. More recently, Dan Brown's *The Da Vinci Code* constructed an elaborate fictional—and anti-Catholic—conspiracy around the cover-up of the alleged fact that Mary bore Jesus' child and raised her in Provence. Brown conveniently disregards the legendary basis of this story: a mysterious boat without helmsman or rudder that supposedly conducted Mary and her companions to the shores of Europe. Medieval legend provided this mode of transport to other saints as well, such as James of Compostela and Andrew. They had probably died in the land of Israel, but their devotees, wanting them and their relics near, insisted that they had been carried to the West by miraculous ships and angelic choirs. If we want to get at the truth about Mary, we need to examine what we know, not invent what we don't know, and refrain from dressing up yesterday's piety as today's revisionism.

The surest truth about Mary Magdalene remains her vision at the mouth of Jesus' tomb, recounted in all the Gospels, starting with Mark. Her vision marks the separation of Jesus from his flesh and his entry into a resurrected existence "like angels" (as Jesus himself described it; Mark 12:18–27; Matthew 22:23–33; Luke 20:27–38), not the reanimated corpse on which resuscitation literalists have insisted.

Mary Magdalene's vision, precisely because it was a vision and not the inspection of an empty tomb, placed Jesus in the realm of heaven with the angels, not in the company of people who had been resuscitated, such as Jairus's daughter and Lazarus. Consequently, after their vision, the women showed no interest in the flesh of Jesus' corpse; only later embellishments on this story have the women or their male colleagues search the tomb. From a material perspective, that poses an inevitable question: What happened to the physical body of Jesus?

Once that question is posed, two answers typically follow: Either Jesus' corpse was resuscitated or somebody took it. The Gospel According to Matthew (27:51–53; 28:11–15) represents both those views, each dependent on the assumption that Jesus' physical corpse and his risen body were one and the same. The two theories, of resuscitation and of a theft, share the same conception of Resurrection. But in the vision of the women, Jesus was no longer there at all, but in Galilee. That is where the young man directed them, and when the women turned away from the tomb, as they were told to do by the young man, they left the question of Jesus' physical body behind them, unanswered. It is conceivable his corpse remained where it lay, although that interpretation can claim no more evidence than the others.

The women's vision implied that the encounter with Jesus in Galilee would also be visionary. In the later Gospels, the variety of accounts of meetings with Jesus shows that the conception of how he was raised from the dead differed strongly from vision to vision. A materialist conception arose by the time of Luke's Gospel and the book of Acts (the companion volume to Luke), according to which Jesus inhabited his own flesh and bone again, and liked to eat (Luke 24:36–43); he physically ascended into heaven at the end of his appearances among his disciples (Acts 1:9–11). But Luke also acknowledged other, clearly visionary encounters (Luke 24:13–35), and told a different story of Jesus' ascension, one in which he disappeared (Luke 24:50–53), his form dissolving as he merged with heaven. In that way, Jesus' continued, spiritual presence in heaven could be conceived.

Saint Paul also taught a spiritual conception of the Resurrection. Human beings are sown, he said, in flesh and bone, and animated by souls, but that existence is transitory. Only spirit can endure death. That is why Paul contrasted the first person, Adam, who became a living soul, to the last person, Christ, who became life-giving spirit (1 Corinthians 15:45). Only a fool, Paul said, could suppose that the corpse sown in the earth was identical to the risen body (1 Corinthians 15:36). Sown in dishonor, it is raised in honor; sown in weakness, it is raised in power: Resurrection gave Jesus "a spiritual body" (1 Corinthians 15:43–44), not his old, physical body. With his own philosophical language and trenchant logic, Paul expressed exactly the visionary conception of the Resurrection conveyed by Mary Magdalene's vision.

⸺

AFTER HER EXPERIENCE at the mouth of the tomb, Mary probably pursued her visionary practices, her anointing, and exorcisms in Magdala, where she must have returned. Galilee harbored many of Jesus' followers at this time; the young man at the mouth of the tomb had directed them back to their native land. But we learn of these disciples indirectly, because Jerusalem takes up the bulk of attention in the pages of the New Testament. The Magdalene source of stories within the Gospels, in addition to conveying Mary's characteristic practices of exorcism, anointing, and vision, refers to the region around the Sea of Galilee with firsthand familiarity, sometimes with a local knowledge of hamlets scholars can't locate anymore. Compared to the difficulties Jesus' disciples faced in Jerusalem, where first Peter and then James (Jesus' brother) drew many followers, Magdala offered a relatively tranquil environment to Mary and those who followed her practice of Judaism in the manner of Jesus.

The tranquillity of Galilee did not last, however. Growing nationalism in Jerusalem broke out into violence during the sixties of the first century. James, Jesus' brother and the most prominent leader of Christianity at the time, was executed by stoning at the instigation of the high priest Ananus in 62 C.E. Violence and opposition to Rome mounted steadily from that point on, and in 66 C.E., the manager of the Temple, Eleazar, refused to accept offerings from Gentiles, the Roman emperor included. Nero—always shrewd and ruthless, even in his most profligate moments—understood that this was tantamount to an Israelite declaration of independence. He dispatched Vespasian and the Legio X Fretensis. The Roman army triumphed. But the fighting was ferocious, and not only in Jerusalem.

Indeed, Vespasian's initial campaign took him and his son Titus through Galilee. Tiberias, near to Magdala, was an inevitable center of fighting, the site of many internecine battles among the Jewish rebels, attacks on the administrative centers of the Romans, and see-saw battles among the would-be leaders of the insurgency. Josephus, a leading participant in the revolt, who defected to the Roman cause after his capture and became a valuable eyewitness chronicler of events, described the occupation of Magdala by the rabble from the surrounding area (*Jewish War* 3.462–542). They made use of rough ramparts, which Josephus himself had installed around the city, and a ramshackle fleet of fishing boats, terrorizing the local residents during their occupation.

Despite their desperate preparations and ruthless tactics, the insurgents were hacked apart on land and on the Sea of Galilee by the professional, well-equipped Romans. But when the battle became pitched, Titus's frenzy was so great that his troops made no distinction between the rebels, who had taken over the city, and the residents, who had opposed war with Rome in the first place. According to Josephus's description, by the time Titus stopped the massacre, the Sea of Galilee near Magdala had turned red with blood, corpses bloated with decay on land and sea, and the air was foul with the stench of rotting flesh. Vespasian joined his son to enjoy the famous victory and to deal with the culprits, and summary execution of the elderly and enslavement of the young was the order of the day.

Mary Magdalene—an unattached woman who belonged to a marginal Jewish sect—was at the mercy of the militants when they occupied the city, and of the Romans when they invaded. Anyone interested in collaborating with the power of the day could have denounced her to the occupier as guilty of the lèse majesté of the hour. By Magdala's definitive capture in 67 C.E., Mary was nearing seventy, an attainable but advanced age by the standards of the time. Because she would have been of no use at all to the great forces of the moment, there is a good chance she died in the anonymity of her native land.

Some followers of Jesus escaped from Jerusalem prior to its fiery destruction by Vespasian's son Titus in 70 C.E. They fled to Pella, on the eastern side of the Jordan River (Eusebius *History of the Church* 3.5.4). Pella became a center of Jesus' movement at this time, and a magnet for any remnants of Mary Magdalene's entourage, as well. There her source was preserved, and it ultimately influenced the Gospels as we read them today. But the woman herself was barely remembered, despite the fact that her importance among Jesus' disciples was universally acknowledged. Forces were at work that would silence Mary even more effectively than the merciless legions of Rome had.

*Chapter Nine*

# THE SCAR

THE GOSPELS PROVIDE only scraps of information concerning Mary Magdalene, but by now I hope to have shown that by sifting through the scant texts available to us and placing Mary in the context of first-century Judaism in Galilee, we can discern vital clues about who Mary was and what she did. The time has come to ask why Mary was very nearly expunged from the Gospels—the very texts she helped shape.

Mary's erasure from the Gospels forms a scar in the historical flesh of Christianity. The excisions that cut Mary out of the texts have removed or damaged vital tissue in the Church's faith and practice—key rituals of exorcism, anointing, and vision. This scar reaches deeper than a blemish: A badly healed wound prevents Christians from moving in ways that are natural to their discipleship.

Mary, the women with her, and the women after her who put her sacramental program into action have been marginalized, limited to strictly ancillary roles within ecclesiastical life. That obscures the power of the rituals Mary pioneered. Women have been sequestered in a male-dominated hierarchy, and that has gradually paralyzed the

Magdalene's sacramental program of expelling demons, healing with oil, and realizing the presence of the risen Jesus.

Yet the cuts that might have excised Mary Magdalene from the Gospels altogether did not actually achieve that result. Her pivotal connection with exorcism, anointing, and vision proved too durable to be erased. By seeing why she was pushed aside, and how that marginalization did not quite come off, we can better understand the influence that she once exerted. Then we can perceive why she was important in her own terms, identify the threat she posed to those who resisted her influence, and tap the continuing power of the rituals she developed.

※

AT THE END OF the Gospel According to Mark, the women at the mouth of the tomb are silent, but we know that they eventually did relate what had happened to them, because their experience is articulated and forms the climax of Mark's narrative. Within the text of Mark, the sources of the Magdalene and Peter are woven together with other oral sources into a single narrative. The Magdalene source must have been considerably compressed during that process, but it lived on in oral form. In Mark's Christian community in Rome during the early seventies of the Common Era, people who had been baptized had access to teachers who spoke on the basis of oral sources of how Mary Magdalene and other disciples experienced the Resurrection. Some of these experiences actually made it into the written texts of Matthew, Luke, and John, but Mark preferred to leave detailed explanation of encounters with the risen Jesus to the personal, oral instruction that followed baptismal immersion.

The Gospels were composed in communities where there was still an oral memory of Jesus. That enabled the written texts to remain succinct, and it resulted in their being very different from one another in content and style. Luke's Gospel puts the existence of sources

that circulated before it was written beyond any real doubt. In a preface to the book, we learn about "eyewitnesses" and "assistants of the word" who provided the material this Gospel weaves into a narrative (Luke 1:1–4):

> *Many have attempted to order a narrative afresh concerning the events consummated among us, just as those who were eyewitnesses from the outset and became assistants of the word delivered them over to us. Accordingly, it seemed to me that I—one who followed after—should also write anew, in everything accurately, in sequence, so that you can recognize the certainty—Theophilus, your Excellency—concerning the things in which you have been instructed.*

The basic picture Luke paints is that people who personally experienced events conveyed their experiences orally to those who taught about Jesus, until those teachings were edited in written form. Each Gospel emphasized its own version of Jesus' story and left a wealth of other material for oral instruction.

Christian teachers had to become skilled in holding back from their story any material that might inflame local opinion against them. As the book of Acts shows, charges of treason against the Roman empire dogged the efforts of those who proclaimed the Kingdom of God, rather than Caesar's kingdom. Nero had unleashed a violent pogrom against followers of Jesus in Rome in 64 C.E. Both Paul and Peter had died in the riot, a combination of mob violence and official torture. Mark's Gospel ends on a note of silence partially because silence was often the best policy in dealing with the Romans; silencing women came to some extent as part of that agenda.

We are at a deep disadvantage compared to ancient readers and hearers of the Gospels when it comes to understanding Jesus and his movement. We have no access to the oral sources that once supplemented the written texts, and as a result it is common to misconstrue the whole purpose of the Gospels by mistaking them for attempts at comprehensive, literal history. No Gospel was written as a biography of Jesus. That is one reason why they differ, why times and places do not correspond from Gospel to Gospel, and why gaps in the story of Jesus' life have been filled in with improbable legends. The Gospels were designed to convey the experience of rebirth by baptism in Jesus' name, not primarily to convey historical information.

Mark's Gospel in particular invited its hearers to make connections beyond the text—between Mary Magdalene and the woman who anointed Jesus, for example. Mark also pointed to further sources of guidance regarding Jesus—for instance, to the truth beyond the silence of the women at the Gospel's close. If we focus only on what was written and insist that the Gospels are only history and that the only information about Jesus is in the Gospels, we ignore the promise of resources beyond the text and thus miss what is actually part of the Gospels' message.

———

Is it impossible for us to recover the actual speech and practice of women such as Mary Magdalene? Feminist theology and textual scholarship have proven a vital force in showing that history is flexible, a work of inferential imagination rather than deduction from scientifically ascertainable data. That correction has become standard in the study of the humanities since the middle of the twentieth century, although it has been slow in being applied within scholarship on Christian origins. I doubt this crucial corner would have been turned at all in the study of the New Testament without the contributions of committed feminist writers.

Nonetheless, the inferences of history need to be distinguished from interpreters' projections. Otherwise, any reconstruction could be dismissed as wishful thinking and therefore would never prove durable enough to stand up to debate. Having freed ourselves from the program of marginalizing Mary Magdalene out of deference to male constructs of authority, it would be a shame to fall into the habit of inventing her in the image of contemporary aspirations for women.

Some feminist theology has suffered a failure of nerve in the face of history, and that has resulted in a setback for interpretation as a whole, as several scholars in the movement have argued. A major movement of correction is currently under way, and deserves critical support. Feminist interpretation came into its own during the seventies and eighties of the last century and with some notable exceptions favored literary techniques, rather than historical analysis. The vogue of "the final form of the text" had a profound impact upon thinking about the Bible, both in academic and in popular circles. In focusing on the literary shape of biblical books and their relationships, this approach resisted the analysis of sources within the Gospels.

This fashion had its merits, because it heightened sensitivity to literary patterns running through texts. But enthusiasts for "the final form" can flatten the texts out as much as Conservative Evangelicals do, and so impede historical insight. Each Gospel becomes an author's literarily consistent story, much as in Fundamentalism each Gospel is flattened into literal proof of Protestant doctrine. Indeed, one leader among feminist biblical scholars has called for a rejection of the approach to "the bible as 'fact.' " As a result, when feminist theologians speak of possible "voices" in texts, they sometimes mean not what Mary Magdalene and other women taught, but their own views of how Christianity could or should be practiced. Both feminist and Fundamentalist interpreters, albeit for different reasons, can prove insensitive to how the Gospels were generated over time from the multiple meanings of the sources that fed into them. The one approach can be two-dimensionally ideological, the other two-dimensionally literary; neither gets at the depth and historical texture of the Gospels or at the reality of Mary Magdalene.

If we look at the Gospels not as monoliths but as the sources that emerged out of diverse streams of tradition that interacted with one another, then we can identify not only their methods of erasing women but also those women themselves as living, historical influences, not ventures in wishful deconstruction.

⸺∞⸺

EVEN WHEN FEMINIST THEOLOGY might seem exaggerated in some of its methods and approaches, it has also left an enduring legacy in pressing upon critical readers inescapable truths about the New Testament that traditional—that is, male-dominated—scholarship has obscured. For example: The Gospel According to Mark effaces women. Almost every female—even Jesus' mother—is deprived of her name. She is regularly called Jesus' "mother" (except when Jesus is identified by his contemporaries as "Mary's son"), although Mark goes on to name Jesus' four brothers and tell us in the same passage that Jesus had sisters (6:3) without telling us how many or who they were.

The mother-in-law of Peter, also deprived of a name, features as a feminine ideal in Mark. She is feverish when Jesus enters her house in Capernaum. He cures her, and she then serves him and his disciples (1:30–31): "But Simon's mother-in-law was recumbent, fevered, and at once they talk to him about her. He came forward, raised her—grasping the hand. And the fever left her, and she was providing for them." Where it concerns women, disciples just want to have lunch. Service emerges as the dominant feminine role in Mark. This Gospel names Mary Magdalene and her companions at its close only from necessity, in order to identify who went to Jesus' tomb according to the oral tradition available. So it admits belatedly that they had been part of the action from a much earlier stage in Galilee (15:40–41).

The erasure of Mary Magdalene in Mark's Gospel results from its apologetic purpose. Written during the formative years of the

Church, Mark's Gospel (as well as the other Gospels) embraced key aspects of the value system of the Roman Empire that oppressed Christians. Although that may seem paradoxical, Christians were neither the first persecuted group nor the last to endorse and amplify the values of their oppressors. Saint Paul's infamous mandate, "the women in the churches will keep silence, because it is not appropriate for them to speak" (1 Corinthians 14:34), reflects more than personal male chauvinism. Men in antiquity generally agreed with him.

In the Rome of Mark's Gospel in 73 C.E., Christians were under intense pressure to make their faith look as little like a threat to conventional Roman virtues as possible. Christians were accused of atheism because they would not call the emperor "God's Son" or honor the gods of Rome. To prove they were no threat to the Roman Empire, Christians tried to make themselves appear, at least in one respect, more Roman than the emperor, his agents, and the Roman aristocracy as a whole. Therefore, they upheld the traditional Roman values of a quiet family life in a stable household. Because the Imperial family honored these values more in breach than in observance, it was easy for even low-class Christians to make a good impression. A well-ordered household became an emblem of Christianity's family values, especially from the end of the first century and onward. Teachers who prepared people for baptism downplayed sharp edges in Jesus' perspective on family and sidelined women who had been prominent among Jesus' disciples. That process and its consequences prove central to understanding Mary Magdalene.

The irony of this development of ancient Christian "family values" is that Jesus had demanded the *renunciation* of family for the sake of his message (see Matthew 19:27–30; Mark 10:28–31; Luke 18:28–30). But by the second century, some of Jesus' teachings had been quietly forgotten or reinterpreted. *The Shepherd of Hermas,* written in Rome almost a hundred years after Mark's Gospel, set aside Jesus' rejection of family ties. The family became the sphere of first recourse in working out the behavior that God required, a haven from persecution, and the prudent conduct of its members was a recommendation of Christianity to the overlords of the Roman Empire.

Hermas, a recently freed slave with a rich visionary life, is told by an angel in his vision that keeping women in check within the domestic household is a principal Christian duty, crucial for salvation (*The Shepherd of Hermas* I.1–II.4):

> *But make these words known to all your children and to your wife, who shall in future be to you as a sister. For she also does not refrain her tongue, with which she does evil; but when she has heard these words she will refrain it, and will obtain mercy. After you have made known these words to them, which the master commanded me to be revealed to you, all the sins which they have formerly committed shall be forgiven them, and they shall be forgiven to all the saints who have sinned up to this day, if they repent with their whole heart, and put aside double-mindedness from their heart. For the master has sworn to his elect by his glory that if there still be sin after this day has been fixed, they shall have no salvation; for repentance for the just has a limit; the days of repentance have been fulfilled for all the saints, but for the nations repentance is open until the last day.*

A man, even a low-class man in control of his household, will win salvation despite sin, and that means he needs to keep his wife and children within the circle of forgiveness that obedience establishes.

Demands for mastery of one's family became a rhetorical strong-arm tactic of Christians, despite their weak political and social position. Everyone in the Roman Empire complained of the debauchery of the elite, and Christians could join in that critique, holding themselves above such practices even during periods when they were persecuted. The servility of women became an emblem of the harmony that derived from following Jesus as one's true lord and master. It is not at all hard to see how Mary Magdalene came to be silenced.

Mark's Gospel was written early enough that Mary's effacement is incomplete. But in the later Gospels, women became more and more ancillary. Likewise, Mary's vision at the mouth of the tomb appeared as purely provisional in the Gospels that followed Mark's. As we are about to see, women were even deprived of the role of going to the tomb to anoint Jesus' corpse.

*Chapter Ten*

# EXPURGATING THE
# MAGDALENE

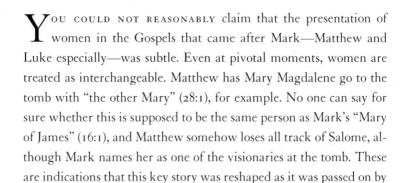

YOU COULD NOT REASONABLY claim that the presentation of
women in the Gospels that came after Mark—Matthew and
Luke especially—was subtle. Even at pivotal moments, women are
treated as interchangeable. Matthew has Mary Magdalene go to the
tomb with "the other Mary" (28:1), for example. No one can say for
sure whether this is supposed to be the same person as Mark's "Mary
of James" (16:1), and Matthew somehow loses all track of Salome, although Mark names her as one of the visionaries at the tomb. These
are indications that this key story was reshaped as it was passed on by
word of mouth prior to the writing of the Gospels—and that reshap-
ing came at a cost to the memory of women.

A well-respected theory, developed in Germany during the nineteenth century and still repeated in standard New Testament text-
books, has it that Matthew is simply an updated edition of Mark, a
direct copy of the original Gospel with additions. But wide variations
between these two Gospels in wording, style, order, and content make
me suspicious of this theory. In my opinion, the differences go far be-

yond slips of a copyist's stylus. We can better account for disparities such as changing the names of the women at the tomb by supposing that each Gospel is a product of interacting oral *and* written traditions.

Mary Magdalene survives Matthew's erasure, but barely. Matthew ignores her whole purpose in going to the tomb. She and the "other" Mary go there not to anoint Jesus but only to see his grave. That change breaks the link with the woman who broke her alabaster jar in order to anoint Jesus. (At least Matthew preserves this narrative |26:6–13|; Luke omits it completely.) The delicate poetics of Mark are discarded: Mary is marginalized, and her deep connection with anointing is submerged.

This break in the link between Mary's ritual anointing and Jesus' Resurrection attenuates her role, but an even deeper reduction in her importance in Matthew, as compared to Mark, follows. Matthew undermines the women's vision at the tomb. Before we read about Mary's experience with her colleagues, Matthew refers to an earthquake that signals Jesus' triumph over death—a legendary event that appears in Matthew alone among the Gospels without leaving a trace in any historical source from the period. It represents a literally seismic shift to a physical rather than visionary belief in Jesus' Resurrection.

Matthew makes the young man at the tomb described in Mark into an agent of this physical event (28:2–4): "And look there happened a great quake, because a messenger |*anggelos* in Greek| of the Lord came down from heaven, came forward, rolled away the stone and sat over it. But his appearance was as lightning and his clothing white as snow. Yet from fear of him those guarding were shaken, and became as dead." The scene in Matthew is no longer purely visionary as in Mark, but a supernatural intervention into the physical world with tangible consequences. The women are completely passive, as if they were "as dead," like the guards.

For all their similarities, each Gospel is unique and develops a poetics all its own. Matthew was composed in Damascus, more than a thousand miles and a cultural world away from Mark's Rome, in a city that—despite its non-Jewish character—Israel's prophets had long associated with the power of God's Spirit. Elisha had healed the Syrian general who came from Damascus (2 Kings 5:1–14), and the Essenes who produced the Dead Sea Scrolls spoke of the city as the place where their teachers had developed their vision of an alternative Israel, brought to earth by an army of angels.

After Jesus' crucifixion and the visions that convinced many of his disciples that he had overcome death, Jesus' Galilean followers faced opposition from the same priestly authorities who had encouraged his execution in response to Jesus' attempt to force a change in Temple worship. Disciples with enough commercial contacts or skills to be mobile settled out of harm's way in cities near Israel, such as Damascus. Damascus was a big pluralistic city with a thriving quarter of Jewish merchants. Ananias, who baptized Paul under prompting by his own visionary experience of Jesus (Acts 9:1–19), had gravitated there in 32 C.E., along with dozens of disciples like him, convinced that visions of Jesus alive and elevated to his Father's Throne fulfilled God's promises to Israel. They didn't think of themselves as "Christians" yet. That word had not yet even been coined. They persistently called the teaching of their resurrected rabbi "the way" (*hodos* in Greek; Acts 9:2; 19:9, 23; 22:4; 24:14, 22), the equivalent of the Rabbinic term *halakhah* (literally, how God commands Israel to "go"). In the years before there was any formal division between Judaism and Christianity, Jesus' followers saw their master as the fulfillment of Israel's destiny, and most of them worked out their peculiar vision in peace with their Jewish neighbors.

By the time Matthew's Gospel was written around 80 C.E., the leaders of the churches in Damascus clearly saw themselves as separate from the synagogues there, and they stopped using the designation "rabbi" altogether (Matthew 23:7–8), but Matthew also shows that the importance of vision had in no way diminished. This is the only Gospel, for example, that speaks of Jesus coming back to earth with his angels to judge all the nations, dividing them up into sheep and goats according to how people had behaved toward one another during their lives (Matthew 25:31–46). Depicted many times in Christian art, it is the classic scene of apocalyptic judgment: eternal punishment for the goats, eternal reward for the sheep. Matthew's poetics pivot on the impact of apocalypse on the material world, just as Mark's poetics pivot on the silent amazement that revelation brings.

It has taken me years to develop a taste for Matthew. Its hard-edged judgment and condemnation of the synagogue leaders of Damascus, together with its insistence that there is no hope for the "goats," lead to Matthew's vilification of "all the people" of Israel, who are portrayed as demanding Jesus' execution from Pilate and saying, "His blood is upon us and upon our children" (Matthew 27:25). Yet with all its anachronism, this Gospel also conveys a sense of vision that is so powerful that it overtakes physical reality and transforms the world. Judgment and trenchant curses heaped on those who do not accept the message of Jesus are part and parcel of Matthew's apocalyptic message. Jesus' Resurrection becomes the model of how all the just will be raised at the end of time. This conception is overtly material in Matthew. Like some Pharisees of the same epoch, the Christian community in Damascus hoped for a physical resuscitation of the dead, not the purely spiritual Resurrection that Jesus, Paul, and Mary Magdalene had taught. The earthquake in Matthew symbolizes how the faithful, starting with Jesus, will be raised from the dead in the same body they had when they were alive: the dogma that Fundamentalists today say is the only correct teaching.

Matthew's materialism derives from the belief that the apocalypse of Jesus, wherever and whenever it occurs, changes physical reality. Vision remains the gateway to revelation, but what counts most for Matthew is the material change in reality that revelation brings. Paul had said that only a "fool" would teach resuscitation of the material body after death (1 Corinthians 15:35–44), insisting that Resurrection needed to be understood spiritually. But Paul finds no place in

Matthew's conceptual universe, and Mary Magdalene's vision appears in the deep shadow of physical apocalypse.

Despite sidelining Mary Magdalene's vision, Matthew does not completely erase her, any more than Mark did. This incomplete erasure underscores her pivotal role as the prime herald of Jesus' Resurrection. Matthew even admits what Mark only implies: after her angelic vision, Mary actually encounters the risen Jesus (Matthew 28:9–10). Matthew's women not only see the angel; they meet Jesus himself as they depart from the mouth of the tomb. Matthew spells out what Mark implies—that the story of the women at the mouth of the tomb points toward a later encounter with Jesus himself.

⸙

LUKE TAKES A DIFFERENT tack from that of Matthew, with poetics that have a literary ring about them. The Gospel opens by acknowledging the oral preachers who provided the sources for the text (Luke 1:1–4). Written around 90 C.E. in Antioch, a more diverse and thoroughly pagan city than Damascus, Luke's Gospel deliberately casts a wider net for these sources than Mark and Matthew do. The purpose of Luke (and its companion piece, the book of Acts, dedicated to the same patron, Theophilus; Acts 1:1; Luke 1:3) was to insist that, despite variety and controversy within Jesus' movement, a single unifying movement of Spirit motivated everything that had happened since the time of John the Baptist's preaching.

Jerusalem symbolizes Christian unity in Spirit for Luke; accordingly, this Gospel portrays the Resurrection in its own way, placing all Jesus' Resurrection appearances in Jerusalem and ignoring any appearances in Galilee. Although Luke does make room for visionary appearances to disciples—preeminently Paul—far from Jerusalem, the dominant conception of Resurrection here is every bit as materialist as Matthew's, but for a different reason. Luke localizes revelation, and the authority revelation brings, in Jerusalem, which is depicted as the unique locus of Jesus' *physical* presence after his Resurrection.

Luke is the first Gospel to have Mary and her companions (whose names change yet again) search the tomb and find it empty (24:2–4): "But they found the stone had been rolled away from the memorial, and entering did not find the body of the Lord Jesus. And it happened while they were at a loss concerning this, and look: two men stood opposite them in gleaming apparel."

Luke produces a certifiably empty tomb, because the women go in and inspect it. Likewise, Luke has the risen Jesus insist on his own physical reality: only in this Gospel does Jesus explicitly say (24:39–43), "See my hands and my feet, that I am myself. Feel me and see, because a spirit does not have flesh and bone just as you perceive I have." Jesus even eats some fish to make his point—and Luke's: the Resurrection is substantial and material, more physical than in any of the other Gospels.

But what is Luke to do with the women's vision, which is never described as anything but a vision, rather than a physical encounter? In this Gospel, Mary's erasure becomes a brutal suppression. Mary Magdalene's whole orientation subverted Luke's materialism. Luke (that is, all those teachers who produced this Gospel, whether as oral teachers or literary editors) reacted fiercely.

The women in Luke don't take part in Jesus' interment, not even implicitly. They only watch and wait through the Sabbath with the ointment they have bought (Luke 23:55–56). But the significance of their ointment—and Mary's connection to the anointing ritual—is lost in Luke, because the entire story about Mary's anointing of Jesus prior to his death, the pivot of the Magdalene source, is excised.

Luke ruptures the connection between Mary's ritual anointing during Jesus' life and her visit to his tomb. The power of an ancient memory nonetheless makes Luke name Mary Magdalene first among the women at the mouth of the tomb. Badly erased, she still is not totally expunged.

Yet for all that Mary's vision remains in Luke, Mary and her companions do not succeed in convincing the other disciples that their vision was authentic; the men reject their testimony as "nonsense" (*leros*, 24:9–12), idle tales from women. Apart from tangible—that is, physical—substance, Luke dismisses vision and women's testimony with a single word.

For Luke's Gospel, only Jesus personally, raised from the dead in flesh and bone (24:39), can explain his resurrected presence among his disciples. The book of Acts (1:3) sets aside a period of forty days, during which the risen Jesus teaches his followers in and around Jerusalem, not Galilee, and no mention of Mary Magdalene appears in this context.

In the midst of notorious disputes among Christians in Antioch (described in Acts 15 and Galatians 2)—between those who practiced circumcision and those who did not, those who avoided meat that had been sacrificed to Gentile idols and those who did not—Luke and Acts insisted that policy could be set only by the apostles in Jerusalem, on the basis of their experience of the Resurrection.

But couldn't that apostolic company have included Mary and her companions? Weren't such women recognized as apostles? Those are realistic possibilities, given what we know about Jesus' movement in its early decades. After all, Paul refers to a woman named Junia as an apostle (Romans 16:7). Why wouldn't someone like Mary Magdalene have had the same status?

Whatever the case in other communities, Luke shuts the door on any such suggestion. Neither Luke nor Acts ever speaks of women apostles; neither relates a personal encounter between Mary and the risen Jesus.

When Luke's male apostles who see the risen Jesus write off Mary's vision, that is no idle dismissal. It is astonishing that this occurs just before another visionary appearance of Jesus, one that Luke *does* accept. Men, and only men, speak of this appearance. A stranger joins two disciples (one named Kleopas) when they are on the way to Emmaus from Jerusalem after the crucifixion. (Recent suggestions that Kleopas's companion might have been a woman stumble on the pattern of male dominance that Luke manifests.) At first, they do not recognize him, but he reveals himself to them as Jesus during a meal—and then becomes invisible (Luke 24:13–35). In Luke, this male-only account completely supersedes the story about Mary and the other women at the tomb.

By including this story, Luke endorsed vision as a partial experience of Jesus' Resurrection, despite the Gospel's materialist bias. That was vital to the plan of Luke and Acts, because all of Paul's three encounters with the risen Jesus were strictly visionary (Acts 9:1–19; 22:6–16; 26:12–18; compare Galatians 1:15–17). Provided these visions were accepted by the apostles in Jerusalem, Luke was also willing to accept them.

But Luke had no use for the visionary precedent that came from Mary Magdalene and her colleagues; it had to be Kleopas and his companion who set the stage for Paul. There is no angelic commission in Luke for Mary and her companions to tell the apostles what they saw. Heavenly messengers simply remind the women of what Jesus himself had already told them when he was alive (Luke 24:6–7): "He is not here, but is raised. Remember how he spoke to you when he was still in Galilee, saying it was necessary for the one like the person to be delivered over into the hands of sinful people and to be crucified and on the third day to arise." Kleopas sets apostolic faith in motion, while Mary is bracketed in parentheses, serving only to hold the place of what Jesus had said earlier, long before her vision.

Luke's Gospel alludes to Mary's intimate knowledge of Jesus' practice of exorcism (8:2), as we have seen. But that obviously doesn't make this Gospel feminist, because referring to women is not at all the same thing as including them as agents in Jesus' ministry and Resurrection. Luke used sources that evidently did convey women's perspectives, but this Gospel's own view is quite different, focused on the unique authority of the male apostles in Jerusalem.

When Luke presents a woman named Mary as choosing "the good part" of a disciple by sitting at Jesus' feet rather than serving him, the Gospel is careful to specify that this is Mary, Martha's sister, not Mary Magdalene (10:38–42). In that way, sitting at Jesus' feet or not, the woman would not be associated with any tradition or source that could compete with apostolic authority in Jerusalem. She does not even speak. But then Jesus' mother, addressed by the angel Gabriel, identifies herself as "the slave of the Lord" (1:38). Luke's dedication to the hierarchy of the Jerusalem apostles, together with a view of the Resurrection that in its own way is as materialist as Matthew's, forced a marginalization of the Magdalene, her vision, her source, and her practice of anointing.

⸙

MARK, MATTHEW, AND LUKE constitute the best available sources concerning Mary Magdalene; they are nearest in time and ethos to the source Mary crafted. Scholars call these Gospels "Synoptic" because they are so similar, they can be printed out in columns and compared with one another. That sets them apart from John's Gospel (to which we shall soon turn) and shows how close they all are to sources such as Mary's. But they also illustrate a program of suppressing Mary's influence. The Synoptic Gospels silence Mary in deference to Christianity's emergent family values, and to prevent her view of Jesus' Resurrection from interfering with their own. They give short shrift to Mary's role in ritual anointing, and they all but wipe out explicit reference to her association with Jesus' exorcisms.

The same Gospels that prove the Magdalene's influence resent her memory and seek to displace it. That ambivalence infected texts that came later, both Christian and Gnostic, and has infected the scholarly and popular evaluation of Mary Magdalene to this day.

## Chapter Eleven

# ORTHODOX AMBIVALENCE
# AND THE GNOSTIC QUEST

A MBIVALENCE SHROUDS MARY Magdalene in Mark, Matthew, and Luke. She threatened the growing conviction among those practicing Christianity that women's authority had to be suppressed, yet Mary's spiritual disciplines of exorcism, anointing, and vision were indispensable to Christian practice. A strained, sporadically broken silence was the result.

Mary moves in the oral shadows of written Gospels, ritually powerful yet muted. As Christianity spread throughout the Greco-Roman world, the strains on this silence increased. Appeals to the tranquillity of a male-ordered household became more and more insistent in Christian literature, but in that same literature women emerged in roles of religious leadership.

This tension crackles through the First Letter to Timothy, which is attributed to Paul but was in fact written some thirty years after his death. This counterfeit letter had several aims, largely related to church organization. It confines women to the role of bearing and rearing children (1 Timothy 2:13–15): "Because Adam was first fashioned, then Eve. And Adam was not deceived, but the misled woman came into transgression. But she will be saved through childbearing, if they remain in faith and love and sanctification with prudence." This is neither the teaching of Genesis nor the theology of Paul, but the party line of the up-and-coming Christian hierarchy that wanted to make sure that, as in a well-run Roman household, men were firmly in positions of leadership throughout the Church and that women did not abandon the roles of wives and mothers.

Yet the same 1 Timothy that stakes out this new doctrine of male dominance also admits that women can undertake the key role of being an "elder" (a *presbuteros* in Greek, from *zaken* in Hebrew). Within Judaism, this term designated a local synagogue leader, but its resonance goes well beyond Jewish custom alone. To this day in several cultures, the gathering of an extended family for a major event such as a wedding includes the designation of a senior relative as the elder of the proceedings. The elder does not personally direct the proceedings, but his presence assures that the event unfolds as it should.

In antiquity, an elder exercised a similar function in a synagogue or a church. The Greek word for *elder* is masculine in gender, and is applied normally to men, but the fact is that 1 Timothy (5:1–2) refers both to the "elderman" (*presbuteros*) and to the "elderwoman" (*presbutera*) leading a congregation.

The earliest known visual image of Christians celebrating a Eucharist, the meal that celebrated Christ's sacrifice and his abiding presence with believers, is the fresco in the Saint Priscilla catacomb in Rome called *Fractio Panis* (*The Breaking of Bread*). Those who take part in the meal, including the person who is breaking and distributing the bread, are women. In this case, the *presbutera* is acting as a priest would act today, and that is no coincidence: The word *priest* in English is a contraction of the term *presbuteros*. In addition to the practices of exorcism and anointing that the Gospels associated with Mary Magdalene, the power of her vision of Jesus risen from the dead made women after her natural leaders of the Eucharist, the celebration of Jesus' heavenly enthronement.

─────

Two conflicting forces lie at the heart of the early Church's fierce ambivalence about women, and they went beyond the scope of usual prejudices in the Greco-Roman world. As we've observed, Christians wanted to appear more Roman than the Romans in the control they exercised over their households. At the same time, they wrestled with the meaning of Paul's principle of an overriding human unity—"There is not a single Jew or Greek, not a single slave or freedman, not a single male or female, because you are all one in Jesus Christ" (Galatians 3:28)—as well as with the simple fact that Jesus had included women such as Mary Magdalene among his closest disciples.

Unknown to the general public and often ignored even in scholarship, the women *presbuterai* exerted a deep influence in the Church until the fourth century of the Common Era. They continued the inheritance of women from the Scriptures of Israel. They led worship, as did another Miriam, the psalmist and sister of Moses who celebrated the exodus from Egypt (Exodus 15:20–21). Like Deborah, prophetess and judge (Judges 4–5), a *presbutera* could guide small communities that were torn apart by persecution and strife. The memory of Huldah, the prophetess in Jerusalem during the seventh century B.C.E., also resonated with the example of leadership that Mary Magdalene set. When King Josiah found a book of the Torah, he confirmed it was indeed the Law of Moses by consulting Huldah (2 Kings 22:8–20) rather than any male prophet. Similarly, Mary Magdalene became the prime herald of the resurrected Jesus as a living spiritual principle and personality.

Mary exerted such authority as the herald of Jesus' Resurrection that some of Christianity's earliest teachers called her "apostle of the apostles." Her role as an ur-apostle in this sense was recognized from the second century. Her role aligns with that of women in the early sources of Rabbinic Judaism; figures such as Imma Shalom and Beruria demonstrate that there was a Judaic tradition of women as authoritative teachers, experts on *halakhah,* and guides to divine Wisdom.

Feminine ministry in its complexity and breadth, authorized by the memory of the Magdalene, surfaces in even the most dogmatic texts of Catholic Christianity during the ancient period. Hippolytus, a famously conservative priest of third-century Rome, designated Mary as the ur-apostle in his commentary on the Song of Songs, a treatise that features the powerful effect of the oil of anointing. Mary Magdalene, the Holy Spirit, and the practice of anointing all converged in ancient Christian practice.

An order of church worship and regulation called the *Didascalia of the Twelve Apostles*—compiled in Syria during the third century on the basis of earlier traditions—explicitly commands, "You shall revere the deaconess in the place of the Holy Spirit" (9.26.6). Women in the ordained role of deaconess actually represented the Spirit in divine worship as far as the ancient Syriac community that produced the *Didascalia* was concerned. The primordial Semitic association between the Spirit of creation and divine Wisdom, both feminine, survived and flourished where Jesus' own patterns of thought and practice were remembered.

Holy Scripture mandated the role of deaconesses according to this source, and Mary Magdalene provided the premier example (*Didascalia* 16.12.4, referring to Matthew 27:55–6): "We have said that the service of a woman deaconess is above all obligatory and necessary, because our Lord and Savior was served by women deaconesses, who are: Mary Magdalene, Mary the daughter of James, and the mother of Joses, and the mother of the sons of Zebedee with other women."

The *Didascalia* stresses this role of women's ministry, even though its dedication to Hellenistic patriarchy caused its authors to stipulate that deaconesses *must* anoint but *cannot* teach (*Didascalia* 15.6.2): "If the women were intended to teach, our Master would have commanded them to teach with us."

Saying that Jesus' "deaconesses" ministered to him implied physical contact. Despite this implication of anointing across the line of gender in Jesus' time, the *Didascalia* advocated none of that during its own period. It guarded against this possibility by insisting that women should be in physical contact *only with other women* (16.12.2): "First of all, when women go down in the water for baptism, it is obligatory that those who go down in the water should be anointed with the oil of unction by the deaconess." The practice of baptism involved sexual apartheid because people entered the water naked, and the deacons or the deaconesses anointed their bodies.

Unction was not only the dab of oil on the forehead and hands at the time of death that it has become in modern Christianity. It involved a full-body application of oil, and the ritual was repeated, both for healing and for sanctification. Prior to baptism, the candidate received "the oil of exorcism," to expel the evil of that person's former life. After baptism came "the oil of thanksgiving," celebrating the Holy Spirit, which inhabited the individual's whole body.

No wonder the *Didascalia* wanted to hold on to the role of the deaconess and insist that she alone represented the Holy Spirit where anointing women was concerned, notwithstanding its desire to exclude women from positions of power and influence. A policy of separating the sexes resulted, gathering force over time. Once Christianity had become a state-sponsored and thus widely accessible institution during the fourth century, the intimacy of esoteric groups in which men might anoint women and women might anoint men was lost. The character of the Church changed dramatically during the fourth century, after Constantine's conversion. The small, sometimes clandestine meetings of Christians liable to persecution, willing in their ecstatic worship to challenge conventional expectations, became large, officially sanctioned liturgical services in basilicas, where the participants consciously shaped their behavior to serve as a model for the Roman Empire. Public decency demanded the sexual apartheid in baptism that quickly became the rule.

Eventually, a distrust of human bodies as such would go beyond sexual apartheid and greatly restrict the practice of anointing—in the extent of flesh that could be touched, the frequency of the rite, and in the clergy authorized to administer it. By the Middle Ages, "extreme unction"—as it came to be called, the term itself indicating the rite's marginalization—had become one of the "Seven Sacraments." Only people at the point of death would receive it, by having their foreheads and hands anointed by an all-male priesthood. (Interestingly, some sacramental manuals called for priests to anoint the area of the kidneys of men |only, of course| when administering extreme unction. That seems to recall the ancient memory of anointing a person's body as a whole.) Women no longer served as clergy, and the repeated full-body application of oil in the ancient church was supplanted by a practice that could only conceive of human bodies as sacred above the eyebrows and on the hands, provided the latter were pure.

By the twelfth century, a legend about Mary Magdalene developed that compensated for the severe restriction in the practice of anointing. Unhampered by conventional morality in her sinfulness, the legendary Mary now acted in a way no decent woman during the Middle Ages could have gotten away with:

*Rising, she reverently approached the couch on which the Saviour was resting and stood confidently behind the Messiah, from whose paths she lamented having wandered. With the tears of her eyes, with which she had once looked after worldly loves, she washed his feet; with her hair, which before enhanced the beauty of her face, she dried them; with her mouth, which she had abused in pride and lasciviousness, she kissed them; and with the perfumes she had bought she anointed them, as once (it grieved her to remember) she had anointed her own flesh to make it more seductive.*

This rich scene, inspired by the first story of anointing in Luke (7:36–50), is here made into an account of Mary Magdalene's anointing of Jesus, an event that climaxed in her "fire of great love"—when she broke her alabaster jar to apply its oil to him at the end of his life, she proved her "intimacy with the Son of God." This is what made her "the special friend of the Son of God and his first servant," as well as "the apostle to the apostles." Their physical intimacy only highlights the contrast with Mary's verbal silence. The Catholic Magdalene has nothing to say, her significance mimed in legend and artistic representation. In order to hear her speak, we must turn to other sources.

⸻

ALONGSIDE THE SOURCES of Catholic Christianity, which silenced Mary and her successors but permitted deaconesses to anoint, Gnostic sources moved in a different direction. Gnostics added a volatile attitude toward sexuality to the ambivalence of early Christians toward women. Some Gnostic communities were celibate and thus had no children of their own. They believed the body's pleasures mired people in a fallen world. Others Gnostics were programmatic libertines, flouting convention in order to transcend this delusional world through orgiastic rites. For many Gnostics of both kinds, Mary Magdalene stood at the apex of those who glimpsed the spiritual reality beyond human flesh: After all, she had seen the risen Jesus.

The Gnostics' ambivalence toward women and sexuality is reflected in their depictions of Mary; even when she is praised, there is criticism, as well. She is authoritative, wise, knowledgeable, and powerful, and, at the same time, submissive, weak, hysterical, and—as *The Gospel According to Thomas* will show us in the next chapter—even physically deficient. Gnostic sources provide fascinating insights into how views of Mary shaped attitudes toward leadership of women in religious communities, feminine identity in the godhead, and the nature of revelation. But, as in the case of Catholic Christianity, context proves crucial to appreciating what Gnosticism has to tell us.

*Chapter Twelve*

# THE BREAKOUT

B ETWEEN THE LATE FIRST century and the end of the fourth century of the Common Era, a powerful religious impulse rippled through the Roman Empire. Gnosticism quested for a single integrating insight into the divine world amid the conflicting religious traditions of the ancient world. Gnostics wanted direct contact with the divine apart from parochial requirements, peculiar customs, and ethnic preferences. Traditional religions talked about transcendence, but they restricted the delivery of their truths to their different constituencies, which were limited and often mutually exclusive, defined by race, history, family, or status. Gnosticism claimed to smash through those barriers, making it the most potent cultural force in this period of the Roman Empire and the most successful effort at the intellectual reform of religion there has ever been. Mary Magdalene became one of Gnosticism's most potent symbols.

Many people in the ancient world—some of them educated, all of them intellectually curious—felt bewildered by the welter of religions around them, each often in open conflict with the others. If you moved from one city to another, the civic god changed; new rites and obligations were required. Civic offerings—a requirement of citizen-ship, if you were lucky and rich enough to be a citizen—were costly.

Judaism rose above a great deal of religious static, offering faith in a single God, who did not change identities, personalities, or names from place to place. Monotheism seemed more consistent with ra-tional philosophy than the soap opera–like cast of thousands that in-habited Mount Olympus and other venues in classical mythology. The attraction of Gentiles to the teaching of Moses and the Prophets proves its appeal within the philosophical and religious syncretism of this period. Non-Jews called "God-fearers" devoted themselves to the God of Israel, worshiping in synagogues and keeping some basic re-quirements of Judaism, enjoying its intellectual and ethical benefits while avoiding its most painful requirements.

But from the perspective of the Hellenistic world, the religion of Israel came from a single people, even if its god claimed to be univer-sal, and coming to Judaism as a proselyte did not make a person into an Israelite. A male who converted, even if he accepted circumcision, could not reverse the course of time and thereby arrange to be cir-cumcised on the eighth day of his life, as the Torah demanded (Gen-esis 17:10–14). Judaism was demanding if you took it seriously: The Torah limited what you could eat and prevented you from worship-ing idols—even the image of the Roman emperor, who by law was owed allegiance as *Divi filius,* "God's Son." The Torah mandated when you could have sexual intercourse as well as with whom, and even the amount of skin you could keep on your penis. To Greco-Roman sensibilities, these practices were not only onerous but also grotesque. Judaism attracted more women than men, but "God-fearers" outnumbered converts in the Hellenistic world.

Mystery religions were demanding in different ways. They offered intimacy with a god or goddess (perhaps Dionysos or Isis) and per-sonal initiation into the divine power of the deity. These initiation rites were expensive and flamboyant. The god Mithra became popular among Roman soldiers who could afford him. In Mithra's cult, the initiate maintained a regime of fasting for weeks and repeatedly immersed himself. At the end of this period of purification, the Mithraic warrior joined in a performance that reenacted on the earth what had happened in the divine realm, when the god Mithra triumphed over and slaughtered the cosmic bull.

This lavish ceremony—with its decorative costumes, dance, carousing, and feasting—took place at night. At its climax, the initiate descended into a pit with an iron grate overhead. A bull was conducted onto the grate and then a priest slit its throat, drenching the initiate with the blood and excrement of the bull's thundering death. When the initiate emerged from the pit, his fellow worshipers cried out that he was *renatus in aeternum* ("reborn into eternity"). All well and good if you could afford the bull (the Mercedes-Benz of sacrificial offerings), the time involved, the feasting, and the equipment— all luxuries few people could pay for or commandeer as a marauding soldier might.

The modern West didn't invent religious diversity; religious pluralism was far greater in the Roman Empire than it is today. Think of Los Angeles or New York, multiply the number of religions, magnify the tensions among them, and add into that mix the pretension of the Roman emperor that he had a divine warrant as God's Son for his authority; then you will have a sense of the profound spiritual rifts that Gnosticism confronted.

Each movement and cult, often named after foreigners like the Egyptian Isis and the Israelite Jesus, proclaimed unique access to the truth and rejected the claims of other religions. Christians even refused to worship the emperor in their zeal for their crucified Savior, and the spectacle of their being torn apart by animals, burned on pyres, and flayed by professional torturers made them seem as obdurate as it made the Romans look vicious.

The power of Gnosticism transformed the face of Greco-Roman

religion: Virtually every religious movement was influenced by it. Gnostic questers pioneered a philosophical approach to religious truth that was based on knowledge rather than faith, practice, or formal organization. The Christian church, the Jewish synagogue, the guild of adepts in the Mysteries find no real counterpart among the Gnostics. They pursued knowledge (*gnosis* in Greek) so intently that they came to be called *gnostikoi*. If the word *knowledgist* existed in English, that would be a good translation, because Gnostics claimed to be "in the know" about the most fundamental reality and to be in contact with the divine. Gnosticism thrived among people educated enough to enjoy philosophical speculation, experimental enough to seek religious experience, and wealthy enough to support experts to teach the ways of knowledge.

Mary Magdalene became emblematic of that transforming guest. Her *gnosis* wasn't just a collection of data or reasoned argument; rather, the knowledge she conveyed involved direct insight into the celestial realm, and brought about an inner transformation in the Gnostic seeker who followed her lead. Gnosticism as a whole was a movement for a self-appointed elite, which strove to transcend the material universe and its corruption. The true Gnostic transcended the shackles of the fallen, physical world and became inured to suffering and pleasure in his or her total dedication to the spiritual world. Each person who found *gnosis* lived thereafter in the assurance of divine favor, saved from the predations of the flesh, incarnated within the realm of Spirit. Entering that realm required guidance, and Mary Magdalene became one of Gnosticism's most articulate guides.

IN ORDER FOR MARY Magdalene to convey her vision of Jesus risen from the dead, her silence had to be broken. Many Gnostics removed the gag that the Gospels imposed, and they taught that she was free of the mold of female subservience to men. In 1896, a manuscript was discovered in Egypt. Entitled *The Gospel According to Mary,* that document has forever changed our understanding of Mary.

*The Gospel According to Mary,* dating from early-third-century Egypt, was used by the prosperous landowners who sustained Gnosticism throughout the ancient period. The *Mary* in the title refers to the Magdalene, and the Coptic text reflects the Gnostic Christianity that thrived in Egypt eighteen hundred years ago.

The Coptic language itself was part of the key to Gnosticism's success in Egypt. The hieroglyphics of ancient Egypt were difficult to write and read, but Coptic put the same language into the phonetic system of the Greek alphabet (with four extra characters). That innovation enabled people with leisure in rural Egypt to read and have read to them recitations of the world's wisdom in their own tongue. They became avid for philosophy, religion, and esoteric knowledge, and Gnosticism packaged them all in a way that ensured its advance on Egyptian soil. Mary's centrality for these seekers has attracted considerable attention from theologians and textual scholars alike.

Following a Gnostic trope, *The Gospel According to Mary* depicts Jesus appearing to his disciples after his death for an extensive period of time. His risen persona doesn't provide reassurance, as he usually does in Gnostic literature. Instead, Jesus' appearance produces anguish. The disciples don't despair because they are bereft. They have the opposite problem. Jesus is all too present, and—as in life—all too demanding. He insists that his followers act in ways that seem unnatural and perilous to them, commanding them to take his message to the Gentiles. He does the same thing in the Gospel According to Matthew and the book of Acts, but in *The Gospel According to Mary,* the disciples respond more fearfully than they do in the New Testament. Jesus' disciples know that it was the Romans who killed him and they realize all too clearly that if they obey him, they court a similar fate. "If they did not spare him," they moan, "how will they spare us?" (*The Gospel According to Mary* 9.10). By the time this Gospel was written, its audience knew that the move to proselytize non-Israelites, although crucial to the emergence of Christianity, had also proved to be a deadly gambit for many of Jesus' closest followers.

Peter is a key figure in *The Gospel According to Mary,* as he is in the book of Acts; in both cases, contact with non-Jews is Peter's central concern. But the Gnostic text—for historical reasons or theological reasons, or some blend of the two—presents a view of how the message of Jesus reached non-Israelites that contradicts the book of Acts, making Mary, rather than Peter, the pivotal disciple who prompted that religious revolution. *The Gospel According to Mary* goes its own way in portraying Peter as more bewildered by Christ's command to approach people outside Israel than he is in Acts 10:9–29. He needs to ask for Mary's advice, because he cannot understand why Jesus would tell him to court mortal danger. Mary does understand, so Peter turns to a woman's authority, despite his male antipathy toward doing so.

While Peter and his colleagues grieve at the prospect of the suffering that awaits them at Gentile hands, Mary intervenes, "greeting them all" and cajoling them to rely on God, who "has prepared us and made us into men" (*The Gospel According to Mary* 9.19–20). The Magdalene emerges as an androgynous hero who strengthens the males in the apostolic company by means of the manhood—the visionary commitment to remain loyal to Jesus despite the risk of martyrdom—that she herself has received from Jesus. To be a "man" in this Gospel is to live in the realm of Spirit, despite the threat of danger in the world of flesh.

Mary kisses her colleagues, "greeting them all." In Coptic, as in Greek, the verb *aspazomai* implies a mouth-to-mouth embrace of fellowship. This gesture of trust among men and women signaled familial intimacy throughout the Mediterranean world. Men kissed men, women kissed women, women kissed men, and vice versa. The "holy kiss" became a key Christian ritual, featuring centrally in both Catholic and Gnostic sources.

But the fact that the verb *aspazomai* is used here should not be misconstrued: It does *not* make Mary an especially sexual figure. Sadly, some modern translators have Mary "kissing" her colleagues, while elsewhere her male counterparts are portrayed as "greeting" each other, although exactly the same term is used. Loose, opportunistic translations of this kind perpetuate the Magdalene's caricature as modern Christianity's favorite vixen.

In *The Gospel According to Mary,* Peter is at a loss without Mary's guidance and the strengthening of her special manhood. He and the apostles have given her a hearing because she is among the select company who experienced the resurrected Jesus. Her kiss is the seal that she belongs in this company, not an invitation to sex. When she speaks of her own revelation, her discourse forms the core of *The Gospel According to Mary* and its content authorizes the apostolic commission to Gentiles in Jesus' name. Mary Magdalene rather than Peter brings about Christianity's emergence in the Hellenistic world.

She speaks very briefly in the text as it stands, because several pages containing her discourse have been physically removed. Yet even in its truncated form, her address offers the clearest evidence we have of how ancient Christianity and Gnosticism conceived of visionary experience. Her words vibrate with a simple grandeur and elegance (*The Gospel According to Mary* 10.6–20):

> *I saw the Lord in a vision and I said to him, Lord I saw you today in a vision. He answered and said to me, You are privileged, because you did not waver at the sight of me. For where the mind is, there is the treasure. I said to him, Lord now does he who sees the vision see it through the soul or through the spirit? The Savior answered and said, He sees neither through the soul nor through the spirit, but the mind which is between the two—that is what sees the vision and is—*

Then the document breaks off for several pages. That excision, apparently inflicted on the text in antiquity, forms yet another scar over the memory of Mary. Yet *The Gospel According to Mary* clearly understands that, in portraying the Resurrection in trenchantly visionary terms (as the perception of the "mind," not of physical eyes or ears or hands), Mary directly contradicted a growing fashion in ancient Christianity that conceived of Jesus as resuscitated from the grave in the flesh.

Whatever Mary goes on to say in the missing part of the document, Peter and Andrew together rebuke Mary after her speech. Their anger—summed up in a rhetorical question—stems both from what she says and from what their paternalism considers her inferior gender (*The Gospel According to Mary* 17.9–19.1): "Has he revealed these things to a woman and not to us?" Mary's articulate insight and her gender upset Peter and his cohort. A woman had experienced a visionary breakthrough that permitted her to see Jesus' desire to reach out to Gentiles before Peter himself did, the same woman whose vision first signaled that Jesus had been raised from the dead. This claim in *The Gospel According to Mary* is quite convincing.

This Gospel reflects not only Mary's theory of vision as she had articulated it from the first century but also the controversies of later periods, using the characters of Peter and Andrew to portray the reaction against Mary within the Catholic Church during the second and third centuries of the Common Era. As theologians became increasingly materialistic in their conception of how Jesus rose from the dead and how all believers were to be resurrected, Mary's vision fell into disfavor.

*The Gospel According to Mary* stood by Mary Magdalene's vision. Here, seeing Jesus is unashamedly a perception of the "mind" (*nous* in both Greek and Coptic). Paul, who shared Mary's view of the Resurrection, also articulated a theology of "mind" that agrees with this (1 Corinthians 14:19). "Mind," for Paul as well as for *The Gospel According to Mary*, was the instrument of lucid vision.

*Mind*, the term used in both Paul and *The Gospel According to*

*Mary,* is the Hellenistic equivalent of "heart" (*livva*) in Aramaic. To appreciate the place of "heart" in the Aramaic language that shaped Mary's experience, we have to imagine thoughts, in addition to feelings and affections, flowing from our bodies, because the *livva* was the locus of insight as well as of emotions and sensations. When Jesus promised that the pure in heart would see God (Matthew 5:8), that was a pledge of bodily transformation, not just insight.

Paul shared Mary's conception of a transforming heart/mind as the key to human existence, but this conception was Mary's before it was Paul's. Knowledge of God for Mary and Paul (as for the Gnostics) could only be spiritual, derived from divine revelation. Just as Paul says in 1 Corinthians 15 that Resurrection is not achieved by flesh or even by soul, but only by Spirit, so he also insists that "the man by soul |*psykhikos* in Greek| does not receive the things of the Spirit, for they are foolishness to him and he can't know, because they are discerned spiritually" (1 Corinthians 2:14). Quoting Isaiah again, Paul specifies the "mind" |*nous* again| as the organ that perceives Spirit (1 Corinthians 2:16): "For who knows the Lord's mind that will advise him? But we have Christ's mind."

For some reason, a simple fact has been passed over in previous scholarship: Paul's conception here agrees with the Magdalene's as expressed in *The Gospel According to Mary.* Paul and Mary agree on "mind" as the locus of revelation, and their agreement is completely coherent with their shared conception of how Jesus was raised from the dead. Mary is the teacher who most likely influenced Peter in the practice of vision, and she also provided Paul (no doubt indirectly) with a visionary theory that he developed in explaining how people come to know God.

Just as Mary's teaching lies silently behind Paul's where Resurrection is concerned, so the centrality of heart or mind represents her contribution to Paul's anthropology of revelation. Mind for Paul discloses Spirit. Mind was also the visionary organ that powered the

Magdalene's recognition of the risen Jesus (John 20:16, discussed below). The importance of *The Gospel According to Mary* only emerges when we read it not in isolation but in its connection with the thought and practice of ancient Christianity as a whole. That principle, too often neglected in the study of Gnostic texts, permits us to perceive the power and continuing force of Mary's vision.

Linking Mary's conception of the vision of the mind with her teaching of the spiritual nature of the risen state yields a final insight. The person she sees with her mind's eye raised from the dead is no longer "flesh" or even "soul," but pure spirit. Jesus no longer corresponds to the categories of this world, but is apprehended as we apprehend God—spiritually. Again, Paul puts Mary's vision into words and into policy (Galatians 3:28): "There is not a single Jew or Greek, not a single slave or freedman, not a single male or female, because you are all one in Jesus Christ."

Paul said that all who believe in Jesus, Jews as well as Gentiles, become children of Abraham, a new "Israel." Jesus was no longer flesh, so that no category of the flesh—not even circumcision as mandated in the Torah—could be used to limit one's understanding of who could benefit from his teaching. Jesus had become a new, spiritual being, a "last Adam" in Paul's words (1 Corinthians 15:45), who poured out the power of Spirit on others, no matter what the conventions of this world might say. What was an intellectual premise for Paul (however deeply felt) was for Mary a direct experience of her rabbi raised from the dead. As the androgynous Mary said in the language of later Gnosticism (*The Gospel According to Mary* 9.19–20), this "has prepared us and made us into men," a new humanity, one in which distinctions of gender and race and religion no longer had any validity.

※

THE CROSSOVER OF IDEAS and traditions between Christianity and Gnosticism alone explains how Mary Magdalene has been understood in the West. During the second century, the Gospel According to John and *The Gospel According to Thomas* had already articulated two crucial ideas that *The Gospel According to Mary* expressed with incomparable clarity during the third century: the nature of Resurrection vision and the Magdalene's androgyny. Taken together, John's Gospel, *The Gospel According to Thomas,* and *The Gospel According to Mary* bring to open expression some of the principal insights and themes of Christian *gnosis.*

By the time the Gospel According to John was produced, around 100 C.E. in Ephesus, the confluence of Christianity and Gnosticism was thriving. John offers the possibility of a new, spiritual birth by being begotten from the "word" of God, rather than from flesh (1:12, 13). Rebirth from water and Spirit happens for John at the moment of baptism (3:3–8). John alone among the Gospels explicitly identifies Satan, the spiritual antagonist who resists this transformation, as "the ruler of this world" (12:31), the realm of flesh. The Gnostic Jesus of John's Gospel triumphs over this enemy by his death: "Courage: I have overcome the world" (16:33).

John's Ephesian audience regarded itself as more philosophical than the well-educated rabbi Nicodemus, who in a scene of almost comic misunderstanding shows himself too literalistic to understand Jesus' teaching about being born again (John 3:1–15). Rabbi Jesus tells him that a person must be born anew to see the kingdom of God. The Greek word used for *anew* can also be understood as "from above" or "again." (This Greek word, *anothen,* corresponds to the English expression of taking a piece of music "from the top.") But poor Nicodemus's imagination is so limited, he finds himself asking how an old man could enter his mother's womb a second time (John 3:4). In John's caricature this "ruler of the Jews" struggles to understand what the baptized Christians for whom this Gospel is designed had long appreciated.

Ephesus was a jewel of Greek culture on the western shore of Asia

Minor. This commercially vibrant center with an active port hosted religious traditions from all over the Mediterranean, as well as innovative movements such as Christianity and Gnosticism and cults of Mystery. Traders transported goods and ideas overland toward the East and by ship south into the Mediterranean from the Aegean Sea, where they bartered for local produce and encountered local primordial traditions of worship and fertility. Ephesus boasted several synagogues, philosophical schools, lecture halls and theaters, temples for Hellenistic deities, a famous brothel, splendid baths and houses, giant tenements, and, by early in the second century, a spectacular library.

John's Jesus—unlike the Synoptics'—"makes" water into wine like the god Dionysos (4:40), whose cult in Ephesus was a powerful influence. Jesus even offers his personal flesh to be eaten and his blood for drinking (6:52–59), much as in the Dionysian Mysteries—but unlike the Gospels of Mark, Matthew, and Luke. John also opens with a poem on the "word" of God (the *logos;* 1:1–18) that echoes Stoic and Platonic ideas at the same time that it resonates with themes at the opening of the book of Genesis. Taken as a whole, this Gospel is a hymn to the cosmic Christ by the Gnostic Church for those with the inner knowledge of how to be reborn in Spirit rather than flesh.

Mary Magdalene's vision of the risen Christ is central to the Gnostic rebirth that John's Gospel offers. Mary is the first person to see Jesus, and in John, she sees Jesus himself, although she is hysterical and doesn't recognize him at first (20:11–18). Only when he speaks her name does she realize that she is speaking to her rabbi, and so she cries out in Aramaic, "*Rabbouni*" (which is to say, "Teacher") (20:16). She must have reached out to Jesus, because he says (v. 17), "Do not touch me, because I have not yet ascended to the father. But proceed to my brothers and say to them, I ascend to my father and your father, my God and your God." Mary departs and is the first person to say, "I have seen the Lord" (John 20:18). It is *her* experience that ultimately teaches the other disciples how to see Jesus as well.

This is by far the most detailed account of Mary's vision in the New Testament, and it disrupts the pattern of her growing marginalization in the Synoptic Gospels. John does undercut the impact of Mary's vision by interrupting the narrative with the race of Peter and his companion to the tomb and their inspection of the site (20:1–10). But this Gospel admits—contrary to what Paul says, and in agreement with what Mark implies and Matthew admits in broad strokes—that Mary Magdalene was the first to see the risen Jesus, and that this experience was part and parcel of her angelic vision.

When Jesus says to Mary, "Do not touch me," it is because his body is now spiritual, no longer to be touched or anointed. But in John, she shouldn't touch him even *prior* to the Resurrection. The physical separation of Jesus from Mary runs through the entire Gospel—expressing a fierce Gnostic ambivalence toward Mary and feminine sexuality.

In the crucial scene of Jesus' anointing prior to his death, John (12:1–8) explicitly names Mary of Bethany, the sister of Martha and Lazarus, as the anointer who is presented anonymously in Mark and Matthew. Having Jesus anointed by a woman whose relatives were present, including a male protector (Lazarus), removes any hint of impropriety from the scene and continues the pattern of the Magdalene's marginalization. John does more than suppress the anointer's identity (as happens in the Synoptics). This Gospel actually switches her identity, making sure that the hands of an unattached woman don't sully Jesus.

In the same way, only Joseph of Arimathea and Nicodemus anoint Jesus' corpse (19:38–42). Mary takes no part whatever in preparing his body for burial, any more than her anointing portends his death. The policy is strictly "hands off" all the way through the Gospel.

Medieval interpretation exploited John's conflation of Mary Magdalene and Mary of Bethany in the interests of a rich legendary elaboration. In this collapsing of two people into one, Mary Magdalene became the sister of Lazarus, and a further conflation made him the "leper" named Lazarus in Luke 16:20. Because prostitutes were believed to give men leprosy during the Middle Ages, it made sense that a single family, blessed by Jesus, should show the way to be relieved of two related ailments.

John alienates rites of unction from Mary because contact with human flesh, even the flesh of Jesus, does not offer the hope of rebirth into the realm of Spirit. (When Jesus' flesh is said to impart eternal life, that is only in the Eucharist, where his flesh is compared to the bread that God gave to Israel in the wilderness by means of Moses; John 6:25–59.) Mary's significance turns on vision alone, and that vision is detailed with exceptional care. Nothing competes with it—not anointing or exorcism. No exorcisms whatever are included in John. That should not surprise us, given all the other Gnostic elements in John that we have seen. If contact with the flesh cannot be trusted enough to have Mary Magdalene anoint Jesus, why should the demons of this world have any place in the story of Jesus?

In John's universe, the world, the flesh, and the devil have no place at all next to the Son of God and those who can perceive him risen from the dead. Consequently, Mary Magdalene's role is both truncated and enhanced. She emerges as a Gnostic visionary, and she continued in that role in the Gnostic tradition as the guardian of the vision of Christ raised from the dead. But her anointing is repressed. We have to put Gnostic and Catholic sources together to understand the whole picture that each side partially obscures: The Catholics wanted Mary anointing in silence; the Gnostics wanted Mary teaching with her hands behind her back. Historically, both sides were wrong. Yet in practice, both preserved vital traces of Mary Magdalene's impact and continuing importance.

⟨⟩

MARY MAGDALENE'S DISTINCTIVE, visionary witness to the Resurrection also comes through in *The Gospel According to Thomas*—but with a new perspective, one that explains her androgynous portrayal

in *The Gospel According to Mary. Thomas* is an anthology of apho-
risms and parables originally from the second century. It was first
compiled in the Syriac language in the ancient city of Edessa in
Syria, a counterpart of Ephesus in terms of its cultural patterns and
vibrant intellectual life. But Gnosticism was an international movement, and *Thomas* was also embraced in Egypt eventually and translated into Coptic, continuing the living legacy of the language of the
hieroglyphics.

In *Thomas,* the "Living Jesus"—the eternal personality whom
death could not contain—speaks wisdom that promises immortality.
The Coptic text includes material presented in the canonical Gospels
as well as teaching culled from oral traditions. *Thomas* focuses so
completely on the wisdom spoken by the Living Jesus in response to
questions from his disciples that it does not include any stories about
Jesus. As the Living Jesus responds to his disciples' problems, doubts,
and entreaties, his epigrammatic wisdom becomes a rich rhythmic
chant—a guide for Gnostic meditation complete with oral cues.

The Gnostics who lived near Nag Hammadi, in Egypt, away from
cities in their rural enclaves, used *The Gospel According to Thomas* as
well as other texts deposited there to deepen their *gnosis. Thomas*
clearly states its purpose, and the aim of Gnosticism as a whole: "The
one who finds the interpretation of these sayings will not taste death"
(saying 1). *Thomas* promises to convey the reality of Resurrection to
the attentive Gnostic, whose goal is to cheat death itself.

Mary Magdalene plays a crucial role in bringing the meaning
of mystical communion with the Living Jesus to expression, and
*Thomas* ratchets up the ambivalence toward her that we have already
seen in John's Gospel. Her visionary insight reaches its height just as
she is denigrated for being a woman.

At the close of *Thomas,* Simon Peter declares that Mary should go
away from the disciples altogether (saying 114): "Let Mary depart
from us." His sexism becomes absolute as he goes on to say, "Females

are not worthy of the life," referring to resurrected, spiritual life. Peter's declaration would mean that Mary—and women in general—
could not be involved in interpreting Jesus' words. They would not
even be included among the disciples who remembered and treasured
Jesus' teaching. But Peter's exclusion of women in saying 114 conveys
an even deeper, more disturbing sense. The right interpretation of
what the Living Jesus says brings life, and the promise never to "taste
death," so that all who are not "worthy of the life" are disqualified as
teachers. Only men could teach, because only men could be "worthy
of the life." Peter's judgment in *The Gospel According to Thomas* implies that men alone could read, understand, and benefit from Jesus'
wisdom, and that Resurrection was for men only; as far as Peter was
concerned, the state of being female rooted a person in this corrupt
world to such an extent that Gnostic escape was impossible.

Peter appears persistently in Gnostic literature as Mary's antagonist. That antagonism may well reflect tension between the increasingly patriarchal hierarchy of Christians who called themselves
Catholic and the attempt of many Gnostic Christians to maintain
Mary's leading role among disciples as a teacher of vision. Because
Peter had been a foundational apostle in great cities such as Jerusalem, Antioch, and Rome, he was a natural symbol of male leadership in Catholic Christianity. The contrast with Mary Magdalene
was inevitable, and Peter's contradiction of Mary emerges as a trope
in Gnostic sources.

That dispute between the types of authority each represented
emerged most clearly between the second and the fourth centuries;
no first-century source represents Peter and Mary at the kind of constant loggerheads typical in some Gnostic literature. More than the
actual teaching of the fisherman from Bethsaida, Peter in *The Gospel
According to Thomas* sometimes represents what many Gnostics
thought of their Catholic counterparts.

But it would be superficial to claim that Simon Peter's intervention, "Let Mary depart from us," and the trenchant, antifemale attitude it articulates reflect only disagreement between *Thomas*'s community and the emerging hierarchy of Catholic Christianity. Peter appears in the Nag Hammadi Library more often than Mary does, and in an unequivocally positive light as a hero of the Gnostic quest. He is much more than a straw man to represent Catholic authoritarianism. Gnostic Christians were not about to cede the rich inheritance of Peter to their Catholic counterparts.

In *The Gospel According to Thomas,* Jesus rebukes Peter's rejection of Mary, but in terms that are the antithesis of some fashionable readings of the text, and which are all the more dramatic for being the book's last words: "Every female who makes herself male will enter the kingdom of heaven" (saying 114). The Coptic text of *Thomas* leaves no doubt about the meaning of these words, because *female* and *male* are the particular words for sexual difference, as in English. Mary is to become a guy. Whenever I read this passage in front of an educated audience, I anticipate an audible gasp. It sounds as though, if Mary wants to enter the kingdom, she needs to grow a penis.

When an audience gasps at these words, they are expressing the perfectly natural revulsion of modern listeners to what seems to be a distorted and perverse view of human sexuality. But there is another reason for their shock. For decades, *Thomas* has been marketed in the United States as if it represented a kinder and gentler Christianity: less hierarchical, more concerned with nature, open to women, anti-authoritarian. One major publisher even sold a "commentary" on *Thomas* written by Bhagwan Rajneesh, the guru of Poona, who for more than a decade espoused a lucrative gospel of Tantric sex and encounter-group psychology with a dash of the Gnostic Jesus mixed in. After he was jailed and deported from the United States, his publisher found another commentator, but the New Age *Thomas* has been a proven seller nonetheless.

This marketing campaign is designed to sell a Gnosticism that never existed, as any open-eyed reading of *Thomas* shows. If you believe, as the community of *The Gospel According to Thomas* did, that "the heaven and the earth came into being" for the sake of James, Jesus' brother (saying 12), that is no less hierarchical than the veneration of Peter as it developed in Rome and elsewhere. If you say, as the "Living Jesus" does (saying 10), that not only earth but also heaven and the heaven above the heavens will be destroyed, that is no less apocalyptic—no less dismissive of the present world and its environment—than what Jewish and Christian seers of the same period said. If you accuse people who want to fast and pray and give alms of committing sin (saying 14), what is that but authoritarian? And finally, telling a woman to grow a penis (however metaphorically) cannot be construed as feminist except by active deception. The soft, liberal, New Age *Thomas* is an artifact of fuzzy analysis and false advertising. This *Gospel* will reveal its secrets only when it is read in its ancient context, not as part of a modern "progressive" agenda.

Primeval androgyny—the conviction that human beings embrace both sexes in their primordial state—is well represented in ancient mythology, including the book of Genesis, Aristophanes, and the Upanishads. *Thomas,* however, sets out *male* androgyny as a condition of future salvation. Females need to become male, but not the reverse.

Sex changes were not considered totally impossible in antiquity, even when they were depicted as unnatural and bizarre. The *Metamorphoses* of Ovid (4.285–389) tells the sorry tale of Hermaphroditus. The inexperienced young man made the unfortunate error of skinny-dipping in a pool guarded by the crazed nymph Salmacis. She was on him like a limpet, and she cried out to the gods never to let the two of them be separated. They indeed became one body, neither woman nor man and yet both, their permanent coitus producing a weak hermaphroditic hybrid.

Obviously, Mary's metamorphosis in *The Gospel According to Thomas* is not intended to be like that of Hermaphroditus and

Salmacis. In fact, it inverts the result of the change. Where Hermaphroditus is weakened, Mary is to be strengthened. But whether you take the language physiologically or spiritually—and I do not think either can be excluded—the fact remains that females here are not merely the weaker sex but the reprobate sex, in need of masculine redemption, the filling of empty space, whether in their souls or in their bodies.

MARY MAGDALENE PRESIDED over the domain of vision in the minds of the many Gnostic practitioners who read John's Gospel, *The Gospel According to Thomas,* and *The Gospel According to Mary* as their Scripture. She inspired visionary disciplines for centuries after her death and became the indispensable guardian of those techniques.

Gnosticism persistently held up Mary as the ideal model of visionary mysticism, in which the Gnostic could know Jesus personally in his living reality after the Resurrection. But at the same time, she stood for female sexuality, which Gnosticism identified with equal persistence as the source of the corruption of the world. The tension between those two poles marks every Gnostic presentation of Mary, with deep consequences for the way she has been viewed ever since in the Christian West.

*Chapter Thirteen*

# THE GODDESS AND THE VIXEN

*T*HE GOLDEN LEGEND of Jacobus de Voragine shows how medieval devotion transmuted both Christian and Gnostic images into its own distinctive piety. At the close of this thirteenth-century text, Mary reaches the apogee of her vision, as a priest sees her levitating to heaven during her hours of meditation. That capacity to transcend her body enables Mary to relocate miraculously from her cave in the cliff of La Sainte-Baum in order to receive Communion in the church at Saint-Maximin at the moment of her death. The *Legend* goes on to record other, postmortem sightings of Mary.

Well before her death, Mary is presented in the *Legend* as the special protectress of a noblewoman, saving both her and her newborn from shipwreck and starvation, appearing to the woman in vision and miraculously transporting her to the city of Jerusalem and back. Mary Magdalene protected pregnant women and became the patron saint of fertility and childbirth.

Gender and vision had both long been linked to Mary Magdalene, so that she fell between flesh and Spirit, the negative and positive poles that charged the religious environment of Gnosticism—and, increasingly, of Christianity. Ambivalence toward Mary, who saw beyond this world and yet also embodied it, made her both a goddess and a vixen. These images have shaped her memory in the West to this day. As a key Gnostic text has a woman in Mary's image say, "I am the whore and the holy one, I am the wife and the virgin." Although Gnosticism and the medieval piety represented by *The Golden Legend* did everything possible to stress Mary's connection with the Spirit rather than flesh, the anointing she had practiced in Galilee—an element of her biography that was never forgotten—bound her irrevocably to the physical life of this world.

For all Gnosticism's stress on the deception of this world, anointing, in fact, remained a central concern in many of its sources. *The Gospel According to Philip,* a third-century Coptic text, goes so far as to say (II.3.74.13–23), "Anointing is superior to baptism, for it is from the word 'anointing' that we have been called 'Christians,' certainly not because of the word 'baptism.'" Taking off from the basic meaning of the term Christ (*khristos* in Greek, "anointed one"), this teaching discovers the essence of Christianity in the spiritual ointment offered by Jesus and his followers. The esoteric meaning of being anointed, a prominent Gnostic sacrament, proves central to the portrayal of Mary Magdalene in Gnosticism and to her legacy in our time.

*The Gospel According to Philip* speaks of salvation as a matter of uniting with one's heavenly image an eternal double provided by God: This is the inner meaning of unction. *The Gospel According to Thomas* (saying 22) also specifies the union of what is above with what is below, the interior with the exterior, as the aim of the Gnostic quest, but *Philip* is more practical. It provides a detailed commentary on this process of union, specifying by means of symbolic language how and where this marriage with a divine image can occur (II.3.67.29–34):

> *The Lord did everything in a mystery, a baptism and a chrism and a Eucharist and a redemption and a bridal chamber. The Lord*

*said, "I came to make the things below like the things above, and the things outside like those inside, I came to unite them in that place."*

The "bridal chamber," the apex in the sequence of mystery, is the "place" where above and below and outside and inside are reconciled, where one merges with one's heavenly counterpart.

*The Gospel According to Philip* never gives a prosaic description of the "bridal chamber," but insofar as a bride is involved, she is definitely associated with Mary Magdalene. The briefest of statements about her in this Gospel has spawned a diverse progeny of interpretations (*Philip* II.3.59.6–9): "There were three who always walked with the Lord: Mary his mother and her sister and Magdalene, the one who was called his companion." The term *companion* has provided an incentive for modern legend: Jesus and Mary were married, or everything but married, and their offspring grew up in France and fed the French royal line—culminating, so one version goes, in Diana, Princess of Wales! (We encounter the inevitable conspiracy theory when an electronic site claims that Diana was murdered to prevent her marriage to a non-Christian.) But the word *companion* does not mean "bride," just as reference to a "bridal chamber" needn't imply a sexual relationship. Some of those who seek evidence to support their view of Mary as Jesus' consort have foisted their conclusions onto *The Gospel According to Philip.*

Gnostics did not talk about sexual intercourse in a roundabout way; bluntness was the rule, especially in agricultural Egypt. The word *companion* (*koinonos*) represents the common Semitic term *chaber,* referring to a companion at meals, rather than in bed. The term is frequently used for male colleagues in the Mishnah, and here, in *The Gospel According to Philip,* it means what Luke's Gospel said in other words: that Mary Magdalene was Jesus' disciple from their early days in Galilee.

Yet the fact remains that Mary's gender, taken in itself, offers the potential that Jesus showed a sexual interest in her. *The Gospel According to Philip* also says—in so many words, most scholars think—that Jesus liked to kiss Mary on the "mouth"; she had to have been a favorite disciple (II.3.63.34–64.5):

> *And the companion of the Savior is Mary Magdalene. But Christ loved her more than all the disciples and used to kiss her often on the mouth. The rest of the disciples were offended by it and expressed their disapproval. They said to him, Why do you love her more than all of us? The Savior answered and said to them, Why do I not love you like her?*

Notice how this reference reminds us that Mary was the woman "companion" and compares her in that status to "the rest of the disciples." That confirms that the term is being used in the sense of *chaber,* colleague. But the real point for many modern interpreters is not the companionship at all, but the kiss.

*The Gospel According to Philip* frequently mentions kissing, an activity that is by no means limited to marriage or moments of sexual intimacy. Then, as now, one could kiss without having intercourse; Jesus kissed his male disciples, and he pointedly observes at the close of this passage, "Why do I not love you like her?" Evidently, he does with Mary what he does with them, only more often and no doubt with greater pleasure. The confusion between kissing and intercourse is not his problem or *The Gospel According to Philip*'s, but a sign of overwrought modern interpretation when sex is involved—or might be involved or could be involved.

In fact, just before Mary Magdalene first appears in this Gospel, *The Gospel According to Philip* comments on the inner, spiritual sense conveyed by the kiss (II.3.59.2–5): "For it is by a kiss that the perfect conceive and give birth. For this reason we also kiss one another. We receive conception from the grace that is in each other."

The grace-conceiving kiss was mouth-to-mouth, as in the old

Galilean custom of greeting. The Gospel According to John details the practice as part of the ritual of earliest Christianity, when the risen Jesus (20:19) greets his disciples with the traditional greeting in Aramaic, *Shelama,* meaning "Peace." A kiss on the mouth often went with this greeting, and John shows that is the case here, because Jesus next "breathes on" his disciples, infusing them with Holy Spirit and the power to forgive sins (20:21–23). The breath of Spirit went with the exhalation of one practitioner into another in an ancient Gnostic practice that stretched from the Gospel According to John through *The Gospel According to Philip.*

Recent popular writing has given a distorted impression of lusty, earth-loving Gnostics in contrast to their allegedly dour counterparts in the early Church. The holy kiss was, in fact, prevalent throughout the practice of Catholic and Orthodox Christianity. Wherever the kiss was practiced, there was the possibility it might look less like one person spiritually conceiving and giving birth to another than like foreplay. Both Gnostics and Catholics were accused by their opponents of promiscuity, their services written off as pretexts for orgies (and even infanticide and cannibalism, as we shall see). Hippolytus, the third-century Roman liturgist, reserved the kiss solely for those already baptized, and set out a period of three years for those who prepared for baptism; during that time, they listened to the liturgy without participating in the Eucharist or the kiss.

*The Gospel According to Philip* explains the kiss in purely spiritual terms, relating the practice to understanding the nature of true intercourse (II.3.78.25–31): "The human being has intercourse with the human being. The horse has intercourse with the horse, the ass with the ass. Members of a race usually are associated with those of like race. So spirit mingles with spirit, and thought consorts with thought, and light shares with light."

By the simple expedient of taking such statements out of their context, you could, of course, claim that this Gospel was intended to promote orgiastic practices. Gnostics have been accused of diverse sexual crimes for centuries. In the late twentieth and early twenty-first centuries, revisionist historians and pop-culture gurus have turned that accusation into a virtue, recommending the alleged sexual freedom of Gnosticism. But *The Gospel According to Philip* militates against that interpretation, because the union it seeks takes place in the symbolic "bridal chamber" (II.3.82.2–24), where one meets Christ as the bridegroom.

Yet *The Gospel According to Philip* does not quite dispel the possibility that Mary and Jesus went beyond kissing. Prior to the scene when the disciples complain about Jesus' favoritism, it says, "As for the Wisdom who is called 'the barren,' she is the mother of the angels" (II.3.63.30–32), explicitly coordinating the Magdalene with Sophia. By calling her "barren," one might think this excludes sexual contact or procreation, until we realize that the book of Isaiah (54:1) promises that one day the barren woman will bear more than her married counterpart by becoming more fecund. In its richly allusive, metaphorical presentation, *The Gospel According to Philip* evokes a host of possibilities but shies away from making firm historical statements.

---

THIS GOSPEL DOES CONTAIN one down-to-earth remark: "No one will be able to know when the husband and the wife have intercourse with one another except the two of them" (II.3.81.34–82.1). The same observation applies to unmarried couples under most circumstances. Because their rituals were private and involved at least the intimacy of a kiss, enemies of the Gnostics frequently accused them of promoting promiscuity. The most infamous accusation comes from Epiphanius, bishop of Salamis, in Cyprus, during the fourth century. He claimed that one Gnostic group engaged in wife swapping and even went to the extreme of consuming semen and menstrual blood within their celebrations of the Eucharist. In spreading this rumor, Epiphanius was adapting a calumny that used to be directed against Christians during the second century, who were accused by pious pagans of engaging in nighttime orgies.

Epiphanius also cited a bizarre variant of the story of Jesus' Transfiguration, which he claimed he'd gotten from a Gnostic group. In this story, Jesus takes Mary Magdalene up a mountain and, in her presence, extracts a woman from his own side—evidently a reenactment of the primordial creation in chapter 2 of Genesis. Then he begins to have intercourse with the woman, ejaculates in his hand, and offers his semen to Mary, telling her, "We need to do this in order to live." Weird though this account is, it agrees with Epiphanius's accusation that this group practiced orgiastic sex (lubricated by anointing and alcohol), coitus interruptus, abortion when physical conception resulted, and the consumption of unwanted fetuses.

How well informed was Epiphanius? His specific charges have not convinced many scholars. But at least he showed, whatever the merit of his particular accusations, that in Gnostic worship actions that skeptics could portray as sexual were involved in the practice of their communal illumination.

THE COMPARISON OF MARY Magdalene to Sophia (Wisdom) lies at the heart of both Gnosticism and Catholic Christianity. But that connection results in deep ambivalence, because divine Wisdom attracted both praise for her powerful knowledge and trenchant criticism for her female sexuality. Sophia's kingdom was, after all, a corrupted realm. The world we live in from a Gnostic perspective constitutes humanity's problem, rather than the key to a solution. Like Sophia, Mary could be portrayed in terms of her involvement with the physical dimension of human life; her devotion to the flesh meant that Sophia/Mary sometimes even sold her sexual wares. The

Magdalene's association with anointing made her contact with fallen flesh undeniable. From there, it was only a short, albeit fateful, step to turn her into a whore.

Catholic sources make the same connections among Mary and Sophia, flesh, and prostitution, so that in the sixth century, Pope Gregory could easily make Mary Magdalene the emblem of sexual penitence in the city of Rome. From Gregory, medieval Europe learned of Mary as the goddess of contrition, who had begun her career in the brothel of this world. The interplay between Gnostic and Catholic theology, the practices that went with them, and Mary's simultaneous sublimation to a goddess and her degradation to a whore can be traced in a chronological reading of some frequently overlooked but compelling texts.

⸺⛬⸺

MARY MAGDALENE OCCUPIED the liminal territory between transgression and enlightenment. The *Pistis Sophia,* a Gnostic text from the fourth century, reflects an awareness of her liminality and uses Mary as a symbol of that awareness. As the title indicates, the *Pistis Sophia* builds on the ancient Gnostic figure of Wisdom (Sophia), the goddess of this world, also called Pistis (Faith). Faith and Wisdom together are divine, yet they are only partial realities. Ancient Gnostics struggled with the perennial issue of how belief and knowledge relate to each other. Each complements the other, but even Faith and Wisdom, when fused, amounted to a flawed and fallen deity. This is expressed in a bizarre variant of the Genesis story of creation in the *Pistis Sophia.*

In this myth, Faith/Wisdom was a divine being who tried to create something entirely on her own in a failed effort to imitate the divine Father's spiritual creation. This explains why physical reality is in the mess that it is. Anything material is by definition an abortive product of Faith/Wisdom's misconceived gambit to produce what she was incapable of producing. Faith/Wisdom became pregnant with the world, but not by intercourse: Her pregnancy was literally hysterical. Her womb swelled due to her envy of the creative power of the divine Father. The universe we live in is all afterbirth without embryo, the failed tissue of Faith/Wisdom's hysterical female ambition.

This basic Gnostic myth of Faith/Wisdom's desperate need for redemption, a restoration to her true place in submission to the divine Father, forms the operating premise of the *Pistis Sophia*. This premise had been long established in Gnostic lore by the fourth century, but the *Pistis Sophia* contributed something new. It connected Mary Magdalene to the image of Faith/Wisdom by portraying Mary as an ideally obedient recipient of revelation. When she questions the risen Jesus, he replies, "Mary, blessed one, whom I will complete in all the mysteries of the height, speak openly, you are she whose heart is more directed to the Kingdom of Heaven than all your brothers" (*Pistis Sophia* I.17; *see also* 24 *and* 25). Mary's questions and the discourses she herself eventually delivers concern both the redemption of Faith/Wisdom and the purification of individual souls. Faith/Wisdom must be freed from the corruption she herself created if her progeny are to receive illumination.

Faith/Wisdom follows a process of restoration in Mary Magdalene's teaching, so that what is described as her compulsion to have intercourse is cured, and she is consequently able to relate to the Father and to the whole divine realm without her former hysteria. Once helplessly enslaved to her sexuality, Faith/Wisdom then takes her place in the divine order again. This pattern also became Mary Magdalene's in the *Pistis Sophia,* and her image as a redeemed prostitute took deep root in Western Catholicism, aided by the influence of Gregory the Great during the sixth century.

In the influential sermon of Gregory the Great, preached in 594, Mary is fully identified with the sinful woman who wiped Jesus' feet in chapter 7 of Luke's Gospel, with Mary of Bethany, and as a prostitute. The aim of this harmonization, however, is not to demean Mary. Rather, she becomes the image of the impatient lover in the Song of Songs, and her desire is compared to the restless love a monk rightly feels for God as he lies on his bed at night. The material linkage of Mary Magdalene to the world of the flesh is beautifully exploited by Pope Gregory to convey the need to transcend this world and discover a cognate passion for the divine. Mary Magdalene revealed the necessity for penance, but also proclaimed its triumph. As Gregory said, "In paradise a woman was the cause of death for a man; coming from the sepulcher a woman proclaimed life to men." Medieval Catholicism would eventually lose the balance of imagery that Gregory achieved, instead highlighting Eve's sin at the expense of the Magdalene's announcement of salvation. This forced Mary out of the realm of Faith/Wisdom to wander in a labyrinth of fallen flesh.

By the thirteenth century, a late form of Gnosticism flourished in the West, chiefly in the South of France and in the Rhineland of Germany. Known as the Albigensians (after the city of Albi in France) or the Cathars (perhaps from the Greek term *katharos,* meaning "pure"), these Gnostics insisted upon a strict separation between this world and the realm of Spirit. That led to their notion that sins of the flesh, while regrettable and to be outgrown before one's death, were only to be expected. Even Jesus as a person of flesh had to be distinguished from the spiritual Jesus, the Christ. But of what sin could Jesus have been guilty?

Mary Magdalene came ready-made as a sinner, given the legends regarding her trade as a prostitute, tales that had circulated for centuries. From there, it was a short step to make her into Jesus' concubine. Their relationship symbolized human weakness and gave Jesus a sin that did not involve him in violence. Pope Innocent III was outraged, although his vehemence may have had more to do with the Cathars' denial of papal authority (as part of the structure of this world) than with their peculiar teaching about Jesus and Mary. Innocent declared a Crusade against the Cathars in 1208, and the result has been called the first European genocide.

Because the Crusade against the Albigensians was of genocidal proportions, it is difficult to ascertain any detail in regard to Cathar theology, although their denial of papal authority and their view of Mary Magdalene are well established. Their belief that they could be "pure" relates to a Gnostic conviction—most obvious in the teachings of Manichaeism—that all matter is evil by definition, so that only the world of Spirit is for the perfect. (Despite speculative claims to the contrary, the Templars were a completely separate organization.) The conduits of the Cathars' ideas included the related Bogomil movement in the Balkans; contact with the syncretism of Muslim, Catholic, Jewish, and Gnostic ideas in Spain also fed their theology. A similar mix produced the medieval Kabbalah of Judaism during the twelfth century in both Spain itself and France.

How precisely the Cathars' dualism of flesh and spirit related to their teaching about Mary can't be specified, but the relationship is probably much as in *The Gospel According to Philip*. This Gospel and the *Pistis Sophia* might even have been sources of their theology, directly or indirectly. The Cathars believed that they could be perfected by a baptism in Spirit with the laying on of hands, and that until then they could enjoy at least some of the benefits of this life, although they frowned on procreation. Accusations of sexual license abound in medieval literature, and the English term *bugger* is said to be a contraction of the name Bogomil. It's impossible to know how far to believe such charges, given their distinctly Epiphanian ring.

The Cathars were eventually wiped out during the course of a succession of persecutions. The Crusaders seemed to triumph over any suggestion that Jesus may have sinned, with Mary or anyone else. Yet three centuries after their Crusade began, Martin Luther continued to countenance the idea that Jesus had a sexual relationship with Mary Magdalene.

The Catholic Church would never question Jesus' chastity, but in one respect the Cathars continue to influence Catholic theology. Pope Innocent and the Crusaders despised the Cathars' heretical idea that Mary Magdalene was the same person as the woman taken in adultery, whose stoning Jesus prevented (John 8:1–11), but the link between Mary and the woman taken in adultery was too good to pass up for long. By the time the thirteenth century had closed, Franciscan preachers were exploring exactly the same theme. In Mel Gibson's recent film *The Passion of the Christ,* this identification is embraced, packaged as if it were part of the Rosary.

Medieval theology didn't limit itself to literal history any more than the ancient Gospels did. Typically modern preoccupations—such as what really happened and what didn't—did not constrain practitioners and believers in antiquity or the medieval period. Some documents, crafted to guide the practice of adepts who sought continuing visions of the risen Christ, abandoned historical concerns almost entirely in their continuing quest for the most authentic visions or insights into the deadliest of all sins. Mary's destiny in the West was to embody the whole spectrum of vision and sin at one and the same time.

*Afterword*

# RELICS OF THE MAGDALENE

CATHOLIC BELIEFS DURING the Middle Ages drew on many streams of thought and practice. In addition to the Gospels, we have seen that the deep polarity between flesh and Spirit in Gnostic sources, the ascetic eroticism of Pope Gregory the Great, the legends of Mary's torrid past and her miraculous travels in Provence, as well as the scandal of the Cathars' teaching all fed the medieval portrait of Mary Magdalene. Diverse though these influences were, Catholic theology proved remarkably resilient despite its many changes.

The emergence of the medieval Magdalene illustrates that resilience. Belief in her was so varied that it tipped into heresy in the judgment of Pope Innocent III, who launched the Albigensian Crusade in response. The Cathars nonetheless vitalized the image of Mary, influencing Catholics and the Protestants who came after them (as well as modern devotees of the Magdalene). Devotion to Mary Magdalene was diverse, but it also expressed the deep conviction that made Catholic theology coherent: Medieval faith was grounded in the assurance that the presence of God's Spirit, focused by devout belief, could transform human flesh.

Mary Magdalene, the converted sinner and sister of Lazarus the leper, was an ideal representative of that conviction; she symbolized the idea that any believer, whatever that person's faults, could, like Mary, become "the sweet friend of God." The legends, pilgrimages, shrines, and ritual practices that grew up around her were all designed to reach ordinary believers in their physical lives, to give their flesh a share of eternity. Most of these beliefs and practices did not endure, many seem superstitious by the standards of modern common sense (not to mention critical history), and all of them have been subject to drastic change. But in the midst of change and reform and revision, the medieval conviction that supernatural Spirit could make all the difference remained consistent. In their confidence that God's Spirit could alter the physical world as well as their own bodies, devotees of Mary during the Middle Ages undoubtedly invented evidence to suit their beliefs. But those inventions were perfectly sincere, and they reflect the passion for Mary Magdalene that continues to grip the modern imagination.

⸳⸳⸳

In December of 1279, the crown prince of the house of Anjou, whose petty kingdom covered parts of France and Italy, ordered an excavation of the church crypt at Saint-Maximin in Provence. One chronicler said that the prince dug with his own hands, working so fiercely that sweat streamed off him. Guided by local Provençal legend, the Angevin prince was convinced he would find the bodily remains of Mary Magdalene interred at Saint-Maximin.

Sacred relics were priceless. It was believed that any small part of a holy person's body conveyed the same sacred power the saint had achieved during life. By the time of Charles of Salerno, as historians today call this Angevin prince, medieval Europe had long embraced Saint Augustine's teaching that a saint's relics effected miraculous healings. This doctrine went beyond the evidence of a few anecdotes;

it was an article of faith, and throughout the Middle Ages, people felt that their experience confirmed their belief.

Augustine taught that when Constantine embraced Christianity, that set in motion the thousand-year rule of those who were true to faith in Jesus, as the Revelation of John (chapter 20) had predicted. That last book in the New Testament, also called the Apocalypse, has fed and framed apocalyptic thought in Christianity ever since it was written. In Augustine's interpretation during the fifth century of the Common Era, the millenarian prediction of the Revelation had truly begun on earth. The power and influence of the Catholic Church during this last interim before the end of all things, which Augustine called the *Christiana tempora*, convinced him that the prophecies of Revelation were unfolding, just as had been predicted.

Logically, that meant that God must already have been transforming human flesh into the holy flesh of eternity. Augustine—a firm materialist in the anti-Gnostic tradition of Catholic Christianity—believed that all people would be resurrected with physical flesh after the thousand-year reign of the saints. The millennium formed the fulcrum between mortality and paradise; the literal flesh of the saints proved by its healing properties that this transition was really happening. Relics of saints amounted to metaphysical data, not just historical curiosities. They brought healing to believers, as Augustine says happened when bits of Saint Stephen's body wrought miracles in and near his city of Hippo in North Africa, conveying the power of the world to come to the physical bodies of those who venerated the relics.

That power manifested itself politically as well as physically. Emperor Constantine himself had ordered the excavation of what is today known as the Church of the Holy Sepulcher in Jerusalem. According to fifth-century legend, the excavators said they found nails there, prompted by Helena, the emperor's mother, who reported a vision of where the true cross lay. Precious as those nails were, Constantine had some melted down and added to the metal of his helmet in order to make himself invincible in battle. Relics projected the force of God's heavenly Kingdom into the uncertainties of this world. Christ was drafted to make the emperor invincible.

Charles of Salerno dug at Saint-Maximin at the time his father, Charles I, was extending the dynasty's power outward from its axis in Provence and northern Italy. The prince would eventually reign over his parts of modern France and Italy as Charles II, and he endowed churches all over his realm for the veneration of Mary Magdalene, his patroness. He also saw to the future protection of his dynasty by having his dead son, Louis of Toulouse, canonized as a saint—ensuring that divine power ran through the veins of his family as well as through the Angevin ground that Mary Magdalene protected.

The Provençal legend that spurred on Charles and his diggers has come down to us in *The Golden Legend* of Jacobus de Voragine. The Dominicans of Charles's time actively used *The Golden Legend* in their preaching against the Cathars, hoping to keep devotion to Mary within orthodox bounds. (Those unconvinced by the preaching and inquisition of the religious arm of the Albigensian Crusade were subject to penalties and executions inflicted by its secular arm.) The identification of the Magdalene with Mary of Bethany, which had been taught since the time of Gregory the Great, had held up without challenge, and it would prevail through the Reformation. Only in 1969 did the revised calendar of the saints authorized by the Second Vatican Council of the Roman Catholic Church acknowledge that Mary of Bethany and Mary Magdalene were two different people. Nonetheless, the conflation of the two women persists in our time.

Mary Magdalene's wealth and promiscuity prior to her conversion were equally legendary, as several examples already cited have indicated. Many more examples have been cataloged, especially by art historians. In this book, I have referred to the best and earliest examples of the main types of portrayal of Mary Magdalene in order to avoid getting lost in the permutations and combinations of these types in the art and literature of the West. The baroque variations, for all their complexity, reflect the stable set of typical portrayals we have encountered.

Mary Magdalene's proselytizing in Provence and her later withdrawal into contemplation prior to her burial in Saint-Maximin were matters of agreement by the time of the royal excavation at Saint-Maximin. Nonetheless, doubt had already been expressed about Mary's levitations as described in *The Golden Legend.* Among Charles of Salerno's contemporaries, faith required tangible proof as validation of visions and legends.

Several pilgrimage sites claimed various parts of Mary's skeleton when Charles of Salerno made his "discovery." Mary's bones had long been venerated at Vézelay, in Burgundy—north of Provence and well outside the Angevin orbit. A monk named Badilus had supposedly stolen the skeleton from under the noses of the Saracens in 749, then removed it from Provence to Burgundy. So how could Prince Charles say that he had found Mary's skeleton? After all, Saint Bernard of Clairvaux had preached the Second Crusade from Vézelay in 1146, and Louis IX—the Crusader king, later canonized a saint—made several pilgrimages to Vézelay during the thirteenth century.

Fortunately for Charles of Salerno, signs testified to the authenticity of the bones in Saint-Maximin. Relics were valued more as metaphysical evidence than as historical fact. Physical authentication in the form of healings and miracles made a bigger impression than arguments about history. The Dominican friars into whose care Charles confided the skeleton produced their *Book of Miracles of Saint Mary Magdalene,* which describes the cures her bones in Saint-Maximin effected, and the relative powerlessness of the bones kept at Vézelay. A Franciscan chronicler recounted a story of a butcher who had gone to venerate Mary Magdalene at Saint-Maximin and got into a fight over how genuine the bones were. He killed his antagonist, but Mary Magdalene assured him in a vision that he would be released from the gallows. She sent a dove to dissolve the chain by which he would have been hung.

Chroniclers sometimes stumbled over themselves in recording the wonders wrought by Mary Magdalene of Saint-Maximin. Charles was kidnapped during his long war with Aragon, and in one account (the *Dominican Legend,* published about a century and a half after the events), he prayed to Mary Magdalene for release and promised to find her relics once he regained his freedom. Unfortunately for that legend, Charles was actually kidnapped *after* he discovered Mary's alleged sarcophagus. Yet the tale's purpose was not plausibility, but the multiplication of supernatural validation for relics.

In the *Dominican Legend,* Mary promises Charles that he will find a written inscription on her sarcophagus, a bit of skin remaining on her skull, where the risen Christ touched her, an amphora containing blood-soaked earth from the foot of the cross, hair turned to ashes, and a plant growing in her mouth, where her tongue had been. The healing potency of these enchantments miraculously proved what skeptics might question.

The relics at Saint-Maximin proved stronger than rational doubt, at least for the pious supporters of the house of Anjou. The prince himself made a golden holder for Mary's skull, inscribed with his name and a prayer for Mary's patronage, and he had Pope Boniface VIII declare these relics authentic. (Boniface diplomatically said nothing against the remains in Vézelay, which Pope Stephen had authenticated by papal bull more than two centuries earlier.) To this day, they are displayed annually on July 22, the feast of Saint Mary Magdalene.

Papal authorization was politically crucial to Charles, and he confided the care of Mary's relics to the Dominicans, papal favorites who had risen to fame because their leader, Dominic Guzman, had joined the Albigensian Crusade to preach against the Cathars. As a result, the cult at Saint-Maximin emphasized Mary's penitence rather than any alleged intimacy with Jesus. A later Dominican inquisitor, Moneta da Cremona, derided the claim among the Cathars that Mary's example authorized preaching by women. In 1297, the Dominicans embraced Mary Magdalene as their patron saint, denying the heretics any similar claim. Charles hewed the line of Dominican orthodoxy and the requirement of private confession introduced earlier by Innocent III, the same Pope who had authorized the slaughter at Béziers and the genocide of the Cathars.

Papal recognition of Mary Magdalene's relics at Saint-Maximin reciprocated Charles's loyalty. Charles's support of Boniface went beyond orthodoxy: He had been instrumental in the Pope's campaign for election.

Charles may have been confident about finding Mary's skeleton because he had arranged for it to be put in the ground. Just seventy-five years earlier, relics said to be Mary's, including a skull, had been looted during the sack of Constantinople by the Crusaders from the West. The word in Latin for the discovery of relics is *inventio,* and Charles's whole story does feel more invented than accurate.

<hr />

CHARLES WOULD HAVE DONE no better if he had dug in Vézelay, or in Magdala, for that matter. Mary Magdalene's relics cannot be found underground, nor will they be disinterred by means of even a plausibly targeted excavation. Her true relics are not physical, and never have been.

Her bones are mixed in with those of thousands of other victims who were hacked to death in Magdala by the Romans in 67 C.E. Likewise, not a single historical source tells us what a biographer would want to know of her life. Even when all the sources are sifted and analyzed and put together with our knowledge of her time and society, they fall short of giving us a conventional biography.

Yet however successful the desire to mute Mary Magdalene's genuine teaching might have been, however much fashion has dominated her presentation in century after century, unmistakable signs of her influence remain. Within the complicated legends of medieval hagiographers and the conspiracy theories of their modern revisionist counterparts, her signature sacraments of exorcism, anointing, and vision persist. Her three gifts of Spirit are the inheritance of Mary Magdalene: dissolving what is impure or evil, offering ointment for sickness and sin, and permitting her followers to perceive the spiritual truth of Resurrection.

The Magdalene inheritance is not for Christianity alone or for Judaism alone. Mary lived before those two religions had separated from each other, and her native Magdala was influenced by the exchange of products and ideas that came from India and China and Nabatea. The pantheon of divinity in the religions of the Indus, Buddhism's meditation in the face of suffering, Arabian mercantilism of a type that Muhammad would later represent—all of these echoed in her mental world.

Mary's sacraments were for those who used them, following the centuries-old practice of women in Galilean Judaism. They did not require hierarchy or dogma, and for that reason her sacraments have survived the imposition of silence that has been Mary's fate in orthodox Christianity. They have made their way, whether in practice or in imagination, through the twists and turns of repression, ignorance, and self-interest in the tortured history of the West.

That is why Mary's life is a sacramental biography. For all the details that texts of the New Testament exclude—in that exclusion opening wide the doors of legend, revision, and uncertainty—her sacraments nonetheless focus the ritual power that Mary Magdalene unleashed during Jesus' life and at his death. In the wordless struggle of exorcism, the silence of anointing, the rapt attention of vision, Mary conveyed the truth of Spirit to those who followed her disciplines, whatever their backgrounds may have been, and she has not ceased to find disciples.

In my visits with Marguerite, I had not realized that sitting in her house, looking out into her garden, I was also visiting the temple of Mary Magdalene. Her temple is manifest wherever her sacraments are embraced. Marguerite's quiet confidence that evil had only to be identified to be dissolved, her resort to the Spirit of God in prayer in times of illness, and finally her persistent question—"Is anyone there? Is there anyone there?"—echoed the practices that Mary Magdalene had crafted with Jesus.

# A Chronology for Mary Magdalene

63 B.C.E.   In the midst of an internecine strife among the Maccabees, Pompey enters Jerusalem and the Temple, claiming them for Rome.

47 B.C.E.   Julius Caesar arranges for the governance of what became known as Syria Palaestina, the Philistine coast of Syria, including Israel.

4 B.C.E.   The death of Herod results in the division of his kingdom: His son Archelaus takes Judah, Herod Antipas inherits Galilee and Perea, while Herod Philip rules Trachonitis.

1 B.C.E.–13 C.E.   The birth of Mary in the fishing town of Magdala and her childhood there.

2–16 C.E.   The birth of Jesus in Galilean Bethlehem and his childhood in Nazareth.

16–21   Jesus' apprenticeship with John the Baptist in Judea.

19   Herod Antipas's construction of Tiberias, near Magdala.

21   The death of John the Baptist and the return of Jesus to Nazareth at the age of eighteen.

24–27   Using Capernaum as a base, Jesus becomes a well-known teacher in Galilee by his twenty-fifth year. Near the beginning of this period, during the year 25, Mary Magdalene meets Jesus for the first time, seeking exorcism, and starts to craft her narratives of Jesus' practice (Mark 1:21–28).

27–31   Herod Antipas's threat forces Jesus to skirt and crisscross Galilean territory and to gather his followers in Syria; Mary returns to Magdala, where she crafts the story of the man with a legion of demons (Mark 5:1–17) and (after the Transfiguration in 30 C.E.) the story of the possessed boy (Mark 9:14–29).

31–32   Jesus' last year in Jerusalem, accompanied by Mary Magdalene and other disciples as well as the Twelve.

35   The meeting of Peter and James and Paul in Jerusalem, and the availability of the earliest sources of the Gospels: Peter's instruction for apostles such

as Paul, and the mishnah of Jesus' teaching, known to modern scholarship as "Q."

37   The removal of Pontius Pilate and Caiaphas from power by the Roman legate Vitellius.

40   The adaptation of Peter's Gospel by James, the brother of Jesus, in Jerusalem.

45   In Antioch, well outside of Palestine, followers of Jesus are for the first time called "Christians."

53–57   Paul writes his major letters to congregations of Christians in Galatia, Corinth, and Rome.

62   The death of James by stoning in Jerusalem, at the instigation of the high priest.

64   The death of Paul and Peter in Rome.

66   The insurrection against Rome is supported by some key authorities in the Temple, and Josephus is dispatched to Galilee, where he organizes resistance in Magdala and elsewhere.

67   Titus defeats the Jewish insurgents in Magdala and the makeshift Jewish fleet off shore. Thousands are slaughtered systematically, making this the likely date of Mary Magdalene's death in her native land.

70–73   The siege and capture of Jerusalem by the Romans, and the burning of the Temple under Titus; the end of the revolt in Palestine; the composition of Mark's Gospel in Rome.

75   Josephus publishes his *Jewish War*.

80   The composition of Matthew's Gospel (in Damascus).

90   The composition of Luke's Gospel and Acts (in Antioch).

93   Josephus publishes his *Antiquities of the Jews*.

100   The composition of John's Gospel (in Ephesus).

# Acknowledgments

No subject I can remember studying has brought me as much encouragement as that of Mary Magdalene has.

Andi Novick, who has attended lectures on a variety of topics at the Institute of Advanced Theology at Bard College, first challenged me to turn my attention to Mary. I demurred, explaining that Mary Magdalene had become a minor industry among scholars of the New Testament and that the critical issues involved might be more technical than public lectures could address. But in deference to the interest in Mary that Andi and I shared, I agreed to convene a small seminar. We read current literature and discussed whether full meetings of the institute might take up the subject.

Those weekly seminars quickly proved me wrong in both of my claims to Andi. The secondary literature amounts to a major industry, not a minor one, and the fact is that the underlying issues involved in approaching Mary Magdalene are accessible and interesting to nonspecialists. That experience pushed me to develop a series of lectures and to deliver them to the institute as a whole.

The lectures were under way as I was working on *Rabbi Paul* for Doubleday, and Kenneth Wapner, my editorial adviser, helped me craft a proposal with Gail Ross, my agent. I was delighted when Michelle Rapkin and Andrew Corbin accepted the proposal for Doubleday, and I turned to writing the book.

Ken was especially helpful, patient, and incisive during the writing of the multiple drafts that were involved. My first draft happened to be in French, since I had been in France when I wrote it, so he had the chore of weeding out Gallicisms. The biggest difficulty came in addressing the wide range of medieval traditions regarding Mary Magdalene without resorting to the kind of exhaustive and exhausting survey that in the end bars the reader from any sense of who Mary was. Ken suggested the format of interweaving discussion of the earliest evidence with connections to later traditions and then helped coordinate the whole.

The result, I hope, will help the reader to treasure the inheritance of Mary Magdalene and to understand where and how her image has been distorted and her message misconstrued. So much has been written about Mary, it's tempting to think that all speculations are equal. While I was finishing this book, a friend showed me correspondence from some years ago between her late father, Professor Robert Gorham Davis, and Cardinal Bernard Law of Boston. Her father took exception to Cardinal Law's confusion of Mary Magdalene with the "sinful woman" in chapter 7 of Luke, although Roman Catholic scholars had long since abandoned that identification. Cardinal Law wrote back to Professor Davis through his secretary, saying that although the idea was false, "there is a tradition with a small 't' in the Church that does allow" for the equation.* There are so many traditions "with a small 't' " that people can become confused by the welter of competing claims and therefore tend to accept those that seem convenient and forget the rest.

My approach, both in specialist work and in books such as *Rabbi Jesus* and *Rabbi Paul,* has been to order traditions chronologically and to explain how meanings unfolded by inferring which statements and actions generated the texts from the ancient world that lie before us. In Mary Magdalene's case, her actions certainly speak louder than words, but I think readers will find some interest in her verbal contribution to the Gospels, as well.

Consultations with colleagues—Jacob Neusner and participants in a faculty seminar at Bard College, Amy-Jill Levine at Vanderbilt University, and Jeffrey Kripal at Rice University—proved productive, and a cherished partner in prose—Marguerite Hayes (another Marguerite)—sifted my words with an exactitude writers long for. At Doubleday, Andrew Corbin helped me see where I might make a series of significant adjustments, and, as usual, he proved to be his intellectually provocative self.

—Lent 2005
Annandale, New York

---

* I am grateful to Professor Lydia Davis for making her father's papers on Mary Magdalene available to me. The letter quoted was written by Cardinal Law's secretary, the Reverend Michael W. MacEwen, and is dated April 22, 1994.

# Notes

### PROLOGUE: MARGUERITE

ix **the "hypothesis" that Mary was the true Holy Grail:** The key work in developing this approach is Michael Baigent, Richard Leigh, and Henry Lincoln, *Holy Blood, Holy Grail* (New York: Delacorte, 1982).

x **major teachers in the New Testament:** An awareness of the variegated sources in the New Testament stands behind my earlier biographies, *Rabbi Jesus: An Intimate Biography* (New York: Doubleday, 2000) and *Rabbi Paul: An Intellectual Biography* (New York: Doubleday, 2004). When I cite these works in this book, I have not included my name in the citation. In addition, *Rabbi Jesus* and *Rabbi Paul* are cited only by short title hereafter.

xi **"the apostle to the apostles":** The broadest survey available is by Susan Haskins, *Mary Magdalen: Myth and Metaphor* (New York: Harcourt, Brace, 1993).

xii **what Gnostic teachers had to say about Mary:** This refers especially to the accounts in the Gospels of Thomas, Mary, and Philip and in the *Pistis Sophia.* My selection is informed by analytic work, such as the anthology and commentary of Antti Marjanen, *The Woman Jesus Loved: Mary Magdalene in the Nag Hammadi Library and Related Documents* (Leiden: Brill, 1996).

xiv **it is tempting for professionals in the study of the New Testament:** Darrell L. Bock, *Breaking the Da Vinci Code* (Nashville: Nelson, 2004), and Ben Witherington, *The Gospel Code: Novel Claims About Jesus, Mary Magdalene, and Da Vinci* (Downers Grove, IL: Intervarsity, 2004), provide good examples.

### I. POSSESSED

2 **In one vivid tale:** Victor Saxer dates Mary's veneration in Ephesus from that time in a monograph that remains fundamental; see *Le culte de Marie Madeleine en Occident* (Paris: Clavreuil, 1959), pp. 10, 21. The Ephesians claimed

to possess her skeleton, which was moved to Constantinople during the ninth century; Susan Haskins, *Mary Magdalen: Myth and Metaphor* (New York: Harcourt, Brace, 1993), p. 108.

2 **In one recent reconstruction:** Marianne Sawicki, *Crossing Galilee: Architectures of Contact in the Occupied Land of Jesus* (Harrisburg, PA: Trinity Press International, 2000), pp. 133–153; this is an otherwise excellent study. Richard Bauckham draws the necessary distinction between Mary and Joanna in refuting Sawicki's conclusion; see *Gospel Women: Studies of Named Women in the Gospels* (London: T&T Clark, 2002), p. 194 n. 356. His criticism of Sawicki for excessive speculation strikes me as overdrawn, since he himself identifies Joanna with the "Junia" mentioned by Paul in Romans 16:7 (pp. 109–202). The only evidence for this claim is the rough similarity between the women's names, and even then Bauckham is faced with how to explain the stark difference in the names of the husbands involved, Chuza and Andronicus. However much Sawicki and Bauckham might disagree and define themselves in terms of that disagreement, their work collectively marks an important turn in the study of women in the formation of the New Testament. I am grateful to them both, even when I disagree with them in regard to particular topics.

5 **he said that he listened to his *daimonion ti*:** A rich discussion can be found in Nicholas D. Smith and Paul Woodruff, eds., *Reason and Religion in Socratic Philosophy* (New York: Oxford University Press, 2000).

5 ***daimonia* could do harm:** Carmen Bernabé Ubieta, "Mary Magdalene and the Seven Demons in Social-Scientific Perspective," trans. Lucía F. Llorente, in *Transformative Encounters: Jesus and Women Re-Viewed,* ed. Ingrid Rosa Kitzberger (Leiden: Brill, 2000), pp. 203–223. Should we see the exorcism of Mary's seven demons as a series of events or a single explosive rout? Luke's spare reference doesn't answer this question directly. The demons are simply described as having "gone out" (*exeleluthei*) of Mary. If a Greek speaker wanted to imply that on one spectacular occasion Jesus expelled them all, it would have been more natural just to say that he cast them out (using the verb *ekballo*), as happens at other points in the Gospels (see Mark 5:1–20; Luke 8:26–39; Matthew 8:28–34). The use of the verb *exeleluthei* and the absence of any reference to a dramatic expulsion of the demons make it seem likely that Mary's demons balked when Jesus commanded them to depart. In a later version of Luke's description, which was appended to the Gospel According to Mark (16:9), the wording was changed in order to describe the demons as having been "cast out" (*ekbeblekei*). This pastiche ending of Mark is much later than the Gospel itself. In the way of many summary references in the Gospels, it irons out the troubling feature of demonic contention with Jesus.

**5 fragments of papyrus that record the ancient craft of exorcism:** Hans Dieter Betz, *The Greek Magical Papyri in Translation, Including the Demotic Spells* (Chicago: University of Chicago Press, 1992).

**6 vaginas made their bodies vulnerable to entry:** Ruth Padel, "Women: Model for Possession by Greek Demons," in *Images of Women in Antiquity,* ed. Averil Cameron and Amélie Kuhrt (Detroit: Wayne State University Press, 1993), pp. 3–19, particularly pp. 11–12.

**6 a man who stayed in his future father-in-law's house could not complain later:** As the text laconically remarks, "He who eats with his father in law in Judea without a witness can not bring a complaint for the cause of non-virginity, because he was alone with her" (Ketuvoth 1:5).

**7 Like Jesus, Mary Magdalene might conceivably have been a *mamzer:*** Since I identified Jesus as a *mamzer* in *Rabbi Jesus* (pp. 3–23), a considerable literature on this subject has emerged: Meir Bar Ilan, "The Attitude Toward *Mamzerim* in Jewish Society in Late Antiquity," *Jewish History* 14, no. 2 (2000): 125–170; Shaye D. Cohen, "Some Thoughts on 'The Attitude Toward *Mamzerim* in Jewish Society in Late Antiquity,' " *Jewish History* 14, no. 2 (2000): 171–174; Sawicki, *Crossing Galilee,* pp. 171–173; Andries van Aarde, *Fatherless in Galilee: Jesus as Child of God* (Harrisburg, PA: Trinity Press International 2001); Chilton, "Jésus, le *mamzer* (Mt 1.18)," *New Testament Studies* 46 (2001): 222–227; Scot McKnight, "Calling Jesus *Mamzer,*" *Journal for the Study of the Historical Jesus* 1, no. 1 (2003): 73–103; Charles Quarles, "Jesus as *Mamzer:* A Response to Bruce Chilton's Reconstruction of the Circumstances Surrounding Jesus' Birth in *Rabbi Jesus,*" *Bulletin for Biblical Research* 14, no. 2 (2004): 243–255; Chilton, "Recovering Jesus' *Mamzerut,*" in *Ancient Israel, Judaism, and Christianity in Contemporary Perspective: Essays in Memory of Karl-Johan Illman,* ed. Jacob Neusner et al. (Lanham, MD: University Press of America, 2005). For an earlier approach, based upon the assumption that a *mamzer* is a bastard in the modern sense, see Jane Schaberg, *The Illegitimacy of Jesus: A Feminist Theological Interpretation of the Infancy Narratives* (San Francisco: Harper & Row, 1987); John J. Rousseau and Rami Arav, *Jesus and His World: An Archaeological and Cultural Dictionary* (Minneapolis: Fortress, 1995), pp. 223–225.

**7 Modern scholarship continues to parry the medieval tradition of portraying Mary as a prostitute:** The hyperbole of these legends is often painful, especially those that emerged during the twelfth century. Honorius Augustodunensis believed that "Mary of Magdala castle" had been wealthy but then slipped into being "a filthy and common prostitute." As Pierre de Celle said, "Out of a prostitute, Christ made an apostle." Both these examples are cited in Haskins, *Mary Magdalen,* pp. 158–159, 192. In a classic study, Elisabeth

Schüssler Fiorenza explains how the confusion arose; see *In Memory of Her: A Feminist Theological Reconstruction of Christian Origins* (New York: Crossroad, 1983, 1992), p. 129. Nonetheless, an attempt has been made to insist that she really is depicted as a prostitute not only by medieval piety, but also by "Luke's own design and subsequent androcentric, misogynistic interpretation"; see Jane Schaberg, *The Resurrection of Mary Magdalene: Legends, Apocrypha, and the Christian Testament* (New York: Continuum, 2002), p. 74 n. 40.

8 **She long remained the ideal icon of mortification among the lay and clerical groups:** See Rudolph M. Bell, *Holy Anorexia* (Chicago: University of Chicago Press, 1985), pp. 171–179. For the examples cited, I am indebted to Katherine Ludwig Jansen, *The Making of the Magdalen: Preaching and Popular Devotion in the Later Middle Ages* (Princeton: Princeton University Press, 2000), pp. 225, 228 (see also pp. 36–46, 124–142).

8 **Mary of Egypt is herself a classic figure of Christian folklore:** For a very clear discussion of a topic that is sometimes made unnecessarily complicated, see Benedicta Ward, *Harlots of the Desert: A Study of Repentance in Early Monastic Sources* (Kalamazoo: Cistercian Publications, 1987), pp. 26–56.

9 ***The Golden Legend* of Jacobus de Voragine:** This book is widely available in the following editions: Christopher Stace and Richard Hamer, *Jacobus de Voragine, The Golden Legend: Selections* (London: Penguin, 1998), pp. 165–172; William Granger Ryan, *Jacobus de Voragine, The Golden Legend: Readings on the Saints* (Princeton: Princeton University Press, 1993), pp. 374–383. For variants of the same story, which made its way all over Europe, see Larissa Tracy, *Women of the Gilte Legende: A Selection of Middle English Saints Lives* (Cambridge: D. S. Brewer, 2003), pp. 68–79; François Halin, "Une vie grecque de sainte Marie-Madeleine BHG 1161x," *Analecta Bollandiana* 105 (1987): 5–23.

10 **the mistake of presuming that women with demons were necessarily promiscuous:** Jane Schaberg argues against dominant interpretations in the West, which have "scrawled . . . the word WHORE" over Mary Magdalene; see *The Resurrection of Mary Magdalene,* pp. 68, 77. Schaberg knows that one way to portray Mary as a prostitute is to ask, "What kind of demons would a woman have?" and then to reply, "Sexual, of course." To guard against that answer, Schaberg wishes to edit Mary's demons out of the available evidence, since the reference to them appears only in Luke (echoed in Mark 16:9, a late addition to that Gospel). In my opinion, however, texts should not be discarded because they have been badly interpreted. Schaberg tends to overcorrect for the "vivid and bizarre postbiblical life" that I agree has been imposed on Mary Magdalene.

10 **the parochial hamlet he had known from his childhood would never accept him as a rabbi:** See *Rabbi Jesus,* pp. 98–102. On the populations of the towns

associated with Jesus, see the discussion since *Rabbi Jesus* (especially pp. 78, 80–82, 95–97, 180) detailed in Chilton, "Review Essay: Archaeology and Rabbi Jesus," *Bulletin for Biblical Research* 12, no. 2 (2002): 273–280.

12 **embracing the complex, rich oral tradition:** See *Rabbi Jesus,* pp. 3–22.

## 2. THE MAGDALENE

15 **the holy relics of flesh transformed by Jesus:** A detailed historical account of the veneration of Mary is given in Victor Saxer, *Le culte de Marie Madeleine en Occident* (Paris: Clavreuil, 1959). His maps document 33 sites between the eighth and tenth centuries, 80 during the eleventh century, 116 during the first half of the twelfth century, 125 during the second half of the twelfth century, 130 during the thirteenth century (until 1278), 196 in the late thirteenth century (after 1279) and during the fourteenth century, and 187 during the fifteenth and sixteenth centuries. The whole study is a brilliant exposition of how medieval piety combined faith, legend, economics, and political ambition.

16 **"that these disgusting dogs were taken and massacred during the feast of the one that they had insulted":** Pierre des Vaux-de-Cernay, *The History of the Albigensian Crusade: Peter of les Vaux-de-Cernay's Historia Albigensis,* trans. W. A. Sibly and M. D. Sibly (Woodbridge, Suffolk: Boydell, 1998), p. 51.

17 **the legend that Jesus and Mary were lovers:** The Grail connection is fleshed out in Lynn Picknett and Clive Thomas, *The Templar Revelation: Secret Guardians of the True Identity of Christ* (New York: Touchstone, 1997), the most immediate source of Dan Brown's novel *The Da Vinci Code* (New York: Doubleday, 2003). But in this vein, see the earlier book by Margaret Starbird, *The Woman with the Alabaster Jar: Mary Magdalen and the Holy Grail* (Santa Fe: Bear, 1993). Among several competent refutations, see Bart D. Ehrman, *Truth and Fiction in "The Da Vinci Code"* (New York: Oxford University Press, 2004).

18 **Jesus took up the protest against Herod Antipas and the forces of Rome:** John the Baptist had objected that Antipas's marriage to his brother's former wife broke a basic law in the Torah. Antipas reacted swiftly to this assault on the status of his marriage—and therefore on the legitimacy of his reign—by beheading John; see *Rabbi Jesus,* pp. 41–63. Luke's Gospel spells out in so many words Antipas's resolve to kill Jesus (Luke 13:31); see *Rabbi Jesus,* pp. 174–179.

18 **He sent them out to preach, heal, and exorcise:** When the New Testament lists the most prominent twelve men among the disciples, the names on the list vary a little (Matthew 10:1–4; Mark 3:13–19; Luke 6:12–16; Acts 1:13). That is not surprising: The people who composed the Gospels a generation after Jesus' death naturally wanted to remember their teachers as among the Twelve.

21 **Jews in Galilee and elsewhere proudly embraced that name for their own daughters:** See, for example, L. Y. Rahmani, *A Catalogue of Jewish Ossuaries in the Collections of the State of Israel* (Jerusalem: Israel Antiquities Authority, 1994); Tal Ilan, *Lexicon of Jewish Names in Late Antiquity: Part I: Palestine 330 BCE–200 CE* (Tübingen: Mohr Siebeck, 2002). Marianne Sawicki has argued that the name Miriam would only have been assigned for nationalistic reasons a generation before Jesus, so that Mary Magdalene "may well have been old enough to be Jesus' mother" when they first met; see "Magdalenes and Tiberiennes: City Women in the Entourage of Jesus," in *Transformative Encounters: Jesus and Women Re-Viewed,* ed. Ingrid Rosa Kitzberger (Leiden: Brill, 2000), pp. 181–202, 192. This suggestion runs up against the occurrence of the names Miriam and even Maria (among other variants) in Jewish inscriptions right through the period, as well as the number of Marys in the New Testament. I agree with Sawicki's inference that Mary was somewhat older than Jesus, for reasons discussed in chapter 1, but Mary's vigorous companionship with Jesus until the end of his life, as well as her influence thereafter, makes it unlikely she was as old as his mother.

21 **Magdala was important both practically and symbolically for Jesus and his disciples:** Richard Atwood, *Mary Magdalene in the New Testament Gospels and Early Tradition* (Bern: Lang, 1993), pp. 21–26; Mendel Nun, "Ports of Galilee," *Biblical Archaeology Review* 25, no. 4 (1999): 18–31, 64. On the sociology of the region, see Richard A. Horsley, "The Expansion of Hasmonean Rule in Idumea and Galilee: Toward a Historical Sociology," in *Second Temple Studies III: Studies in Politics, Class and Material Culture,* ed. Philip R. Davies and John M. Halligan (Sheffield: Sheffield Academic Press, 2002), pp. 134–165. Nazareth, where Jesus grew up, was a fifteen-mile walk west and south from Magdala. Nazareth was much smaller and poorer than Magdala.

The site of Magdala has fallen victim to the ravages of nature, politics, and modern warfare; see Jane Schaberg, *The Resurrection of Mary Magdalene: Legends, Apocrypha, and the Christian Testament* (New York: Continuum, 2002), pp. 47–64. Rising groundwater, forced up by recently built dams at the southern end of the Sea of Galilee, has jumbled ancient remains beneath the ruined site. Bombings have also damaged ancient archaeological remains.

Schaberg's hopes of renewing excavation of the site have run up against the complicated cross-claims of the Israeli government, Franciscan proprietors, and Palestinians who have traditionally lived there. So while Capernaum—the site of Peter's home with his in-laws—is a neatly labeled model dig (with a Disneyesque touch in a modern church built there), Magdala has been closed to research, much as Mary Magdalene has been concealed with clichés about women.

Historical sources say more than archaeology can at the moment. Josephus, born around 37 C.E., knew Magdala from personal experience; his writings detail the cultural context of the town in a way the Gospels do not. Magdala itself became a service town for Tiberias, Antipas's new capital. Josephus later attempted to organize Galilean resistance to the Romans from a base in Magdala during his brief and disastrous career as a Jewish general in Galilee between 66 and 67 C.E.; see Gohei Hata, "Imagining Some Dark Periods in Josephus' Life," in *Josephus and the History of the Greco-Roman Period: Essays in Memory of Morton Smith,* ed. Fausto Parente and Joseph Sievers (Leiden: Brill, 1994), pp. 309–328. He referred to the place by its Greek name, Taricheae, derived from the word for salted fish; the town had become a city, specializing in a preserved product that could be exported, and even boasted its own hippodrome as well as a stadium (Josephus *Jewish War* 2.596–647). With a market as big as nearby Tiberias, *fish* spelled wealth and splendor. This extensive trade, the key to Magdala's success, made the town notorious for its association with Gentile culture.

22 **"Jesus Christ, God's Son, Savior":** In the way of acronyms, a liberty with spelling was involved. In the actual word for fish, there is an *o* before the *u, ikhthous,* while the acronym yields *ikhthus.*

22 **He chose a spot along the Sea of Galilee:** See Josephus *Jewish War* 2.168; Moshe Dothan, *Hammath Tiberias,* 2 vols. (Jerusalem: Israel Exploration Society, 1983–2000); *Rabbi Jesus,* pp. 91–93; Jonathan L. Reed, *Archaeology and the Galilean Jesus: A Re-examination of the Evidence* (Harrisburg, PA: Trinity Press International, 2000); Chilton, "Review Essay: Archaeology and Rabbi Jesus," *Bulletin for Biblical Research* 12, no. 2 (2002): 273–280.

22 **the Jews who moved to the city were the flotsam of Galilee:** After two wars with the Romans, however, rabbis who contributed to the Mishnah eventually settled in Tiberias during the second century and it became "the center of Jewish life and the spiritual capital not only of Jewish Palestine, but also of the Diaspora" (see Dothan, *Hammath Tiberias,* vol. I, p. 4).

23 **To call Jesus "the Nazarene" naturally evokes Nazareth as his native village:** This geographical meaning is also expressed in the Gospels by another designation, "Nazorean" (Nazoraios in Greek, Natsoraya in Aramaic), which does not rhyme with Magdalene. The use of Nazorean predominates in the Gospels of Matthew, Luke, and John, while Mark uses only Nazarene. See the still-worthwhile article by Hans Heinrich Schader in *Theological Dictionary of the New Testament,* ed. Gerhard Kittel, trans. Geoffrey W. Bromiley (Grand Rapids: Eerdmans, 1978), pp. 874–879. In the Talmud and other Rabbinic sources, Jesus is called "the Notsri," an evident play on Nazaraya and Natsoraya. Notsri means someone who "keeps" or "hinders": Jesus and his

followers kept their own traditions, and therefore hindered other Israelites on this view.

### 3. SECRET EXORCISM

25 **Mary was so wealthy:** David Mycoff offers an excellent treatment of such stories in *The Life of Saint Mary Magdalene and of Her Sister Martha* (Kalamazoo: Cistercian Publications, 1989).

26 **narrators relished tales of demonic possession:** Josephus, the first-century historian, described a Jewish exorcist named Eleazar, whose success was proven when the departing demon—as commanded—knocked a vessel of water over on its way out. In this wonderful story, Eleazar used a root, approved by Solomon, attached to a ring; he applied it to the possessed man's nose and drew the obliging demon out of his nostrils (Josephus *Antiquities* 8.46–48). Apollonius of Tyana, born slightly later than Saint Paul and north of Paul's native Tarsus, in Asia Minor, dispatched a demon into a statue, and then the statue collapsed (Philostratus *The Life of Apollonius of Tyana* 4.20): The adolescent who had been possessed was cured of his crude behavior, including the habit of exposing himself in public. When we analyze these sources, we see that compared to other practitioners, Jesus was not a run-of-the-mill exorcist. He exorcised Mary seven times, so the first six sessions did not completely dispel her demons. This is part of an unusual pattern in the Gospels that reveals a great deal about the difficulty Jesus had with many of his exorcisms, the meaning he attached to them, and how other people reacted to him.

27 **the positive energy of God's purity:** See Chilton, *Jesus' Baptism and Jesus' Healing: His Personal Practice of Spirituality* (Harrisburg, PA: Trinity Press International, 1998), 58–97; Scot McKnight, *A New Vision for Israel: The Teachings of Jesus in National Context* (Grand Rapids: Eerdmans, 1999), pp. 15–69.

27 **this teaching appears shortly after the reference to Mary's possession:** Even the most skeptical of commentators have agreed that Jesus himself made this statement. It passes muster with what John Meier has called "the criterion of embarrassment"—you can more easily imagine Rabbi Jesus saying this than pious followers making it up and attributing it to him; see John P. Meier, *A Marginal Jew: Rethinking the Historical Jesus,* vol. 1 (New York: Doubleday, 1991), pp. 168–171. Observing the possible embarrassment caused the early Church by teachings like this one (and Jesus said many other things that have cast an embarrassing light on the doctrines of later times) is like being surprised ourselves, only at one remove. Once you have observed the reaction, you need to see what provoked it; otherwise, all you are doing is registering puzzlement,

not furthering insight. Looking beyond our surprise or the early Church's embarrassment, why should Jesus speak of this problem of abortive exorcism? That is the question that demands a plausible answer.

28 **a possession that an incautious exorcist might make repeatedly worse:** Showy exorcists, both ancient and modern, have often reinforced the sense that unclean spirits are powerful, opening the way for fresh possessions, and thus more requests for exorcisms. That spiral is good for business and fine for demons, but bad for those who suffer from possession. For vivid illustrations of modern practice, see Mario Cuneo, *American Exorcism* (New York: Doubleday, 2001).

28 **Petrarch called her "the sweet friend of God" (*"dulcis amica dei"*):** Susan Haskins, *Mary Magdalen: Myth and Metaphor* (New York: Harcourt, Brace, 1993), pp. 192, 196–197.

29 **Beelzebul, god of the underworld:** W. Herrmann, "Baal Zebub," in *Dictionary of Deities and Demons in the Bible,* eds. Karel van der Toorn, Bob Becking, and Pieter W. van der Horst (Leiden: Brill, 1999), pp. 154–156. The form "Baal Zebub," meaning "Lord of the flies," deliberately distorts the original "Baal Zebul," or "Lord, the prince." That was how the Hebrew Bible demoted a god of the underworld into the ringleader of demons. There is evidence from Qumran that exorcists were, in fact, willing to invoke Beelzebul's help; see Douglas L. Penny and Michael O. Wise, "By the Power of Beelzebub: An Aramaic Incantation Formula from Qumran (4Q560)," *Journal of Biblical Literature* 113, no. 4 (1994): 627–650.

30 **Mary's companionship with Jesus would not have been permitted:** Haskins, *Mary Magdalen,* pp. 196–197, quoting Honorius Augustodunensis.

30 **the false claim that women had no place within the leadership of Jewish worship and learning:** The response that modern Christians had coming can be found in Amy-Jill Levine, "Lilies of the Field and Wandering Jews: Biblical Scholarship, Women's Roles, and Social Location," in *Transformative Encounters: Jesus and Women Re-Viewed,* ed. Ingrid Rosa Kitzberger (Leiden: Brill, 2000), pp. 329–352. Professor Levine writes (pp. 343–344), "Unsupported and insupportable historical views of a misogynistic, essentialist, atavistic Judaism lead naturally to theological speculation. The bad history reflected in these numerous citations culminates in a theology that at best can be labelled obscene." See also Mary R. Thompson, *Mary of Magdala: Apostle and Leader* (New York: Paulist, 1995), pp. 81–95.

32 **male and female together reflected the reality of the divine image:** Jane S. Webster, "Sophia: Engendering Wisdom in Proverbs—Ben Sira and the Wisdom of Solomon," *Journal for the Study of the Old Testament* 78 (1998): 63–79;

Notes

*Rabbi Jesus,* pp. 145–146; Karen L. King, ed., *Women and Goddess Traditions in Antiquity and Today* (Minneapolis: Fortress, 1997). This conception was also pivotal within Jesus' teaching on marriage; see Mark 10:2–12. The wide range of estimates for dating Proverbs is detailed in R. N. Whybray, *The Book of Proverbs: A Survey of Modern Study* (Leiden: Brill, 1995). My own chronology falls well within that range.

4. MARY'S SIGNATURE

34 **The Gospels emerged a generation after Jesus' death:** Early Christian tradition agreed that the earliest of the Gospels, Mark, was not composed by one of the disciples of Jesus. Papias (the learned and garrulous bishop of Hierapolis, in Asia Minor) described Mark as the secretary or amanuensis of Peter, who preached an oral gospel. This story has had a rich afterlife. See Eusebius *History of the Church* 3.39.15–16; Raymond Brown, *An Introduction to the New Testament* (New York: Doubleday, 1997), pp. 158–161. Papias's assumption that individual authors did not compose the Gospels agrees with the consensus of modern critical scholarship.

35 **Peter was especially involved with preparing converts for baptism:** Acts 10:34–43 provides an outline of the narrative of Peter's oral gospel, as has been widely recognized since the contribution of C. H. Dodd, *The Apostolic Preaching and Its Developments* (London: Hodder & Stoughton, 1944) and *According to the Scriptures: The Sub-Structure of New Testament Theology* (London: Nisbet, 1952). Because sources are reconstructed on the basis of inference, there is no universal agreement concerning their number or extent. But Dodd's work set the stage for a growing consensus among critical scholars. Fashions of study such as Fundamentalism and Structuralism discredited source analysis and an interest in history during the 1970s and 1980s, but these basic tenets have made a fine comeback since the 1990s, especially in Europe. See *Journal of Biblical Literature* 112 (1993): 146–148, review of the seminal work of Matti Myllykoski, *Die letzten Tage Jesu: Markus und Johannes, ihre Traditionen und die historische Frage* (Helsinki: Suomalainen Tiedeakatemia, 1991).

35 **Mary Magdalene also emerges as the author of a source of stories that bear her oral signature:** In a groundbreaking study, Thorleif Boman credited women for a source within the Gospel According to Luke in particular; see *Die Jesus-Überlieferung im Lichte der neueren Volkskunde* (Göttingen: Vandenhoeck & Ruprecht, 1967), pp. 123–137. In my opinion, the likely center of this circle of women was Joanna (Luke 8:3). She had access to members of the Herodian court, which explains the specific and sometimes sympathetic reference to them

Notes

in both the Gospel According to Luke and the book of Acts. See Carla Ricci, *Mary Magdalene and Many Others: Women Who Followed Jesus,* trans. Paul Burns (Minneapolis: Fortress, 1994), pp. 43–46, 69–72, 154–156.

The hypothesis that there was an exorcistic source within the Gospels was developed by Etienne Trocmé in *L'Evangile selon saint Marc* (Geneva: Labor et Fides, 2000) and *La formation de l'évangile selon saint Marc* (Paris: Presses Universitaires de France, 1963), pp. 42–43.

35 **these three stories amount to a manual of how to cope with unclean spirits:** These are the three most detailed accounts of exorcism in the Gospels. Each of the three is also represented in Matthew and Luke, but Mark's is the earliest written form available. For that reason, Mark is the point of departure for establishing the Magdalene source, fully reproduced in the Appendix.

36 **a small building fitted with benches:** For further description and a diagram drawn by James F. Strange, see *Rabbi Jesus,* pp. 96–97.

37 **The slip back and forth between plural and singular:** Chilton, "Exorcism and History: Mark 1:21–28," *Gospel Perspectives* 6 (1986): 253–271.

40 **no commentator has been able to draw the line between the story's symbolic meaning and the literal event it depicts:** Chilton, "Friends and Enemies," in *The Cambridge Companion to Jesus,* ed. M. Bockmuehl (Cambridge: Cambridge University Press, 2001), pp. 72–86, and *Rabbi Jesus,* pp. 168–173, where the context of the events in the deadly threat to Jesus from Herod Antipas explains the political symbolism of this exorcism. The sequel to the exorcism (Mark 5:14–17) is also discussed in those pages of *Rabbi Jesus.*

40 **he saw Satan fall like lightning from heaven:** Joel Marcus, "Jesus' Baptismal Vision," *New Testament Studies* 41 (1995): 512–21; *Rabbi Jesus,* pp. 174–179.

41 **"except by prayer":** Some ancient manuscripts of Mark's Gospel attest the addition of "and fasting." Fasting was certainly a part of Jesus' spiritual discipline, but it does not feature as a part of his exorcistic technique, except here. Most textual critics have concluded that the phrase was added later, as practices of the early Church influenced the way Mark was copied in Greek; see William Lane, *The Gospel According to Mark* (London: Marshall, Morgan & Scott, 1974), pp. 335–336.

42 **where other disciples and their sources are concerned:** The collection of Jesus' sayings known as "Q," the mishnah his apostles assembled after his death, has been parsed so thoroughly that some scholars believe they can tell you to the fraction of a verse what was in it and what was not. See James M. Robinson, Paul Hoffmann, and John S. Kloppenborg, eds., *The Critical Edition of Q* (Leuven: Peeters, 2000). I demur from this claim of certitude, although I agree that Jesus'

mishnah, an oral source, influenced the Gospels; see *Pure Kingdom: Jesus' Vision of God* (Eerdmans: Grand Rapids and London: SPCK, 1996), pp. 107–115.

James, the brother of Jesus, led a circle of disciples that seems to have been the source of passages in the Gospels that concern worship in the Temple, where James headed up Jesus' movement after the crucifixion; see B. D. Chilton and J. N. Neusner, eds., *The Brother of Jesus: James the Just and His Mission* (Louisville: Westminster John Knox, 2001).

43 **Rabbis of this period also characterized another mystic:** *Rabbi Jesus,* pp. 41–63, 83–102, 150–196, 303.

44 **her own bloody battle with a demon:** Katherine Ludwig Jansen, *The Making of the Magdalen: Preaching and Popular Devotion in the Later Middle Ages* (Princeton: Princeton University Press, 2000), p. 300.

44 **"the messianic secret"** Heikki Räisänen, *The "Messianic Secret" in Mark* (Edinburgh: Clark, 1990). As he rightly says (p. 171) of the exorcisms in chapter 1 and chapter 5, "The people however do not appear to hear, and the secret does not break out," and he makes a comparison to the heavenly voices of 1:11 and 9:7 (p. 172). This difference between what demons say and what people hear also launched my approach.

### 5. NAMELESS ANOINTER

47 **The same kind of incompatibility emerged:** *Rabbi Jesus,* pp. 168–171, 174–196.

48 **by offering sacrifice on Mount Zion in the way that the God of Israel desired:** Ibid., pp. 174–212.

49 **She would have observed the planning in Bethany:** Ibid., pp. 213–247.

49 **oiling skin was a routine ritual in Jesus' movement:** Anointing was commonly practiced in Judaism as a whole during this period. Anointing was much less unusual than sending out the disciples or the extraordinary, aberrant exorcisms that are recorded in detail, and for that reason, the Gospels do not dwell on the practice, although they do attest it. See Tal Ilan, "In the Footsteps of Jesus: Jewish Women in a Jewish Movement," in *Transformative Encounters: Jesus and Women Re-Viewed,* ed. Ingrid Rosa Kitzberger (Leiden: Brill, 2000), pp. 115–136. The Talmud of Jerusalem (Shabbat 14:3–4) provides several examples of the permission to engage in anointing on the Sabbath for purposes of celebration and of healing. Ilan (p. 129) takes this as evidence of "the large number of women who practiced the art of healing."

50 **Mark's Gospel provides the earliest, most richly textured account of this ritual event:** *Rabbi Jesus,* pp. 248–268.

50 **Mark's Gospel withholds her actual identity:** Elisabeth Schüssler Fiorenza wrote a pathbreaking book that features this passage in its title; see *In Memory of Her: A Feminist Theological Reconstruction of Christian Origins* (New York: Crossroad, 1983, 1992). Her work stands as a classic among feminist studies of the New Testament. Professor Schüssler Fiorenza wrote at a time, however, when literary approaches were sometimes pursued to the exclusion of asking basic historical questions. In the present case, the result is that she overlooks a key feature of the text and therefore assumes the woman was always anonymous. Tal Ilan seeks to correct this problem in feminist interpretation in "Paul and Pharisee Women," in *On the Cutting Edge: The Study of Women in Biblical Worlds—Essays in Honor of Elisabeth Schüssler Fiorenza,* eds. Jane Schaberg, Alice Bach, and Esther Fuchs (New York: Continuum, 2004), pp. 82–101.

52 **medieval interpreters correctly surmised:** Valerie I. J. Flint cites the example of the Ruthwell Cross in Scotland from the seventh or eighth century, showing Mary with *ungentum,* which had magical associations from the time of Gregory of Tours; see *The Rise of Magic in Early Medieval Europe* (Princeton: Princeton University Press, 1991), p. 260. See also Brendan Cassidy, ed., *The Ruthwell Cross* (Princeton: Princeton University Press, 1993).

52 **She, by name and by action, embodies the connection between Jesus' interment and the angelic announcement:** Other women are present at the interment and at the mouth of the tomb; only Mary Magdalene is in both places, according to Mark.

### 6. "THY NAME IS AS OIL POURED FORTH"

55 **Women featured prominently among practitioners of anointing:** See Tal Ilan, "In the Footsteps of Jesus: Jewish Women in a Jewish Movement," in *Transformative Encounters: Jesus and Women Re-Viewed,* ed. Ingrid Rosa Kitzberger (Leiden: Brill, 2000), pp. 115–136, and *Mine & Yours Are Hers: Retrieving Women's History from Rabbinic Literature* (Leiden: Brill, 1997), pp. 105, 230–232. Matthew Morgenstern has commented upon an Aramaic text of exorcism that involves anointing; see "Notes on a Recently Published Magic Bowl," *Aramaic Studies* 2, no. 2 (2004): 207–222.

55 **this service included financial support:** In the case of Lydia in Philippi (Acts 16:11–15), support was more than financial. She personally accommodated Paul in Philippi and provided him with crucial contacts; see *Rabbi Paul,* pp. 151–152. Neither Lydia nor the Magdalene is just a patroness or donor in the presentation of Luke and Acts. Their support went beyond financial largesse. Mary Magdalene—evidently less wealthy than Lydia, the dyer known

for her purple cloth—physically traveled with Jesus, despite the risks of travel on foot and without any guarantee of food or lodging. During these expeditions, even a wealthy supporter had more to do than just open his or her purse, and there is no indication that Mary was wealthy. "Serving" or "ministering" meant work with one's hands for the immediate needs of the fellowship, and labor for the Kingdom.

**56 In the synagogue, Rabbi Jesus did not quote the familiar words:** The most accurate version of what he said is contained not in the Greek manuscripts of Luke but in a version called the Old Syriac Gospels. Written in Syriac, a sister language to Aramaic, the Old Syriac Gospels sometimes contain primitive traditions that are older than the Greek Gospels. See *Rabbi Jesus,* pp. 97–102, 300. See also Chilton, *God in Strength: Jesus' Announcement of the Kingdom* (Freistadt: Plöchl, 1979; reprint, Sheffield: JSOT, 1987), pp. 157–177.

**57 perhaps a merchant dealing in olive oil from Galilee:** Oil, because it was a fluid, was held particularly to convey uncleanness, so that having pure oil in one's household was vital to maintaining the laws of kashrut. In his histories, Josephus refers to the purity of Galilean oil in contrast to Hellenistic products: See *Life* 74–75; *Jewish War* 2.591–592; *Antiquities* 12.120.

**58 rules that sought to govern whether an Israelite from one social group:** Mishnah Qiddushin 4:1–2 makes these rules explicit:

> Ten descents came up from Babylonia: (1) priest, (2) Levite, (3) Israelite, (4) impaired priest, (5) convert, and (6) freed slave, (7) *mamzer,* (8) *Netin,* (9) silenced |*shetuqi*|, and (10) foundling. Priest, Levite, and Israelite intermarry among one another. Levite, Israelite, impaired priest, convert, and freed slave intermarry one another. Convert, freed slave, *mamzer, Netin,* silenced, and foundling all intermarry among one another. These are silenced—everyone who knows his mother but does not know his father; and foundling—everyone who retrieved from the market and knows neither his father nor his mother. Abba Saul called a "silenced" |*shetuqi*| "to be examined" |*beduqi*|.

For an explanation of this system, see "Recovering Jesus' *Mamzerut,*" in *Ancient Israel, Judaism, and Christianity in Contemporary Perspective: Essays in Memory of Karl-Johan Illman,* eds. Jacob Neusner et al. (Lanham, MD: University Press of America, 2005); *Rabbi Jesus,* pp. 12–22, 64–69, 133–134.

**59 stamped her as a woman of ill repute:** See Dom David Hurst, *Gregory the Great: Forty Gospel Homilies Translated from the Latin* (Kalamazoo: Cistercian Publications, 1990), pp. 187, 198 (from Homily 25). The Latin manuscripts, from Barcelona, Cambridge, and Paris, are specified by Hurst on p. 3.

*Notes*

59 **Critical scholarship since 1517 has formally refuted the confusion:** The scholar who showed the problems involved in the identification was Jacques Lefèvre d'Etaples, in a study entitled *De Maria Magdalena et triduo Christi disceptatio*. Unscrambling the confusion was a major accomplishment of the Reformation, and it ran into violent, sometimes deadly, opposition from Catholic authorities; see Victor Saxer, *Le culte de Marie Madeleine en Occident* (Paris: Clavreuil, 1959), pp. 4–6. In *Rabbi Jesus* (pp. 133–134), I discussed the significance of the incident, and provide a shortened version of the treatment here. In *The Resurrection of Mary Magdalene: Legends, Apocrypha, and the Christian Testament* (New York: Continuum, 2002), p. 102, Jean Schaberg claims to be unable to determine whether or not *Rabbi Jesus* identifies Mary Magdalene with the woman in chapter 7 of Luke's Gospel. My book never in any way asserts that they were the same person. Professor Schaberg's assessment and my own largely agree, except in regard to Mary's connection to the ritual of anointing. Scholars occasionally claim to disagree with one another more than they actually do, which can give nonexperts the impression of more volatility within a field than there really is.

59 **went on to pursue him as a heretic in 1523:** This episode is detailed in James K. Farge, *Orthodoxy and Reform in Early Reformation France: The Faculty of Theology in Paris, 1500–1543* (Leiden: Brill, 1985), pp. 170–177.

60 **The Testament of Job:** In referring to Job's "patience" (James 5:11), the New Testament appears to have the *Testament of Job* in mind, rather than the biblical book. Like Elijah (*Testament of Job* 52:8–12), this Job is even taken up in the divine Chariot that represents God's presence at the end of his life. *Merkavah* mysticism is introduced in *Rabbi Jesus* with reference to critical discussion, pp. 41–63, 157, 161–165, 190–196, 269–289, 306–307.

61 **the "Spirit," the "Creation of the Heavens," and "The Paternal Splendor":** See R. P. Spittler, "Testament of Job (First Century B.C.–First Century A.D.): A New Translation and Introduction," in *The Old Testament Pseudepigrapha*, vol. 1, ed. James Charlesworth (Garden City, NY: Doubleday, 1983), pp. 829–868. The actual texts of this document are quite late, and no one would want to take everything about the *Testament of Job* literally, but the fact that it attests mystical legends about women cannot be refuted.

61 **Job's three daughters are said in Rabbinic literature to have settled:** See H. C. Kee, "Satan, Magic, and Salvation in the Testament of Job," in *Society of Biblical Literature Seminar Papers* (Missoula: Society of Biblical Literature, 1974) vol. 1, pp. 53–76; Schaberg, *The Resurrection of Mary Magdalene*, p. 312, citing Pesiqta de Rab Kahanah 7, Exodus Rabbah 17:4, and Ruth Rabbah 1:5.

62 **a woman came up behind him and touched him:** *Rabbi Jesus*, p. 179.

63 **One involves a deaf-mute (Mark 7:31–37) and the other a blind man (Mark 8:22–26):** *Rabbi Jesus,* pp. 130–131.

63 **the woman applies her unction of saliva seven times:** See Sotah 1:4, 16d and—more generally—Shabbat 14:4.

64 **Life on the other side of death was an existence "like angels":** This conception, less material than that of many Jewish teachers during the first century, and of many Christians in ancient times and today, was too much for Luke's Gospel. There the key wording is changed from "like angels" to "angelic" (*isangeloi;* Luke 20:36) in an attempt to leave room for a theory of survival in the Resurrection. But Jesus' nonmaterialist teaching is categorical, and it comes through clearly. See *Rabbi Jesus,* pp. 236–237.

64 **Love of God *was* love of neighbor, and vice versa:** *Rabbi Jesus,* pp. 242–244; Christopher D. Marshall, *Beyond Retribution: A New Testament Vision for Justice, Crime, and Punishment* (Grand Rapids: Eerdmans, 2001); Robin W. Lovin, *Christian Ethics: An Essential Guide* (Nashville: Abingdon, 2001).

69 **our inability to specify how intimate Mary and Jesus were in sexual terms:** This is the conclusion in *Rabbi Jesus,* pp. 142–145, 269–270, with which Professor Schaberg agrees almost verbatim (*The Resurrection of Mary Magdalene,* pp. 314–317, 330–335), although earlier in her book she captiously promises to disagree with my "patriarchal" position on this point (p. 102).

### 7. TRANSFIGURATION AT THE TOMB

72 **How could anyone end a story by saying "they were afraid, because—"?** In Greek, the phrase is expressed as *ephobounto gar.* The word *gar* regularly occurs in writings of the period and throughout Mark's Gospel in what linguists call the postpositive position. That is, it is the second element in a clause, introducing an explanation, the way the word *because* does in English. In every other occurrence in the Gospel, the expected explanation follows the use of *gar,* so its absence here deliberately produces a feeling of truncation.

72 **Pious scribes frequently harmonized the texts of the Gospels:** Additional material they appended to Mark's Gospel (both a "shorter ending" tacked on to verse 8 and a "longer ending" that extends for a good ten verses) refers to personal appearances of the risen Jesus that are comparable to what can be read elsewhere in the New Testament. When you read these additions and compare them to the accounts in the other Gospels, you quickly see that they amount to no more than a boiled-down mixture of stories from Matthew and Luke, and they have been recognized since the eighteenth century as pasted-on afterthoughts. They represent a failed effort to make this Gospel look like the others.

The reference to Mary Magdalene in Mark 16:9, for example, as the woman "from whom he had thrown out seven demons" alludes to what is said in Luke 8:2. But Mark doesn't speak of that exorcism at all, so the ending refers back to what the original Gospel doesn't even say. That is a sure sign of a pastiche, designed to make an unusual Gospel more conventional by the standards of a later time. Once all the texts of the New Testament circulated as a single canon of Scripture, it was natural for scribes to harmonize and homogenize what the different documents said. By becoming aware of tendencies of that kind, scholars can then distinguish the individual character of each document from the style of copyists, which is the purpose of textual criticism.

The desire to patch together this ending shows that the distinctive voice of Mark was lost on later readers due to the copyists' desire to make all the Gospels sound as much alike as possible. Sadly, modern editions of the New Testament in English sometimes go the way of this homogenization and thus ignore the clear findings of textual study based on the earliest manuscripts. Mark ended with the silence of the women; any reading of the Gospel that fails to cope with that is faulty.

73 **An iron spike with an attached piece of wood:** Craig Evans, *Jesus and the Ossuaries* (Waco, TX: Baylor University Press, 2003), pp. 98–103. The nail had been driven into a hard knot of olive wood and could not be removed at burial as the others evidently were.

73 **According to usual burial practice:** See Rachel Hachlili, "Burials, Ancient Jewish," in *The Anchor Bible Dictionary,* ed. David Noel Freedman et al. (New York: Doubleday, 1992), vol. 1, pp. 798–994.

73 **the claim, fashionable for more than a century, that Jesus' body was tossed:** John Dominic Crossan has recently propagated this description in chapter 6 ("The Dogs Beneath the Cross") of *Jesus: A Revolutionary Biography* (San Francisco: HarperSanFrancisco, 1994), pp. 123–158, but it comes from the century-old work of Alfred Loisy. Loisy's scholarship could not have taken into account Yochanan's ossuary, and he typified foibles of his time in ignoring Judaic evidence for the burial of crucified people. Crossan tries to explain away this evidence in favor of a sensationalist image, which is more to his liking. The postmodern period, in its enthusiasm for theory, has allowed of too much explaining away, instead of accounting for the data at hand. I have detailed this problem in *Rabbi Jesus,* pp. 270–272, 308. In *Jesus and the Ossuaries* (p. 101), Evans also contradicts Crossan, as does Jane Schaberg in *The Resurrection of Mary Magdalene: Legends, Apocrypha, and the Christian Testament* (New York: Continuum, 2002), pp. 239–240. On pp. 280–281, Professor Schaberg agrees with my reconstruction of the basic elements of Jesus' interment, although she

does not discuss the location I have suggested, which is based on the discovery of the ossuary of Caiaphas (*Rabbi Jesus*, pp. 214–215, 270–272).

74 **The story of the resuscitation of Lazarus in John 11:1–44:** *Rabbi Jesus*, pp. 179 (citing Ebel Rabbati 8:1, an additional tractate of the Talmud), 244–246. In *The Theology of the Orael Torah: Revealing the Justice of God* (Montreal: McGill-Queen's University Press, 1999), Jacob Neusner brilliantly analyzes the theological and literary relationships among the Mishnah, the Talmud of Jerusalem, and the Babylonian Talmud (as well as other texts). For the evidence of women's role in lamentation, see Kathleen Corley, "Women and the Crucifixion and Burial of Jesus," *Forum* 1 (1998); Marianne Sawicki, *Seeing the Lord: Resurrection and Early Christian Practices* (Minneapolis: Fortress, 1994). Precedent for such customs goes all the way back to the patriarch Jacob, in his command to his sons to bury him with his fathers (Genesis 49:29). Jesus' burial, including the likely site, is described in *Rabbi Jesus*, pp. 269–272.

75 **Crucifixion was a punishment that only the Roman authorities themselves:** Gerald O'Collins, "Crucifixion," in *The Anchor Bible Dictionary*, ed. Freeman et al., vol. 1, pp. 1207–1210.

75 **the observance of the Sabbath:** Mark knew that the authorities of the Temple, fearful of the impact of Jesus' intervention in the Temple, had decided to act prior to Passover (Mark 14:1–2). A later liturgical tradition turned Jesus' last meal with his disciples into the Seder of Passover (Mark 14, 12–15), but that reflects the emerging practice of Eucharistic observance, and its cooptation of Passover, rather than plausible history. If the priests and their associates feared "a riot of the people" (*thorubos tou laou;* Mark 14:2), why would they have awaited the arrival of Passover, along with its tens of thousands of pilgrims, to arrest Jesus? For an account of how differing datings of the Last Supper evolved in association with different liturgies, see Chilton, *A Feast of Meanings: Eucharistic Theologies from Jesus Through Johannine Circles* (Leiden: Brill, 1994); *Jesus' Prayer and Jesus' Eucharist: His Personal Practice of Spirituality* (Valley Forge, PA: Trinity Press International, 1997).

76 **one ancient manuscript of the New Testament (the Codex Bezae):** It is named after Theodore Beza, the sixteenth-century reformer, who gave this unusual fifth-century Greek manuscript to the University of Cambridge.

76 **the Church of the Holy Sepulcher:** Bishop Cyril of Jerusalem made his city into a prosperous religious destination: Pilgrims were promised they could walk in the final footsteps of Jesus. The bishop mapped the Via Dolorosa, which marks the so-called Stations of the Cross—key stages in Jesus' passion and death. Those stations are imitated to this day in churches all over Christendom. They encourage meditative devotion in overcoming one's selfish attachment to

well-being by following the example of Jesus, but they have also been manipulated to mount one of the most effective advertising campaigns for pilgrimage that has ever been devised. But Cyril's program for the honor of his city and the worship of Christ crucified does not stand up well to historical or archaeological considerations. The Church of the Holy Sepulcher probably doesn't mark the place of Jesus' grave.

The legend that it does began when Emperor Constantine ordered the destruction of a temple dedicated to Venus just outside Jerusalem; a burial cave was discovered during the subsequent excavation. The excavators convinced themselves they had discovered Jesus' tomb. Later, it was said that Constantine's mother, Helena, had a vision confirming the site, which—investigated on her order—was found to contain bits of what was said to be the cross and some nails.

Whatever you make of this story, the best archaeological opinion estimates that during the first century (before two sieges, fires, and demolitions by the Romans—in 70 and in 135 C.E.) the city wall ran north of the site on which the Church of the Holy Sepulcher was built. It would therefore have been inside the city, where Jewish practice prohibited cemeteries, and there is no evidence of a cemetery at that site during the first century, although a couple of skeletons of indeterminate date were uncovered. But the force of legend is hard to resist, and even Protestant scholars in recent years have abandoned their earlier skepticism to embrace this factoid of fourth-century pilgrimage propaganda, which Cyril exploited with incomparable skill.

By the fourth century, this church was inside the city again, as it is today, puzzling theologians of the time. Why did the women have to walk or travel there? One later copyist of Mark solved this problem by having the women "walk into" the tomb (*eisporeuesthai;* from the codex known as "W," now at the Smithsonian) instead of walking out of the city. Scribes in antiquity, like some scholars even today, find it easier to change the meaning of texts than to break with tradition. See John J. Rousseau and Rami Arav, *Jesus and His World: An Archaeological and Cultural Dictionary* (Minneapolis: Fortress, 1995), pp. 112–118; see also *Rabbi Jesus,* pp. 269–272. For a similar position from an Evangelical point of view, see J. A. Thompson, *The Bible and Archaeology* (Grand Rapids: Eerdmans, 1962), pp. 347–349. Thompson observes that "Protestant scholars have not been greatly interested to preserve the reputation of the traditional site of Calvary" (p. 348). This is to be contrasted with the view expressed twenty years later, which claims the Holy Sepulcher site is "almost certainly correct"; see Harold W. Mare, "Jerusalem, New Testament," in *The New International Dictionary of Biblical Archaeology,* ed. E. M. Blaiklock, R. K. Harrison, and D. R. Douglass (Grand Rapids: Zondervan, 1983), pp. 261–265.

77 **Mark's Gospel intentionally highlights the mystical qualities of these encounters with the divine:** Rudolf Otto's *The Idea of the Holy: An Inquiry into the Non-Rational Factor in the Idea of the Divine and Its Relation to the Rational,* trans. John W. Harvey (London: Oxford University Press, 1923), remains a classic in this field, although personally I am more attracted to Evelyn Underhill's *Mysticism: A Study in the Nature and Development of Man's Spiritual Consciousness* (London: Methuen, 1911). Both these authors influenced Thomas Merton deeply; see *The Seven Storey Mountain* (New York: Harcourt, Brace, 1948). Among the works of current authors, those of Matthew Fox are the most influential as well as the soundest; see *The Coming of the Cosmic Christ: The Healing of Mother Earth and the Birth of a Global Renaissance* (San Francisco: Harper & Row, 1988).

79 **The whole Gospel According to Mark is designed as a program:** It is well known that the Aramaic word *abba* means "father," but too little known is the fact that it can also mean "source." By utilizing the Aramaic term to refer to their own inner experience of baptism, Greek Christians showed that they did not in any way think of the term as referring to literal paternity when God was involved; see *Rabbi Jesus,* pp. 41–63. As I recently remarked to a friend who is a classicist, I am happy to speak of Jesus as "unique," in the sense that every parent knows that each and every child one cares for is unique. When theologians press the term *unique* to mean that Jesus is *exclusively* God's child, they undermine the meaning of baptism in Jesus' name, which is designed to realize the same relationship to God that Jesus developed. It should go without saying that the term *bar* in Aramaic, like *ben* in Hebrew, may be used inclusively of females and males. Yet some New Testament scholars today have taken to writing "[*sic!*]" after "son," as if it were a mistake, so it would seem that even the obvious has to be stated.

## 8. ECSTATIC VISION

81 **Moses and Elijah, prophets who:** Chilton, "Not to Taste Death: A Jewish, Christian and Gnostic Usage," in *Studia Biblica 1978,* vol. 2, ed. E. A. Livingston (Sheffield: JSOT, 1980), pp. 29–36.

84 **What causes their astonishment?:** In her recent book *The Resurrection of Mary Magdalene: Legends, Apocrypha, and the Christian Testament* (New York: Continuum, 2002), Jane Schaberg talks of all the experiences of Mary Magdalene as necessitating the "empty tomb" as the jolt (pp. 282–291) that it took to make her vision happen. In my opinion, that vastly underestimates the force of meditative practice, as well as reducing varied texts to a single simplistic mean-

ing. Because part of the argument of her book is against the "conflation" of passages and of people, Schaberg's own harmonization is glaring. She goes on to say (p. 284), "But I do not think this commits me to the belief that the Resurrection must be thought of as the resuscitation of a corpse; rather, it is compatible with a lost or stolen corpse, and compatible with exaltation/ascent, and compatible with the mystery of the unknown fate of the corpse, and compatible with the destruction of the corpse." She apparently agrees with what I say in *Rabbi Jesus* (p. 273): "When the women turned from the tomb of Jesus, directed away from any search for Jesus' corpse by their vision of the white-robed youth, the question of what became of his physical body was left open forever." Had Professor Schaberg observed that they make no search in Mark's text, so that the "empty tomb" is moot there, she would have saved herself complication.

84 **He said he could not even tell whether he was "in the body or outside the body":** 2 Corinthians 12:2–4; *Rabbi Paul,* pp. 114–116, 119, 203, 228.

87 **Several of these are unmistakably male fantasies:** Scorsese's *The Last Temptation of Christ* (1988) misses the subtlety of the novel of the same name (1951) by Nikos Kazantzakis. On the other hand, Dan Brown's novel *The Da Vinci Code* (New York: Doubleday, 2003) represents its "factual" predecessors quite faithfully.

90 **James, Jesus' brother and the most prominent leader of Christianity at the time:** The stoning of James occurred during the interregnum of the Roman governors Festus and Albinus (Josephus *Antiquities* 20.9.1 §§ 197–203), and Ananus was removed from office as a result of popular protest; see B. D. Chilton and J. N. Neusner, eds., *The Brother of Jesus: James the Just and His Mission* (Louisville: Westminster John Knox, 2001).

### 9. THE SCAR

94 **The Gospels were composed in communities where there was still an oral memory of Jesus:** Well into the second century, an early Christian teacher named Papias said he always preferred the "living voice" of those who taught about Jesus to any written Gospel; see Eusebius *History of the Church* 3.39.

96 **No Gospel was written as a biography of Jesus:** This point was well expressed by Elisabeth Schüssler Fiorenza in her landmark study, *In Memory of Her: A Feminist Theological Reconstruction of Christian Origins* (New York: Crossroad, 1983, 1992), p. 102: "The Gospels, then, are paradigmatic remembrances, not comprehensive accounts of the historical Jesus but expressions of communities and individuals who attempted to say what the significance of Jesus was for their own situations." The resulting erasure of women is an im-

portant theme in Jane Schaberg, *The Illegitimacy of Jesus: A Feminist Theological Interpretation of the Infancy Narratives* (Sheffield: Sheffield Academic Press, 1995).

96 **If we focus only on what was written:** See Antoinette Clark Wire, "Rising Voices: The Resurrection Witness of New Testament Non-Writers," in *On the Cutting Edge: The Study of Women in Biblical Worlds—Essays in Honor of Elisabeth Schüssler Fiorenza,* ed. Jane Schaberg, Alice Bach, and Esther Fuchs (New York: Continuum, 2004), pp. 221–229. In her article, Wire writes (p. 229), "By taking seriously those who are speaking, we could learn how to tune in and hear these and other rising voices." That is precisely the program here, a continuation of Professor Wire's prescient approach in *The Corinthian Women Prophets: A Reconstruction Through Paul's Rhetoric* (Minneapolis: Fortress, 1990).

96 **Feminist theology and textual scholarship have proven a vital force in showing that history is flexible:** See Elisabeth Schüssler Fiorenza, *But She Said: Feminist Practices of Biblical Interpretation* (Boston: Free Press, 1992). She spells out her approach on p. 93 in a way that both engages and rejects historical inquiry:

> A reconstructive historical model seeks to reshape our historical and theological self-understanding by displacing the androcentric reconstructions of early Christian origins that marginalize or eliminate women and other nonpersons from the historical record. It does so by interrogating the rhetorical strategies of androcentric biblical texts in order to subvert them. For it is in and through such interrogations that the "reality" which the text marginalizes and silences is brought to the fore. As I will now go on to explain, although I agree fully that historical inquiry involves inference, it seems to me that attempting to change historical judgments by means of rhetorical subversion might not only fail to convince, but wind up entrenching positivist reactions.

97 **Some feminist theology has suffered a failure of nerve in the face of history:** In addition to Professor Wire's work, referred to heretofore, see the criticism of Professor Fiorenza's theoretical perspective by Dr. Tal Ilan in *Mine & Yours Are Hers: Retrieving Women's History from Rabbinic Literature* (Leiden: Brill, 1997) and in "Paul and Pharisee Women," in *On the Cutting Edge,* ed. Schaberg, Bach, and Fuchs, pp. 82–101, and the major series Feminist Companions to the New Testament and Early Christian Writings, edited by Amy-Jill Levine with Marianne Blickenstaff (Edinburgh: Clark, 2001–2004).

97 **The vogue of "the final form of the text" had a profound impact upon thinking about the Bible:** See G. T. Sheppard, "Canonical Criticism," in *Dictio-*

*nary of Biblical Interpretation,* ed. John H. Hayes (Nashville: Abingdon, 1999), pp. 164–167.

97 **one leader among feminist biblical scholars has called for a rejection of the approach to "the bible as 'fact'":** Elisabeth Schüssler Fiorenza, *Wisdom Ways: Introducing Feminist Biblical Interpretation* (Maryknoll, NY: Orbis, 2001), p. 41. In her earlier work, Professor Fiorenza did invoke a social scientific model of history (defining history as inference rather than deduction). Having passed through a period in which she severely criticized historical work generally, she now does make more room for it here, albeit in a qualified way (p. 145): "However, insofar as historical studies do not sufficiently problematize the positivist assumption that kyriocentric source-texts are descriptive and reliable evidence for socio-historical reality, their focus on women's history remains caught up in the marginalizing tendencies of the kyriocentric text, which subsumes women under male terms." That is because she is committed to a programmatic reading, which is at odds with historical assessment; see her statements: "Whether you are a believing bible reader or a reader who appreciates the bible as a cultural treasure, becoming a feminist interpreter means shifting your focus from biblical interpretation construed as an ever better explanation of the text to biblical interpretation as a tool for becoming conscious of structures of domination and for articulating visions of radical democracy that are inscribed in our own experience as well as in that of texts" (p. 3); ". . . a feminist biblical Wisdom interpretation is best understood as a spiritual practice in the open space of Divine Wisdom through which, like the wind, the Spirit blows as it/s/he wills" (p. 77); "In short, the transformation of the scientific-positivist ethos of biblical studies into a rhetorical-ethical one creates a grassroots democratic space in which feminist and other readers/hearers can participate in defining and debating the meaning and significance of a biblical text in contemporary social-political locations and cultural-religious rhetorical situations" (p. 97).

97 **when feminist theologians speak of possible "voices" in texts:** A recent study of the Gospel According to John makes this explicit; see Satoko Yamaguchi, *Mary and Martha: Women in the World of Jesus* (Maryknoll, NY: Orbis, 2002) p. 142: "And the old stories should be accompanied by new stories too. In retelling old and new stories I hope we emancipate our spirituality from later doctrinal interpretations of the Bible as well as from a modern Western dualistic mind-set that exclusively identifies Western culture with the 'pure' Christian tradition." She puts into practice Fiorenza's observation (*Wisdom Ways,* p. 148): "From its inception, feminist interpretation has sought to actualize biblical stories in role-playing, storytelling, bibliodrama, dance, and song."

99 **Saint Paul's infamous mandate:** See Wire, *The Corinthian Women Prophets; Rabbi Paul,* pp. 214–216.

99 **Jesus had demanded the *renunciation* of family for the sake of his message:** The New Testament proves that some Christians departed from Jesus' attitude by the end of the first century: The relationships of family were portrayed as providing an opportunity for enacting the love one had learned from Christ (see 1 Peter 2:18–3:7).

### 10. EXPURGATING THE MAGDALENE

102 **But wide variations between these two Gospels:** For a representative example of the textbook presentation, see Mark Allan Powell, *Fortress Introduction to the Gospels* (Minneapolis: Fortress, 1998). I develop an alternative reading of the evidence, accounting for variations that the standard theory cannot accommodate, in *Targumic Approaches to the Gospels: Essays in the Mutual Definition of Judaism and Christianity* (Lanham, MD, and London: University Press of America, 1986) and in *Profiles of a Rabbi: Synoptic Opportunities in Reading About Jesus* (Atlanta: Scholars Press, 1989). See also Holly E. Hearow, *The Magdalene Tradition: Witness and Counter-Witness in Early Christian Communities* (Collegeville, MN: Liturgical Press, 2004).

103 **a legendary event that appears in Matthew alone among the Gospels:** This is actually the second reference to the earthquake in the Gospel According to Matthew. At the time of the crucifixion, this Gospel says (yet again, uniquely; 27:51–53): "And look: the curtain of the Temple was split from top to bottom in two, and the earth quaked, and the rocks were split, and the tombs were opened and many bodies of the holy ones who slept were raised; they came out from the memorials after his raising and entered into the holy city and were manifested to many." Matthew is not clear about its own chronology, so you can't tell when exactly this earthquake (unmentioned by historians of the time) was supposed to have occurred. Presumably, it coincides with the moment of Jesus' Resurrection, because Matthew's conception is that this Resurrection marks an apocalyptic breakthrough that shows how all believers will be raised.

104 **Ananias, who baptized Paul:** *Rabbi Paul,* pp. 48–71.

105 **But Paul finds no place in Matthew's conceptual universe:** This is one reason that makes me think the originating community was Damascus, rather than Antioch (another contender). Damascus—with its deep and ancient connection with Judaism—was the kind of city in which one might have heard of Jesus saying things such as "Whoever looses one of the least of these decrees and teaches people that way will be called least in the kingdom of the heavens"

(Matthew 5:19). That is a likely swipe at Paul, appearing only in Matthew; those who heard Matthew read would have known very well that the word *paulus* in Latin means "little" or "least." This Gospel is categorically pro-Law, and yet vociferous in its condemnation of Pharisees and synagogue leaders, as one would expect, if Christians in Damascus were influenced by the Essenes, who had been well ensconced in the city.

106 **Matthew's women not only see the angel; they meet Jesus himself as they depart from the mouth of the tomb:** Their response reflects this Gospel's view of what people should do to acknowledge Jesus as God's Son (Matthew 28:9–11): "They came forward and seized his feet and worshipped him. Then Jesus says to them, Do not fear. Depart, report to my brothers so that they go away into Galilee, and there they will see me." This encounter evokes worship, exactly the response of the eleven apostles (28:16–17), who heed the women's instructions and go to Galilee, where the risen Jesus commissions them to baptize "all the Gentiles" in the name of the Father, Son, and Holy Spirit and promises them his visionary presence until the end of the world (28:16–20). The eleven male leaders are solely authorized to take up this commission, but Mary Magdalene and the "other Mary" are the pioneers of the apostolic experience, and the issue of doubt is not associated with them as it is with the eleven (28:17). The eleven reflect how Christian teachers presented baptism in Damascus: an initiation into Spirit brought by the blinding lightning of vision just before the thunderclap of a final judgment, at which time all humanity would be held accountable before God.

108 **notorious disputes among Christians in Antioch:** *Rabbi Paul,* pp. 100–170.

108 **Paul refers to a woman named Junia as an apostle:** Ibid., pp. 3, 272.

108 **Neither Luke nor Acts ever speaks of women apostles:** Barnabas, like Paul, does make it onto the list of those called "apostles" in Acts (Acts 14:4, 14), and a named woman is called "disciple" in Acts 9:36.

109 **all of Paul's three encounters with the risen Jesus were strictly visionary:** *Rabbi Paul,* pp. 48–71.

109 **Heavenly messengers simply remind the women of what Jesus himself had already told them:** It is interesting that there are *two* heavenly emissaries now, and that they are called not "youths" or "angels," which would have accorded with Mark and Matthew, but *andres,* the term for adult males.

109 **referring to women is not at all the same thing as including them as agents:** The confusion between the topic of women and the perspective of women is elegantly developed by Elisabeth Schüssler Fiorenza in *Jesus and the Politics of Interpretation* (New York: Continuum, 2000), reviewed in *Anglican*

*Theological Review* 83, no. 4 (2001): 886–887. A particularly effective critique of previous scholarship on Luke is available in the work of Ann Graham Brock, *Mary Magdalene, the First Apostle: The Struggle for Authority* (Cambridge: Harvard University Press, 2003), pp. 36–40.

110 **the Gospel is careful to specify that this is Mary, Martha's sister:** Chilton, "Opening the Book: Biblical Warrants for the Ordination of Women," *Modern Churchman* 20 (1977): 32–35. It is interesting that Luke does not name the place involved as Bethany, and that may hint at change introduced editorially into the tradition presented here. Originally, Mary Magdalene might conceivably have been at issue.

110 **They give short shrift to Mary's role in ritual anointing:** If anointing was pleasing to Jesus and a regular practice within his movement, as we have seen, why is the memory of anointing so sparsely represented in the New Testament? James, the brother of Jesus and leader of his movement in Jerusalem, was described by the first Christian historian, Hegesippus, as refusing the use of oil; see Eusebius *History of the Church* 2.23. Like the Essenes, with whom James shared several interests, he evidently regarded oil as polluting. The letter attributed to James (5:14–16) sets out a practice of laying hands on people who are ill and anointing them, but it restricts this practice to "elders" (*presbuteroi* in Greek, from which the English word *priest* derives). When ordinary Christians pray for healing, no oil is to be involved.

James was a powerful man in earliest Christianity, its single most influential authority during his lifetime; see B. D. Chilton and J. N. Neusner, eds., *The Brother of Jesus: James the Just and His Mission* (Louisville: Westminster John Knox, 2001). Because he generally avoided the use of oil, it was natural that believers thought of Jesus as being similarly ascetic, although—as we have seen—some references to oil and anointing do remain in the Gospels. Mary's effacement in the Gospels and the downplaying of her anointing is not explicable on the basis of simple sexism. She also represented practices that did not accord with other teachings in primitive Christianity. The seesaw influences of Mary and James lie at the root of Christianity's ambivalent attitudes toward oil over the centuries.

This ambivalence nearly submerged Mary Magdalene and her anointing, and almost erased the evidence of Jesus' dedication to the practice, as well. Her anointing was his also: focusing the Holy Spirit on the body of the person anointed. From this perspective, anointing was the opposite of polluting—contrary to what the Essenes and James taught. Paul also insisted, in terms reminiscent of Mary's teaching, on the connection of anointing, Spirit, and Resurrection (Romans 1:3–4; 2 Corinthians 1:22).

## 11. ORTHODOX AMBIVALENCE AND THE GNOSTIC QUEST

111 **First Letter to Timothy:** Timothy helped Paul write some of his letters and also gathered correspondence together after the apostle's death. That opened the door for later writers (after 90 C.E.) to take up the Pauline cause, as they conceived it, by writing letters in Paul's name to Timothy (and to Titus), which are known collectively as the Pastoral Epistles. These issues are addressed in *Rabbi Paul,* pp. 246–266.

112 **Those who take part in the meal:** See Dorothy Irvin, "The Ministry of Women in the Early Church: The Archaeological Evidence," *Duke Divinity School Review* 45, no. 2 (1980): 76–86; Damien Casey, "The 'Fractio Panis' and the Eucharist as Eschatological Banquet," *Theology @ Mcauley: An E-Journal of Theology* 2 (2002). When the fresco was first uncovered during the nineteenth century, scholars assumed that all the participants in the depiction must have been male. When Irvin showed that could not be the case, some scholars denied that a Eucharist was at issue. As Casey points out, the challenge of Irvin's contribution is that it uncovers anachronisms in thinking about liturgy as well as women's ministry. Whether all the figures in the fresco are women remains a matter of debate, to a large extent owing to the condition of the work.

113 **Christians wanted to appear more Roman than the Romans:** This policy is summed up in the rhetorical question, "But if anyone does not know how to lead one's own house, how shall he care for God's church?" (1 Timothy 3:5), an attitude that contradicts Paul's own theology; see *Rabbi Paul,* pp. 90, 119, 190.

114 **women in the early sources of Rabbinic Judaism:** See Tal Ilan, *Mine & Yours Are Hers: Retrieving Women's History from Rabbinic Literature* (Leiden: Brill, 1997).

114 **Hippolytus, a famously conservative priest:** See Ann Graham Brock, *Mary Magdalene, the First Apostle: The Struggle for Authority* (Cambridge: Harvard University Press, 2003) pp. 2, 15. The reference in Hippolytus (*Song of Songs* 24–26) speaks of the women at the tomb as all being female apostles sent to the male apostles, and over time this characterization was applied to Mary in particular, as most prominent among the women. In this case, Hippolytus probably reflects and supports a second-century motif.

114 **An order of church worship and regulation called the *Didascalia of the Twelve Apostles:*** F. Nau, *La Didascalie des douze Apôtres* (Paris: Lethielleux, 1912); R. Hugh Connolly, *Didascalia Apostolorum* (Oxford: Clarendon, 1929). For a succinct description of the relationship among the various orders of the ancient church, see W. Jardine Grisbrooke, *The Liturgical Portions of the Apostolic Constitutions: A Text for Students* (Brancote, Nottinghamshire: Grove, 1990).

115 **Unction was not only the dab of oil on the forehead and hands at the time of death:** Paul Bradshaw and Carol Bebawi, *The Canons of Hippolytus* (Bramcote, Nottinghamshire: Grove, 1987), Canon 19, and Burton Scott Easton, *The Apostolic Tradition of Hippolytus* (New York: Macmillan, 1934), vol. 1, p. 5; vol. 2, pp. 21–22.

117 **This is what made her "the special friend of the Son of God and his first servant":** David Mycoff, *The Life of Saint Mary Magdalene and of Her Sister Saint Martha* (Kalamazoo: Cistercian Publications, 1989), lines 240–251, 876–903, 1959–1961.

## 12. THE BREAKOUT

119 **Gnostics wanted direct contact with the divine:** Riemer Roukema, *Gnosis and Faith in Early Christianity: An Introduction to Gnosticism,* trans. John Bowden (Harrisburg, PA: Trinity Press International, 1999); F. Stanley Jones, *Which Mary? The Marys of the Early Christian Tradition* (Atlanta: Society of Biblical Literature, 2002); Karen L. King, *What Is Gnosticism?* (Cambridge: Belknap, 2003).

120 **These initiation rites were expensive and flamboyant:** Although this field of study is in considerable ferment today, the classic work remains Franz Cumont, *The Mysteries of Mithra,* trans. T. S. McCormack (New York: Dover, 1956). For a sensible guide through the thicket, see David Ulansey, *The Origins of the Mithraic Mysteries: Cosmology and Salvation in the Ancient World* (New York: Oxford University Press, 1989).

123 **The *Mary* in the title refers to the Magdalene:** In fact, a couple of recent scholars have inserted *Magdalene*—or (worse still) the Aramaic *Magdala*—into the title of this Coptic work, apparently trying to capitalize on the spike in modern interest in the Magdalene. Occasionally, such ploys are part of a fashion to date *The Gospel According to Mary* much earlier than scholarship has established, and to treat it as if it were somehow a primitive Aramaic source, although remains have been found only in Coptic and Greek. Among many useful treatments, see Jean-Yves LeLoup, *The Gospel of Mary Magdalene,* trans. Joseph Rowe (Rochester, VT: Inner Traditions, 2002); Karen L. King, *The Gospel of Mary of Magdala: Jesus and the First Woman Apostle* (Santa Rosa: Polebridge, 2003); Anne Pasquier, *L'Evangile selon Marie: Texte établi et présenté* (Québec: Université Laval, 1983), a book that merits an edition in English. Although the insertion of Magdalene or Magdala into the title of this Gospel is inaccurate and perhaps opportunistic, it is more a minor annoyance than a serious deception. After all, in this Gospel, Mary engages her risen teacher on the pre-

cise topic of how the vision of him raised from the dead is possible, so it is pretty obvious that she must be the same pivotal figure of all the Resurrection accounts in the canonical Gospels—Mary Magdalene. That inference is sound, even though it does not warrant changing the ancient title of the Gospel.

124 **Peter is a key figure in** *The Gospel According to Mary,* **as he is in the book of Acts:** To that extent, *Mary* and Acts agree, and their common portrayal of Peter—not Paul—as the true starting point of a deliberate extension of Jesus' message to Gentiles is historically accurate. See Acts 10:9–48, 11:5–17, 15:7–11; *Rabbi Paul,* pp. 94–99.

In Acts, Peter's reluctance to consort with Gentiles comes from his concern for purity. When he is offered unclean food in a vision, Peter responds that nothing unclean has ever entered his mouth (Acts 10:14). In *The Gospel According to Mary,* personal fear disturbs Peter; he shares the anguish of the apostles as a whole that the Gentiles will treat them no better than they did Jesus.

These two sources disagree even more profoundly over the degree of Peter's competence in the domain of vision. His personal apparition in Acts resolves the issue of how he and believers generally should behave toward non-Israelites. As he sees unclean animals lowered from heaven in a linen sheet of cosmic dimensions, a voice tells him that what God has purified, he should not treat as unclean. Consequently, he agrees to visit the house of a Gentile, the Roman centurion named Cornelius. In *The Gospel According to Mary,* Peter is bereft of personal vision; it apparently assumes that Peter's vision in Joppa came later, portraying Mary Magdalene as his spiritual guide prior to his apparition.

126 **A woman had experienced a visionary breakthrough that permitted her to see Jesus' desire to reach out to Gentiles before Peter himself did:** Yet by the time Peter himself later had a vision in the city of Joppa—the vision Acts relates, of all the four-footed beasts of the planet, the reptiles of the earth, and the birds of the air in a surreal image, derived from the book of Ezekiel (Acts 10:12–14)—he had learned from Mary that he was seeing with his mind, not his eyes. He knew the vision did not concern literal animals, but contact with people who were non-Israelites. That pivotal moment, when Peter authorized contact with Gentiles, was the culmination of a visionary path Mary Magdalene had set him on. The same woman who helped Peter see the risen Jesus in the first place guided him to the visualization of what this Resurrection meant in terms of letting it be known to non-Israelites. *The Gospel According to Mary* is of deep historical value in permitting us to see that Peter's vision was not spontaneous, contrary to what Acts implies, but arose as a result of apostolic controversy over contact with Gentiles and Mary Magdalene's guidance.

126 **As theologians became increasingly materialistic in their conception of how Jesus rose from the dead:** During this period, Irenaeus, bishop of Lyons (in today's France)—having inherited the millenarian theology of his teachers in Asia Minor—preached a physical Resurrection of the flesh; see *Against Heresies* 2.29; 4.18; 5.7–16, 36. Despite what Paul had clearly said in 1 Corinthians 15, Irenaeus called anyone who did not go along with this millenarian literalism a heretic. The Catholic Church of this period largely defined itself by its opposition to Gnosticism, and therefore by a stubborn assertion of the value of the flesh, even if that meant contradicting Saint Paul.

127 **the *livva* was the locus of insight as well as of emotions and sensations:** For example, Job conceives of his own death as climaxing in a moment of insight. When his flesh is stripped away, he shall nonetheless see God—as his redeemer. The removal of the flesh—even by the painful steady drip of mortal suffering—brings Job to the moment he can perceive God with all that he has left of his being, his "heart" (see Job 8:10; 19:23–27). For Job and for the Prophets—in fact, for Hebrew and Aramaic speakers generally in the ancient world—the heart was what a person thought and felt with. Modern English still preserves a bit of this conception; we speak of loving with one's whole heart (no doubt influenced by Deuteronomy 6:5), and the feeling of love is often experienced in one's chest and gut, whatever we may claim to know of psychology and physiology.

This is a case where Paul's familiarity with the world of Aramaic Judaism, as well as the Hellenism he was born into, makes him a reliable guide when it comes to mapping the overlap between Hellenistic and Semitic conceptions. Paul spelled out how he saw Spirit at work in relation to "heart" in Aramaic and "mind" in Greek (1 Corinthians 2). If one asks how we can know what God has prepared for us, Paul says, the answer is that Spirit alone is able to convey divine purposes, but that mind alone decodes that truth.

Paul develops his position in detail by quoting a passage from Isaiah (Isaiah 64:4, cited verbatim in 1 Corinthians 2:9) that speaks of truths beyond human understanding that God has readied for those who love him. Paul goes on to say (2:10–11): "God has revealed them to us through the Spirit; for the Spirit searches all things, even the depths of God. For who among men knows the things of man except the spirit of man which is in him? So also no one has known the things of God except the Spirit of God." As Paul sees human relations, one person can know what another thinks and feels only on the basis of their shared "spirit." Spirit is the name for what links one person with another, and by means of that link, we can also know what God thinks, what the divine feels. The Spirit at issue in knowing God, Paul goes on to say, is not "the spirit of the world," but "the Spirit which is of God" (1 Corinthians 2:12). The human spirit that is the medium of ordinary human exchange becomes the vehicle of divine revelation as soon as God is involved.

127 **Just as Mary's teaching lies silently behind Paul's where Resurrection is concerned:** The Nag Hammadi Library, the principal source of ancient Gnostic writings, actually begins with *The Prayer of the Apostle Paul,* which addresses Christ by saying, "You are my mind: bring me forth! You are my treasure: open for me!" (I.1.6–7). This agrees with *The Gospel According to Mary.* There are also echoes of Mary's conception in *The Sophia of Jesus Christ* (III.4.98.9–22); *The Dialogue of the Savior* (III.126.16–23; III.134.20–135.5); *The Thunder, Perfect Mind* (VI.2.18.9–10); *The Paraphrase of Shem* (VII.1.5–15); *The Second Treatise of the Great Seth* (VII.2.64.9); *The Teachings of Silvanus* (VII.4.103.1–10). Wherever possible, I have followed the system of citation presented in James M. Robinson, ed., *The Nag Hammadi Library in English* (San Francisco: Harper & Row, 1978). This is the most widely used translation of the ancient library of Gnostic books discovered in Egypt in 1945, and it also includes *The Gospel According to Mary.*

128 **not even circumcision as mandated in the Torah:** *Rabbi Paul,* pp. 173–196.

129 **By the time the Gospel According to John was produced:** Ernst Käsemann, *The Testament of Jesus: A Study of the Gospel of John in the Light of Chapter 17,* trans. Gerhard Krodel (Philadelphia: Fortress, 1978). More recently, April D. De Conick has pursued these ideas further in " 'Blessed Are Those Who Have Not Seen' (Jn 20:29): Johannine Dramatization of an Early Christian Discourse," in *The Nag Hammadi Library After Fifty Years: Proceedings of the 1995 Society of Biblical Literature Commemoration,* eds. John D. Turner and Anne McGuire (Leiden: Brill, 1997), pp. 381–398. See also Käsemann's article "The Structure and Purpose of the Prologue to John's Gospel," in *New Testament Questions of Today,* trans. W. J. Montague (Philadelphia: Fortress, 1979), pp. 138–167, which similarly finds a sequel in Chilton, "Typologies of Memra and the Fourth Gospel," *Targum Studies* 1 (1992): 89–100.

129 **Ephesus was a jewel of Greek culture on the western shore of Asia Minor:** An earthquake in 23 C.E. makes the population estimate of 100,000 hazardous, but there is no doubting the importance of the city; see L. Michael White, "Urban Development and Social Change in Imperial Ephesos," in *Ephesos, Metropolis of Asia: An Interdisciplinary Approach to Its Archaeology, Religion, and Culture,* ed. Helmut Koester (Valley Forge, PA: Trinity Press International, 1995), pp. 27–79, 46–47.

130 **John's Jesus—unlike the Synoptics'—"makes" water into wine like the god Dionysos:** The story itself (2:1–11) doesn't claim Jesus "makes" the water

into wine; only the Johannine flashback does that. The story itself is a parable of purification, in which people celebrate with water as they would with wine; see Brooke Foss Westcott, *The Gospel According to St. John,* vol. 2 (London: Murray, 1908), pp. 333–347; Raymond E. Brown, *The Gospel According to John (XIII–XXI)* (Garden City, NY: Doubleday, 1970), pp. 979–1017; Charles H. Talbert, *Reading John: A Literary and Theological Commentary on the Fourth Gospel and the Johannine Epistles* (New York: Crossroad, 1992), pp. 248–264; *Rabbi Jesus,* pp. 182–185.

131 **When Jesus says to Mary, "Do not touch me":** The command has been understood as a theological statement that underscores, in Raymond Brown's words, "the permanent nature of his presence in the Spirit"; see *The Gospel According to John (XIII–XXI),* p. 1015. We can think of the same idea in simpler terms borrowed from Paul that speak of the "spiritual body" of the risen Jesus. That accords better with the visionary nature of Mary's experiences in all the Gospels and with Jesus' teaching in the Synoptic Gospels concerning those raised from the dead and the angels.

131 **John (12:1–8) explicitly names Mary of Bethany:** I have argued that the resuscitation of Lazarus in John's Gospel is historical, and Jesus' intimacy with Mary and Martha has caused me to infer they were related to him; see *Rabbi Jesus,* pp. 24–25, 234–247.

131 **Because prostitutes were believed to give men leprosy:** Katherine Ludwig Jansen, *The Making of the Magdalen: Preaching and Popular Devotion in the Later Middle Ages* (Princeton: Princeton University Press, 2000), pp. 149–167, ·174. As Professor Jansen also observes (p. 176), this belief rationalized the treatment of Jews, who were segregated in much the same way prostitutes and lepers were in medieval Europe, because prostitution and money lending were held to go together. Just as John's Lazarus and Luke's were mixed up, so the Mary of Luke 10:38–42 has been identified with Mary Magdalene since the Middle Ages. As I have indicated, medieval legend might be quite right in the last case.

133 **In *Thomas,* the "Living Jesus":** The document begins, "These are the secret sayings that the Living Jesus said, and the Twin, Judas Thomas, wrote them." My special thanks are due to Professor J. M. Plumley of Cambridge University, who taught me Coptic in 1974 and permitted me to work from photographs of the original manuscripts from Nag Hammadi. The Coptic manuscripts of the work come from the fourth century, but fragments in Greek establish that the work was written during the second century. Its reliance on all the canonical Gospels shows that *Thomas* must have been composed after the first century; see Chilton, "*The Gospel According to Thomas* as a Source of Jesus'

Teaching," *Gospel Perspectives* 5 (1985): 155–175. For a good version of the Coptic text, and a translation with notes and a good bibliography, see Marvin Meyer, *The Gospel of Thomas: The Hidden Sayings of Jesus* (San Francisco: HarperSanFrancisco, 1992). Further references are available in Meyer's *Secret Gospels: Essays on Thomas and the Secret Gospel of Mark* (Harrisburg, PA: Trinity Press International, 2003), and in Stephen J. Patterson, *The Gospel of Thomas and Jesus* (Sonoma, CA: Polebridge, 1993).

133 **Thomas promises to convey the reality of Resurrection to the attentive Gnostic:** Richard Valantasis, *The Gospel of Thomas* (London: Routledge, 1997); Stevan Davies, *The Gospel of Thomas: Annotated and Explained* (Woodstock, VT: SkyLight Paths, 2002).

134 **That antagonism may well reflect tension between the increasingly patriarchal hierarchy of Christians who called themselves Catholic:** Throughout the ancient period, the term *katholikos* derived from the phrase *kath holes,* which means, "across the whole." Catholic teachers tried to define a literally wholistic Christianity that all civilized people could embrace. The patriarchalization of ordained ministry, an imitation of the hierarchies of Roman power, was a by-product of the attempt to make the Church as respectable and unified as possible.

135 **Peter appears in the Nag Hammadi Library more often than Mary does:** A document called the *Apocalypse of Peter* even has Peter complain about those "who name themselves bishop and also deacons, as if they have received their authority from God.... These people are dry canals" *(Apocalypse of Peter* VII.79.24–30). Far from being a symbol of opponents in the Church, the Peter of Gnosticism could protest *against* ecclesiastical power.

135 **Bhagwan Rajneesh, the guru of Poona:** Bhagwan Rajneesh, with Amrit Pathik and Satya Deva, *The Mustard Seed: Discourses on the Sayings of Jesus Taken from the Gospel According to Thomas* (New York: HarperCollins, 1978). See the article by Gail Hinich Sutherland in *American National Biography* 18 (New York: Oxford University Press, 1999), pp. 85–86.

136 **Primeval androgyny:** Wendy Doniger O'Flaherty and Mircea Eliade, "Androgynes," in *The Encyclopedia of Religion,* vol. 1, ed. Mircea Eliade (New York: Macmillan, 1987), pp. 276–281; Mircea Eliade, *Mephistopheles and the Androgyne: Studies in Religious Myth and Symbol,* trans. J. M. Cohen (New York: Sheed and Ward, 1965), pp. 103–124.

137 **But whether you take the language physiologically or spiritually:** There is evidently a strong aspect of symbolic meaning here, as in the *First Apocalypse of James* from Nag Hammadi (V.41.15–19): "The perishable has gone up to the imperishable, and the element of femaleness has attained to the element of this

maleness." *The Gospel According to Thomas* earlier indicates the purpose of Mary's sex change—however conceived—and teaches how the change is accomplished. The risen Jesus' entire aim involves becoming one with the heavenly counterpart that people are searching for in their lives (saying 22):

> When you make the two one, and when you make the inner like the outer and the outer like the inner, and the upper like the lower, and when you make male and female into a single one, so that the male will not be male nor the female be female, when you make an eye in the place of an eye, a hand in place of a hand, a foot in place of a foot, an image in place of an image, then you will enter the kingdom.

Divine androgyny is more male-looking than female-looking, as the close of this Gospel shows, but its final result is nonetheless androgyny, because "the male will not be male nor the female be female." The whole process occurs within a total reconciliation with one's heavenly image, the divine template from which humanity was created. Marvin Meyer makes a game effort at saving *Thomas* from its own words in "Making Mary Male: The Categories 'Male' and 'Female' in the Gospel of Thomas," *New Testament Studies* 31 (1985): 554–570. But after all his labors, even he has to admit, in a classic understatement, "the specific use of gender categories may be shocking to modern sensitivities" (*The Gospel of Thomas*, p. 109). For a full account of Meyer's position, see *Secret Gospels*, pp. 76–106.

### 13. THE GODDESS AND THE VIXEN

138 **The Golden Legend of Jacobus de Voragine shows how medieval devotion:** Christopher Stace and Richard Hamer, *Jacobus de Voragine, The Golden Legend: Selections* (London: Penguin, 1998), pp. 165–172; William Granger Ryan, *Jacobus de Voragine, The Golden Legend: Readings on the Saints* (Princeton: Princeton University Press, 1993), pp. 374–383. For discussion of the motifs mentioned here, see Katherine Ludwig Jansen, *The Making of the Magdalen: Preaching and Popular Devotion in the Later Middle Ages* (Princeton: Princeton University Press, 2000), pp. 36–46, 298–299.

139 **"I am the whore and the holy one, I am the wife and the virgin":** *The Thunder, Perfect Mind* VI.2.13.13–14, in *The Nag Hammadi Library in English*, ed. James M. Robinson (San Francisco: Harper & Row, 1978).

139 **"Anointing is superior to baptism":** Elsewhere, Christ's whole purpose is to anoint with an ointment that is described as "the mercy of the father who will have mercy on them" (*The Gospel of Truth* I.3.36.15–25), and anointing also

conveys Holy Spirit, much as we have seen already in the *Didascalia (The Apocryphon of John* II.1.6.25–30). Similarly, the First Letter of John in the New Testament (1 John 2:20, 27) speaks of anointing as the source of sanctity and wisdom for all believers. *The Gospel of the Egyptians* III.2.44.24–25 includes a similar statement.

140 **The briefest of statements about her in this Gospel has spawned a diverse progeny of interpretations:** Hans-Martin Schenke, *Das Philippus-Evanglium (Nag-Hammadi-Codex II, 3)* (Berlin: Akademie, 1997), p. 270; Wesley W. Isenberg, "The Gospel According to Philip," in *The Nag Hammadi Library in English,* ed. J. M. Robinson (San Francisco: Harper & Row, 1978), pp. 131–151; Martha Lee Turner, *The Gospel According to Philip: The Sources and Coherence of an Early Christian Collection* (Leiden: Brill, 1996); R. McL. Wilson, *The Gospel of Philip: Translated from the Coptic Text, with an Introduction and Commentary* (London: Mowbray, 1962); Jacques E. Ménard, *L' Evangile selon Philippe* (Paris: Letouzey & Ané, 1967).

140 **Jesus and Mary were married, or everything but married, and their offspring grew up in France and fed the French royal line:** There are many versions of this legend, none of which is sufficiently cogent or grounded in evidence to merit being called a theory. For those who wish to pursue what can be said in this vein, the best single volume, in my opinion, is Lynn Picknett and Clive Thomas, *The Templar Revelation: Secret Guardians of the True Identity of Christ* (New York: Touchstone, 1997), although other books of this genre have already been mentioned here.

141 **The confusion between kissing and intercourse is not his problem or *The Gospel According to Philip*'s:** Elaine Pagels has described the significance and context of the kiss; see "Ritual in the *Gospel of Philip,*" in *The Nag Hammadi Library After Fifty Years: Proceedings of the 1995 Society of Biblical Literature Commemoration,* eds. John D. Turner and Anne McGuire (Leiden: Brill, 1997), pp. 280–291, 282:

> And although we cannot say what precise ritual form Philip may have in mind, he does mention divestiture of clothing (75.20–26), descent into water (64.24; 72.30–73.1; 77.1–10), and immersion as the threefold name ("father, son, and holy spirit") is pronounced over the candidate (67.20–22) apparently followed by chrismation (69.5–14; 67.4–9), and the kiss of peace (59.1–6), and concluded by participation in the eucharist.

Pagels goes on to say, "Nothing in Philip's allusive and poetic references to these ritual elements is incompatible with the ritual that Hippolytus, describing what is probably a conservative form of Roman practice some 70 to 80 years later, relates in detail." Although this dating places *Philip* too early, the conclusion is sound.

141 **The grace-conceiving kiss was mouth-to-mouth, as in the old Galilean custom of greeting:** *Rabbi Jesus,* pp. 43, 82, 104, 133–134, 182, 259.

142 **The holy kiss was, in fact, prevalent throughout the practice of Catholic and Orthodox Christianity:** Hippolytus of Rome, who also wrote during the third century, sets out the practice of the kiss as part of the traditional liturgy; Paul Bradshaw and Carol Babawi, *The Canons of Hippolytus* (Bramcote, Nottinghamshire: Grove, 1987), Canon 18 (forbidding women to kiss men, in a restriction of the practice, a regulation that grew over time).

142 **Both Gnostics and Catholics were accused by their opponents of promiscuity:** Stephen Benko, *Pagan Rome and the Early Christians* (Bloomington: Indiana University Press, 1984), pp. 54–78.

142 **Hippolytus, the third-century Roman liturgist, reserved the kiss solely for those already baptized:** Burton Scott Easton, *The Apostolic Tradition of Hippolytus* (Cambridge: Cambridge University Press, 1934), vol. 2, pp. 17–18.

143 **The most infamous accusation comes from Epiphanius:** See Philip R. Amidon, *The "Panarion" of St. Epiphanius, Bishop of Salamis: Selected Passages* (New York: Oxford University Press, 1990), translating *Panarion* 26.1.1–26.17.9. Epiphanius refers to a lost document he calls *Greater Questions of Mary.* For an assessment of the plausibility of the charges, see Silke Petersen, *"Zerstört die Werke der Weiblichkeit!" Maria Magdalen, Salome und andere Jüngerinnen Jesu in christlich-gnostischen Schriften* (Leiden: Brill, 1999), pp. 127–131; Jeffrey Kripal, "The Apocryphon of the Beloved," in *Homosexuality and Religion, Part III: Christianity and Comparative Reactions,* ed. K. C. Serota (Annandale, NY: Bard College, 2004), pp. 1–30; Anneti Marjanen, *The Woman Jesus Loved: Mary Magdalene in the Nag Hammadi Library and Related Documents* (Leiden: Brill, 1996), p. 191.

145 **in the sixth century, Pope Gregory could easily make Mary Magdalene the emblem of sexual penitence in the city of Rome:** In chapter 6, I discussed the brilliant sermon in which Gregory connected this imagery to his interpretation of the Song of Songs and the longing for God in the monastic life. In developing his theme, Gregory seems to assume that his basic portrayal of Mary is already a matter of tradition; his innovation lies in his specifically exegetical connections. See Dom David Hurst, *Gregory the Great: Forty Gospel Homilies Translated from the Latin* (Kalamazoo: Cistercian Publications, 1990), pp. 187, 198 (Homily 25).

146 **"Mary, blessed one, whom I will complete in all the mysteries of the height":** Carl Schmidt, ed., *Pistis Sophia,* translation and notes by Violet MacDermot (Leiden: Brill, 1978), vol. 1, pp. 17–21, 24–27, 30–32, 33–34.

146 **In the influential sermon of Gregory the Great:** Hurst, *Gregory the Great,* Homily 25, pp. 187, 198. As sources, Hurst cites the Maurist text of Migne's *Patrologia Latina,* ms. 69 at Corpus Christi College in Cambridge (eighth century), ms. 12 in the Archivo Capitular de la Catedral de Barcelona (eighth century), and ms. 12254 in the Bibliothèque Nationale (ninth century).

147 **By the thirteenth century, a late form of Gnosticism flourished in the West:** Malcolm Lambert, *The Cathars* (Oxford: Blackwell, 1998); René Weis, *The Yellow Cross: The Story of the Last Cathars' Rebellion Against the Inquisition, 1290–1329* (New York: Vintage, 2002); René Nelli, *Ecritures Cathares,* ed. Anne Brenon (Monaco: Rocher, 1995); Malcolm Barber, *The Cathars: Dualistic Heretics in Languedoc in the High Middle Ages* (Harlow, Essex: Longman, 2000); Roelof van den Broek, *Studies in Gnosticism and Alexandrian Christianity* (Leiden: Brill, 1996), pp. 157–177 ("The Cathars: Medieval Gnostics?").

147 **From there, it was a short step to make her into Jesus' concubine:** This motif has been discussed in chapter 2 and is documented in a contemporary source; see Pierre des Vaux-de-Cernay, *The History of the Albigensian Crusade: Peter of les Vaux-de-Cernay's Historia Albigensis,* trans. W. A. Sibly and M. D. Sibly (Woodbridge, Suffolk: Boydell, 1998), p. 51.

148 **(Despite speculative claims to the contrary, the Templars were a completely separate organization):** Helen Nicholson, *The Knights Templar: A New History* (Phoenix Mill, Gloucestershire: Sutton, 2001), pp. 240–244; J. M. Upton-Ward, *The Rule of the Templars: The French Text of the Rule of the Order of the Knights Templar* (Woodbridge, Suffolk: Boydell, 1992).

148 **three centuries after their Crusade began, Martin Luther continued to countenance the idea that Jesus had a sexual relationship with Mary Magdalene:** *D. Martin Luthers Werke, kritische Gesamtausgabe* (Weimar: Böhlau, 1893), vol. 2, no. 1472, April 7–May 1, 1532, p. 33, a remark best taken as a reflection on how people viewed Jesus, rather than as a categorical assertion. But the idea has a life of its own; see Margaret George, *Mary, Called Magdalene* (New York: Viking, 2002).

149 **the woman taken in adultery, whose stoning Jesus prevented:** This is a late addition to John's text, not a part of the original Gospel. Scribes were so uncertain where it belonged that some added it at different places in John (or to Luke!); see Bruce M. Metzger, *A Textual Commentary on the Greek New Testament* (Stuttgart: United Bible Societies, 1971), pp. 219–222. The crime of condoning adultery was alleged by one of the Crusaders, a cardinal named Raynaldus, in his thirteenth-century *Annales Ecclesiastici;* see S. R. Maitland, *History of the Albigenses and Waldenses* (London: Rivington, 1832), pp. 392–394.

149 **By the time the thirteenth century had closed, Franciscan preachers were exploring exactly the same theme:** Jansen, *The Making of the Magdalen,* p. 148, citing a sermon by Luca da Padova.

151 **Mary Magdalene, the converted sinner and sister of Lazarus the leper:** This picture of Mary is a hybrid of biblical passages, as I indicated in chapter 12. It conflates Mary Magdalene with Mary of Bethany, who had a brother named Lazarus (John 11:1–12:8), and then conflates him with the sore-ridden Lazarus who appears in Luke (16:19–31). His sores, in turn, are taken to make him a leper. From the point of view of historical study, this sort of free association is not convincing, but it illustrates the power of medieval imagination to use biblical passages to express its conviction about the transformative power of God's Spirit. "The sweet friend of God" is Petrarch's phrase, discussed in chapter 3; see Susan Haskins, *Mary Magdalene: Myth and Metaphor* (New York: Harcourt, Brace, 1993), pp. 192, 196–197.

151 **ordered an excavation of the church crypt:** Varying assessments of Charles's dig, along with documentation, can be found in Victor Saxer, *Le culte de Marie Madeleine en Occident* (Paris: Clavreuil, 1959), pp. 218–219; Haskins, *Mary Magdalen,* p. 108; Katherine Ludwig Jansen, *The Making of the Magdalen: Preaching and Popular Devotion in the Later Middle Ages* (Princeton: Princeton University Press, 2000), pp. 36–115, 308–315. Jansen suggests Charles might have been inspired by legends, perhaps taught him by his mother, Beatrice of Provence.

152 **Relics of saints amounted to metaphysical data, not just historical curiosities:** See B. D. Chilton and Jacob Neusner, *Trading Places: The Intersecting Histories of Judaism and Christianity* (Cleveland: Pilgrim, 1996), pp. 203–209. Augustine refers to Saint Stephen's healings in *City of God* 22.8.

152 **Precious as those nails were, Constantine had some melted down and added to the metal of his helmet:** Socrates Scholasticus, *Ecclesiastical History,* 1.17, who noted that some of the precious metal was also added to the bridle of the emperor's horse.

153 **Mary Magdalene's wealth and promiscuity prior to her conversion were equally legendary:** Marjorie M. Malvern, *Venus in Sackcloth: The Magdalen's Origins and Metamorphoses* (Carbondale: Southern Illinois University Press, 1975); Ingrid Maisch, *Maria Magdalena, Zwischen Verachtung und Verehrung: Das Bild einer Frau im Spiegel der Jahrhunderte* (Freiberg: Herder, 1996).

154 **Nonetheless, doubt had already been expressed about Mary's levitations**

**as described in *The Golden Legend*:** David Mycoff, *The Life of Saint Mary Magdalene and of Her Sister Martha* (Kalamazoo: Cistercian Publications, 1989), lines 2299–2326. Such doubt is not surprising, since levitation was by this time associated with witchcraft.

154 **Mary's bones had long been venerated at Vézelay:** This had been going on since the eighth century, according to the monks there; see Saxer, *Le culte de Marie Madeleine en Occident,* pp. 50, 53, 69, 70. As Saxer points out, the claim is not verifiable until the twelfth century.

156 **Just seventy-five years earlier, relics said to be Mary's, including a skull, had been looted during the sack of Constantinople:** If there is a Templar connection in the development of Mary's legend, this sorry episode may be the root of it. They were active participants in the sack of Constantinople in 1204, then still the capital of the Roman Empire and the seat of the patriarch of the Orthodox Church. The financial motivation for this atrocity was the repayment of financiers back in Venice, but the relics kept in Constantinople offered another attraction. Venice itself had profited centuries earlier by receiving the remains of Saint Mark, famously smuggled out of Alexandria in a barrel of pork.

156 **Her bones are mixed in with those of thousands of other victims who were hacked to death in Magdala:** I describe the final battle of Magdala in chapter 8, on the basis of Josephus *Jewish War* 3.462–542.

157 **The Magdalene inheritance is not for Christianity alone or for Judaism alone:** I have to disagree with Jane Schaberg's description of "Magdalene Christianity" or "Magdalene christianity"; see Jane Schaberg, "Magdalene christianity," in *On the Cutting Edge: The Study of Women in Biblical Worlds—Essays in Honor of Elisabeth Schüssler Fiorenza,* eds. Jane Schaberg, Alice Bach, and Esther Fuchs (New York: Continuum, 2004), pp. 193–220. As she rightly says (p. 210), "Magdalene christianity was not Christianity but a developing form (one of many) of first-century c.e. Judaism." But since that is the case, we should avoid conflating Mary with religious categories that came after her. "Magdalene inheritance" seems to me a better description of her legacy.

# Appendix

*The Magdalene Source in the Synoptic Gospels*
*(A Direct Translation from Luke and Mark)*

And there were some women who had been healed from evil spirits and ailments—Mary who was called Magdalene, from whom seven demons had gone out, and Joanna, Khuza's wife (Herod's commissioner), and Susanna and many others who provided for them from their belongings. [Luke 8:2–3]

And they proceed into Capernaum. At once on the Sabbaths he entered into the synagogue and taught. And they were overwhelmed at his teaching, because he taught them as having authority, and not as the letterers. And at once there was in their synagogue a person with an unclean spirit. He cried out and said, We have nothing for you, Nazarene Jesus! Have you come to destroy us? I know who you are—the holy one of God! Jesus scolded it and said: Shut up, and get out from him! The unclean spirit convulsed him, sounded with a big sound, and got out from him. And all were astonished. Result: they argued together, saying, What is this? A new teaching with authority? Even the unclean spirits he directs, and they obey him. And his fame went out at once everywhere, into all the surrounding land of Galilee. [Mark 1:21–28]

And they came to the opposite side of the Sea, into the area of the Gerasenes. He got out from the boat, and at once there met him from the tombs a person with an unclean spirit. He had the habitation among the tombs, and no one was any longer able—even with a chain—to bind him. (For many times he had been bound with fetters and chains, and the chains were torn apart by him, and the fetters smashed, and no one was capable of subduing him. And all night and day he was among the tombs and in the hills, shouting and wounding himself with stones.) He saw Jesus from a distance, and ran and worshipped him, and shouting with a big sound he says, I have nothing for you, Jesus Son of the highest God! I adjure you by God, do not torment me! Because he had been saying to him, Unclean spirit, get out from the person! And he interrogated him, What is your name? And it says to him, Legion is my name, because we are many. And they summoned him a lot, so that he would not dispatch them outside of the area. Yet there was there by the hill a big herd of pigs grazing. They summoned him and said, Send us into the pigs, so that we may enter into them. And he permitted them. The unclean spirits got out and entered into the pigs, and the herd rushed over the cliff into the sea, about two thousand, and they were choked in the sea. |Mark 5:1–13|

And a woman who had a flow of blood twelve years (and had suffered a lot from many physicians and had expended everything that was hers and had not improved, but rather got worse) had heard things concerning Jesus. She came in the crowd from behind, touched his garment. Because she was saying that: If I touch even his garments, I shall be saved. And at once the fountain of her blood dried up, and she knew in the body that she was cured from her plague. Jesus at once recognized in himself the power gone out from him and turned back in the crowd; he was saying, Who touched my garments? And his students were saying to him, Look at the crowd pressing you around, and you say, Who touched me? And he glared around to see the woman who had done this. But the woman was afraid and trembling: she knew what had happened to her. She came and fell before him and said all the truth to him. But he said to her, Daughter, your faith has saved you; depart in peace and be healthy from your plague. |Mark 5:25–34|

From there he arose and went away into the regions of Tyre. He entered into a home, and wished no one to know. And he was not able to be hid, but at once there heard about him a woman whose little daughter had an unclean spirit. She came, fell at his feet (but the woman was Greek, Syro-Phoenician by race), and asked him so that he would throw the demon out of her daughter. And he was saying to her, Let the children be satisfied first, because it is not fair to take the bread of the children and to throw it to the dogs. But she replied and says to him, Indeed, Lord: even the dogs under the table eat from the scraps of the children. He said to her, Because of this word, Depart: the demon has gone out from your daughter. She went away to her house, and found the child thrown upon the stretcher, and the demons having gone out. |Mark 7:24–30|

He again went out from the regions of Tyre and came through Sidon to the Sea of Galilee in the middle of the regions of Ten Cities. And they carry to him a deaf and mute person and they summon him so that he might lay the hand on him. He took him away from the crowd privately and put his fingers into his ears, spat and touched his tongue. He looked up into heaven and sighed and said to him, *Ephatha* (that is, Be opened up). And his hearings were opened, and the bond of his tongue was loosed, and he spoke clearly. He ordered them strictly so that they would speak to no one, but as much as he ordered them, they announced rather all the more. And they were overwhelmed beyond all measure, saying, He was done everything well: he even makes the deaf hear and the dumb speak. |Mark 7:31–37|

And they come into Bethsaida, and they carry to him a blind person and summon him, so that he would touch him. He took hold of the blind person's hand and carried him away outside the village; he spat into his eyeballs, laid hands on him and interrogated him, You looking at anything? He looked up and was saying, I am looking at people, because I see them as walking trees. Then he laid hands on his eyes again; and he directed his gaze and was restored and perceived everything clearly. And he delegated him into his house, saying, Do not even enter the village. |Mark 8:22–26|

They came to the students and saw a big crowd around them and letterers arguing with them. At once all the crowd saw him and were completely astonished; they ran and greeted him. And he interrogated them, What are you arguing about with them? One from the crowd answered him, Teacher, I brought my son to you, who has a dumb spirit. And wherever it seizes him, it tosses him down, and he foams and gnashes his teeth and shrivels. And I talked to your students, so they would throw it out, and they were not capable. He answered them and says, Faithless generation, how long will I be for you? How long will I endure you? Bring him to me! And they brought him to him. The spirit saw him and at once convulsed him up; he fell upon the ground and rolled, foaming. And he interrogated his father, For how much time has it happened like this to him? But he said, From infancy, and often it throws him into even both fire and water, to destroy him. But if you can, help us—feeling for us! But Jesus said to him, "If you can"—everything is possible to one who believes! At once the father of the child shouted and was saying, I believe: help my unbelief! But Jesus saw that a crowd was running together, and scolded the unclean spirit, saying to it, Dumb and deaf spirit, I direct you, get out of him and no longer enter into him. It shouted and convulsed a lot, and got out; and he became as if dead. Result: many said that he had died. But Jesus held his hand fast and raised him, and he arose. He entered into a house and his students interrogated him privately, Why were we not able to throw it out? And he said to them, This sort can go out by nothing except by prayer. |Mark 9:14–29|

He was in Bethany in the home of Simon the scabby, recumbent, and there came a woman who had an alabaster of genuine, expensive nard ointment. Smashing the alabaster, she poured over his head. But there were some angry among themselves. Why has this waste of the ointment happened? Because this ointment could have been sold for more than three hundred denarii and given to the poor! And they were upbraiding her. But Jesus said, Leave her: why are you making problems for her? She has done a fine deed with me. Because you always have the poor with yourselves, and whenever you want, you can do them good, but me you do not always have. She acted with what she had; she undertook to oil my body for burial. Amen I say to you, wherever the message is proclaimed in the whole world, what she did will also be spoken of in memory of her. |Mark 14:3–9|

But there were also women perceiving from a distance, among whom were Mary the Magdalene, Mary the mother of James the less and Joses, and Salome, who when he was in Galilee followed him and provided for him, and many others who had gone up with him to Jerusalem. It already became evening, and since it was preparation (that is before Sabbath), Joseph from Arimathea—a reputable councilor who also expected the kingdom of God himself—came and dared to go into Pilate, and implored the body of Jesus. But Pilate was surprised that he had already died, and, summoning the centurion, interrogated him, Did he die long ago? He knew from the centurion and granted the corpse to Joseph. He purchased linen, took him down, wrapped him in the linen and placed him in a tomb which was carved from rock and rolled a stone upon the opening of the tomb. Yet Mary the Magdalene and Mary of Joses perceived where he was placed. |Mark 15:40–47|

And when Sabbath elapsed, Mary the Magdalene and Mary of James and Salome purchased spices so they could go anoint him. And very early on the first of the Sabbaths they come upon the tomb when the sun dawned. And they were saying to one another, Who will roll the stone away from the opening of the tomb for us? They looked up and perceived that the stone had been rolled off (because it was exceedingly big). They went towards the tomb and saw a young man sitting on the right appareled in a white robe, and they were completely astonished. But he says to them, Do not be completely astonished. You seek Jesus the crucified Nazarene. He is raised; he is not here. Look—the place where they laid him. But depart, tell his students and Peter that he goes before you into Galilee; you will see him there, just as he said to you. They went out and fled from the tomb, because trembling and frenzy had them. And they said nothing to any one; they were afraid, because— |Mark 16:1–8|

# Index

Page numbers beginning with 163 refer to notes.

# Index

116–17, 131, 132, 139, 145, 157, 175, 177, 188, 206
  by nameless woman, 50, 51, 52–53, 206
  olive oil used in, 54, 57, 176
  in physical healing, 49, 55, 63
  as prominent Gnostic sacrament, 139, 196–97
  with saliva, 63
  sensuality of, 65–69
  Spirit conveyed by, x, 56, 57, 65, 67–68, 69, 114, 188, 196–97
  with tears, 58–59, 60
  women's practice of, 55, 57, 60, 63, 115, 131
Antioch, 106, 108, 160, 186
*Antiquities* (Josephus), 22, 160, 170, 176, 183
*Apocalypse of Peter,* 193
Apollonius of Tyana, 170
Aramaic Scriptures, 12
Aristophanes, 136
Augustine, Saint, 151–52
Augustodunensis, Honorius, 165

Babylonian culture, 25
Babylonian Talmud (Bavli), 74, 78
Badilus (monk), 154
baptism
  anointing rituals in, 115, 116
  anointing and, 139
  Gospel study as preparation for, 34, 35, 51, 79, 85, 87, 96
  holy kiss after, 142
  as immersion in Spirit, 79, 182, 187
  oral instruction after, 87, 94
  sexes separated in, 115–16
Barnabas, Saint, x, 187
Barrabas, 49
Bauckham, Richard, 164
Bavli (Babylonian Talmud), 74, 78
Beatrice of Provence, 200
Beelzebul, 29, 30, 43, 171
  *See also* Satan
Bernard of Clairvaux, Saint, 154
Beruria, 114
Beza, Theodore, 180
Béziers, Crusaders' massacre at, 16
Bogomil movement, 148
Boman, Thorleif, 172

Boniface VIII, Pope, 155, 156
*Book of Miracles of Saint Mary Magdalene,* 154
*Breaking of Bread, The (Fractio Panis),* 112, 189
Brock, Ann Graham, 188
Brown, Dan, 88, 167, 183
Brown, Raymond, 194
Buddhism, 157
bull, Mithraic sacrifice of, 121
burial practices, 73–74, 75–76, 179, 180, 181

Caiaphas (high priest), 49, 76, 160, 180
Capernaum, 1, 159, 168
  buildings of, 10–11
  exorcism at, 24, 36–38, 41–42, 44, 77, 86, 203
  as fishing town, 10, 36
Caravaggio, Michelangelo Merisi da, 20
Cardinal Virtues, 26
Casey, Damien, 189
Cathars, 147–48, 149, 150, 153, 155
  *See also* Albigensians
Catholic Church
  Gnosticism opposed by, 134–35, 147–49, 152, 192
  holistic approach of, 195
  Mariolatry of, viii
  Mary Magdalene misidentified by, 59–60, 177
  patriarchy of, 134, 195
  penitential disciplines of, 16
  on Resurrection, 126, 192
  saints authorized by, 153
  sevenfold sins/virtues of, 26
Celle, Pierre de, 165
Chariot of God (*Merkavah*), 60–61, 64, 77–78, 80, 81, 177
Charles I, King of Naples and Sicily, 153
Charles of Salerno, 151, 153, 154, 155, 156, 200
childbirth, impurity of, 4
Christianity
  ambivalence toward women in, viii–ix, xii, 111–18
  charismatic/prophetic strand of, 42
  doctrinal disputes within, 108, 134–35, 147–49, 152, 186–87, 192

# Index

# Index

on renunciation of family, 99–100, 186
Resurrection of, xi, 2, 24, 52, 63–64,
    65, 70, 71–73, 77, 80, 82–90, 103,
    104, 105–6, 113–14, 123, 125–28,
    131, 134, 152, 157, 178, 182–83, 187,
    192
sexual behavior allegations and,
    16–17, 68–70, 88, 140–41, 142, 144,
    148–49
as son of God, 78, 79–80, 182
spiritual evolution of, 40, 41, 56, 79,
    85, 128
Temple intervention of, 48–49, 104,
    180
temptations of, 48
Transfiguration of, 33–34, 36, 41, 77,
    78, 79, 81, 85, 86, 144, 159
travels of, 1, 10, 40, 47–48, 49, 68, 159,
    176, 203–6
twelve apostles of, 18, 40, 48, 49, 57,
    167
on unclean spirits, 4, 5, 26–27, 30,
    44–45
visionary appearances of, 51, 85, 86,
    106–7, 108–9, 127, 191; see also
    Jesus, Transfiguration of
visionary experiences of, 48, 78–79
washing of feet of, 58–59, 60
water/wine, transformation of, 130,
    193–94
on Wisdom, 31–32
woman's anointing of, 50, 52–53,
    58–59, 60, 72, 131–32, 175, 206
*Jewish War* (Josephus), 91, 160
Joanna (wife of Khuza), 1, 2–4, 164,
    172–73, 203
Job, 60–61, 177, 192
Job, Book of
    on perception of God, 192
    8:10, 192
    19:23–27, 192
John, First Letter of, 197
John, Gospel According to, 110, 133
    anointing scene in, 131–32
    on disciples, 10
    on Eucharist, 132
    Hellenic religion and, 130
    on Jesus' prevention of stoning, 149
    on Jesus' touch of Mary Magdalene,
        15

kiss of peace in, 142
on Mary Magdalene's vision of risen
    Jesus, 127–28, 130–31, 132, 137
Mary Magdalene vs. Mary of Bethany
    in, 131–32, 200
Nazorean designation used in, 169
Samaritan woman in, 58
sources of, 34, 129, 160, 199
on spiritual rebirth, 129, 130
Synoptic Gospels vs., 110
    1:1–18, 129, 130
    1:44, 10
    3:1–5, 129
    4:5–42, 58
    4:40, 130
    6:25–59, 132
    6:52–59, 130
    8:1–11, 149
    11:1–12:8, 200
    12:1–8, 131
    12:31, 129
    16:33, 129
    19:38–42, 131
    20:1–10, 131
    20:11–18, 127–28, 130
    20:17, 15
    20:19, 142
    20:21–23, 142
John, Saint, 19, 41, 77, 78
John the Baptist, Saint, 18, 56, 78, 79,
    106, 159, 167
Joseph of Arimathea, 52, 75, 76, 131, 206
Josephus, Flavius, 22, 73, 91, 160, 169,
    170, 176, 183, 201
Josiah, King, 113
Jubilees, Book of, 78
Judaism
    anointing practices of, x, 49, 54–55,
        61–62, 174
    burial practices of, 73–74, 75, 179, 180,
        181
    Christian separation from, 104–5,
        157
    converts to, 120
    feminine Spirit in, 30–32, 171
    on harmful spirits, 5
    Kabbalah of, 148
    monotheistic appeal of, 120
    mystic symbols in, 60, 61, 77–78
    purity laws of, 4, 7, 69, 73–74, 120, 191

# Index

# Index

© SIGRID ESTRADA

BRUCE CHILTON is the Bernard Iddings Bell Professor of Religion at Bard College in Annandale-on-Hudson and priest at the Free Church of Saint John in Barrytown, New York. He is the author of many scholarly articles and books, including the widely acclaimed *Rabbi Jesus* and *Rabbi Paul.*

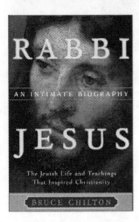
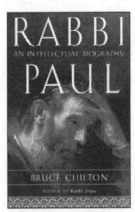

Printed in the United States
by Baker & Taylor Publisher Services